— MEXICAN ANARCHISM AFTER THE REVOLUTION —

MEXICAN ANARCHISM AFTER THE REVOLUTION

DONALD C. HODGES

UNIVERSITY OF TEXAS PRESS
AUSTIN

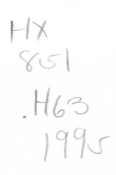

HX
851
.H63
1995

Requests for permission to reproduce material from this work should be sent
to Permissions, University of Texas Press, Box 7819, Austin, TX 78713-7819.

∞ The paper used in this publication meets the minimum requirements of
American National Standard for Information Sciences—Permanence of
Paper for Printed Library Materials, ANSI Z39.48-1984.

Library of Congress Cataloging-in-Publication Data
Hodges, Donald Clark, 1923–
Mexican anarchism after the revolution / Donald C. Hodges. — 1st ed.
p.   cm.
Includes index.
ISBN 0-292-73093-4 (alk. paper). — ISBN 0-292-73097-7 (pbk.).
1. Anarchism—Mexico—History—20th century.   2. Mexico—Politics
and government—1910–1946.   I. Title.
HX851.H63   1995
335'.83'09720904—dc20   94-20488

To
Mónico Rodríguez
and to my loyal friends in Mexico,
Ross Gandy
and
Juan de Dios Vargas Sánchez

For the great majority of mankind are satisfied with appearances, as though they were realities, and are often even more influenced by the things that seem than by those that are.

MACHIAVELLI, *DISCOURSES*, I:25

CONTENTS

PREFACE

The research for this study of Mexican anarchism covers a period of almost two decades. I began my research during a sabbatical year from September 1974 to September 1975 in Cuernavaca, the capital of Morelos. In October I made my first contact with Mexican anarchists in the Grupo Informe de Cuernavaca.

Juan de Dios Vargas Sánchez, a former student activist at the National University in Mexico City, volunteered to be my Virgil and living passport into Morelos's anarchist underground. After studying for the priesthood and participating in the student days of rage in Mexico City and in local self-defense committees, he decided to throw his lot with the Grupo Informe. A partisan of urban and rural guerrilla warfare, he armed himself in 1973 in defense of squatters' rights in the Colonia Rubén Jaramillo some eleven miles south of Cuernavaca and took an active role in the 1976 armed recovery of communal land claimed by residents of Cuernavaca's proletarian neighborhood, El Salto de San Antón. In 1977, persuaded by its commitment to a new revolution, he joined the Communist party of Mexico.

Vargas introduced me to Mónico Rodríguez Gómez, my principal informant for the shadowy history of local organizers and anarchists from the 1930s to the early 1960s. Since his testimony lies at the heart of the present study, a few words should be said about his reasons for cooperating with me. The reader is entitled to know whether Rodríguez's anarchism slanted his narration. Considering that Rodríguez had a vested interest in the reconstruction of history in his own image, the reader may reasonably wonder about the credibility of his coverage of events that took place some four decades ago.

My first meeting with Rodríguez occurred at his workshop in Chiconcuac, Morelos, in July 1975, after which I visited him repeatedly until my last trip to Mexico in 1983. In each of those sessions, which lasted from three to four hours, Rodríguez became emotionally distraught to the point of incoherence. They all ended on the same note: he would burst into tears and involuntary sobbing from the painful memories he had evoked. It was the correspondence that I began in November 1991 that enabled me to check his oral history with a written account and to piece together the unrelated fragments of a puzzle that until then had eluded me.

In the half-dozen letters I have since received, Rodríguez has filled in the lacunae, corrected some of the memory lapses from our earlier conversations, and resolved the inconsistencies in his differing reports of the same events. Gravely ill from a series of strokes in 1992, he nonetheless replied to my detailed questions concerning the secret history of Mexican anarchism after the Revolution.

Although Rodríguez had a personal interest in highlighting his role in the events, he acknowledged a revolutionary duty to transmit what had actually happened and its lessons for posterity. He had dedicated his life to a cause for which his family had to suffer and he was not disposed to sacrifice historical truth in the vainglorious search for immortality through the printed word.

My relationship to Rodríguez became closer with each successive interview. By the time of our second conversation in December 1977, he no longer had to take Vargas's word to endorse me as an anarchist fellow-traveler. In March 1976 my book on the Latin American Revolution appeared in a Mexican translation. The blurb revealed that I had interviewed revolutionary leaders in Peru at the height of the antioligarchical campaign in 1969, in Bolivia at the inauguration of its first soviet-type Popular Assembly in May 1971, in Chile a few months before and after Salvador Allende's inauguration, in Uruguay during the electoral campaign of the Broad Front in 1971, and that in the course of my research I was arrested and imprisoned by military intelligence in Montevideo on charges of aiding and abetting Uruguay's urban guerrillas.

Rodríguez had other reasons to confide in me. In February 1977 my book with Abraham Guillén, *Revaloración de la guerrilla urbana*, appeared with a Mexican publisher. A Spanish Civil War veteran, political exile from the Franco dictatorship, and mentor of the urban guerrillas in Argentina, Uruguay, and Brazil in the late 1960s, Guillén was widely known as an anarcho-Marxist.

Aristotle says in *Politics* that one should not expect from a given inquiry more precision than it is capable of giving. Since in the case of hidden or secret histories the evidence is scant and mostly circumstantial, that is all one should expect. To dispute such evidence as inconclusive is not to dismiss it. Otherwise, there will be no shadowy history to supplement the established one. If disputable evidence is better than no evidence, then the story should be told and the informants held accountable for their retroprojections.

The history of what has happened is the principal subject matter of a worldly philosophy concerned with grasping the reality behind appearances, the deeds that contradict what people say they are doing or have already done or promise to do. In the spirit of Machiavelli, I take for granted that one cannot uncover political reality by taking people's words and beliefs at face value, that logical action plays a relatively minor role in human behavior, that history is often a record of confused attempts to achieve incompatible goals, that the outcomes of human action are frequently unforeseen and seldom correspond to people's motives or intentions, that political success is often a matter of luck, that fraud and conspiracy are fundamental factors of political life with or without conscious deception, that political labels typically conceal more than they reveal, and that a conceptual apparatus based on these premises is fundamental to penetrating the surface of political events. Such are the premises of this inquiry into the silent processes of a popular resistance marginalized by scholars and by Mexico's mainstream press and media.

ACKNOWLEDGMENTS

To Abraham Guillén, the Spanish anarchist and mentor of urban guerrilla warfare, for awakening me to the pervasive influence of anarchism throughout Latin America. To Mónico Rodríguez Gómez of Chiconcuac, Morelos, for his memoirs and secret history of Mexican anarchism and communism in the states of Puebla and Morelos from 1930 to the present. To Renato Ravelo, Rodríguez's son-in-law and author of *Los jaramillistas*, for giving me a copy of Rubén Jaramillo's missing Plan of Cerro Prieto. To Juan de Dios Vargas Sánchez of Cuernavaca, for hard-to-find documents of guerrilla organizations, for the many interviews he arranged with former participants in the armed uprisings in Morelos in the 1940s and the 1950s, and for introducing me into Rodríguez's inner sanctum. To Valentín Campa Salazar, veteran labor leader and presidential candidate of the Mexican Communist party in 1976, for data concerning the first workers' strike against the public sector in Mexico and for his account of how the Communist Youth in 1970 evolved into the underground September 23 Communist League. To the editor of the Caballito publishing house, Manuel López Gallo, for publishing my first book on Mexico and for encouraging this sequel. To the Austrian anarchist Leo Gabriel and his Grupo Informe de Cuernavaca, for documentation concerning the September 23 Communist underground. To Dr. Ross Gandy of Cuernavaca, Morelos, for his vivid depictions of Mexico's social problems and keen grasp of Mexican politics. To Dr. David Ronfeldt of RAND, Inc., for a telephone interview concerning the missing links in his published account of the political struggle at the sugar complex at Atencingo. To Prof. Barry Carr of the History Department at La Trobe University, Bundoora, Australia, for helpful comments and criticism of different drafts of the manuscript. To Prof. John Hart of the History Department of the University of Houston, for insights into the historian's craft and for help in cleaning up the final draft and bringing it to life. To Richard Phillips of the Latin American Collection at the University of Florida in Gainesville, for making available materials otherwise unavailable. To my former students at the Escuela Nacional de Estudios Profesionales (ENEP-Aragón-UNAM) in Mexico City's mammoth slum of Nezahualcóyotl, for drawing my attention to the anarchizing current within the student movement. To Florida State University, for underwriting two full sabbatical years in Mexico in 1974–1975 and 1979–1980, and six extended field trips to Mexico from 1968 to 1983. To the *Canadian Journal of Latin American and Caribbean Studies*, for permission to reprint reworked versions of my articles, "The Plan of Cerro Prieto: The Peasant-Worker Movement in Morelos (1942–1962)," no. 31 (Spring 1991), and "The Political Heirs of Ricardo Flores Magón," no. 33 (Spring 1992). To Roxane Fletcher, for numberless editorial tips aimed at improving the manuscript and making it more readable. To Cathy Butler, for her patience and perseverance in feeding the manuscript through the word processor. And to all those who, in one way or another, helped me to finish this book after twenty fitful years of trying to document the history of Mexico's popular resistance to presidential despotism.

— MEXICAN ANARCHISM AFTER THE REVOLUTION —

INTRODUCTION

On 10 January 1978 Mónico Rodríguez, the only living reminder of the anarchist conspiracies in the states of Puebla and Morelos during the 1930s and the 1940s, and Valentín Campa, the indomitable leader of Mexico's railroad workers with the longest prison record for a Mexican Communist since World War II, faced one another for the first time since Campa's last prison stint from 1960 to 1970. The place was number 13, Calle del Taller, Chiconcuac, Morelos, Rodríguez's home. Rodríguez had invited Campa to explain the recent change in line of the Partido Comunista Mexicano (Mexican Communist party, PCM) and its response to the electoral reform of 1977. At the same time, as one of the party's top leaders, Campa hoped to entice Rodríguez into rejoining the party he had abandoned on the eve of their last encounter in 1958.

Campa had no inkling of the profound political differences that divided them. From conversations with him that afternoon, I learned that he had known Rodríguez as a professional party organizer during the late 1950s, but had mistakenly assumed that Rodríguez was a Marxist-Leninist like himself. In fact Rodríguez had disguised his anarcho-communism under a Marxist veneer and had joined the party as the only viable organization even nominally committed to communism. Like Rubén Jaramillo, his anarchist precursor in Morelos, Rodríguez stood for decentralized power in the form of soviets, or workers' and peasants' councils, and credited anarchism for its defense of workers' self-management and an independent policy vis-à-vis the state.

When we arrived in Chiconcuac, some thirty miles southwest of Cuernavaca, we were introduced to local members of Rodríguez's group. Among them was Edmundo Raya, head of the Communist Youth in 1956, who had quit the party about the same time as Rodríguez. Of the many questions addressed to Campa, his were the most strident. The party had sold out the workers, Raya insisted, as Campa too had maintained during the years of his expulsion from 1939 to 1963. Had Campa forgotten the PCM's role as fellow-traveler of Mexico's ruling party throughout this period? Had not Campa repeatedly argued against the PCM's surrender of its independence through popular, national, and democratic fronts with the middle classes and so-called progressive sectors of the bourgeoisie? And why should Raya support the party's electoral pretensions, which would assuredly compromise his revolutionary principles and tie him even closer to the political system?

Campa had been seduced, Raya argued, by the party's change of face during the 1960s, when it adopted a new, seemingly revolutionary, program. Its talk of a new revolution could lead nowhere, he said, as long as the party hoped to reform the 1917 Constitution. A merely electoral strategy without simultaneous preparations for armed struggle, Raya concluded, could never dislodge the ruling party from power. Occasionally, Rodríguez would add a word, but it was apparent from his periodical nodding that he agreed with Raya's explosive comments.

Campa conceded that the party's record was appalling. Even so, he defended the party on the grounds, first, that it was an integral part of the international Communist movement, second, that it was the only organized vanguard of the proletariat in Mexico, and third, that the best way to change it was by reforming it from within. He added that Fidel Castro agreed with the party's program for a new revolution and that the party had played a prominent role in defending the Cuban Revolution.

The discussion dragged on until the early hours of the morning. In the end, nobody was convinced by Campa's arguments except me and my companion, Juan Vargas, the anarchist and PCM militant responsible for hosting Campa and scheduling the meeting with Rodríguez. However, the party's self-dissolution by quotas has since convinced me that Raya was right. In 1981, in a merger with four other parties on the Left, the PCM dropped the name "communist" to become a bona fide socialist party, a strategy reaffirmed in 1987 in a merger with another left-wing party. Then, in 1989 this new party joined forces with the Democratic Current in the ruling circles to float a neopopulist party committed simply to a "democratic revolution."

That such a discussion could take place at all, and with a top executive of the Communist party pressed to defend himself, testifies to the continuing relevance of anarchism after the Revolution. Like Jaramillo before him, Rodríguez had been targeted by the party's bureaucrats in Mexico City as an ideal "catch" for extending its influence in the state of Morelos.

But Campa failed in his mission, and Rodríguez's group is still actively independent while carrying the torch abandoned by the PCM.

The perennial criticism of anarchism is that it is utopian, which is to say politically inconsequential. But whatever may be the case elsewhere, this is not true of Mexico. There, an indigenous and libertarian form of communism maintained itself independently of the Communist party while simultaneously acquiring a niche within it. Although the party's historians claim that this anarcho-communist deviation was effectively suppressed by the mid-1920s, it was never expunged entirely.

Despite pretensions to Marxist-Leninist orthodoxy, Campa exemplified in thought and deed the lurking presence of Mexican anarchism. In his first job as a pipe fitter for a Tampico oil company in 1920–1921, he became exposed to native anarchist traditions. By 1922 he had immersed himself in anarchist literature, which admittedly transformed him into a revolutionary. Not until 1927 did he become a member of the PCM. However, his persistent opposition to the party's reformist and opportunist policies suggests a carryover from his anarchism.

Unlike Campa, Rodríguez joined the Communist party in the expectation of carrying on anarchist work within it. When that effort failed after two decades as a party militant, he tried his luck elsewhere. But in or out of the party, both men distinguished themselves by championing the independent interests of the working class. Each contributed in a unique way to some of the most important labor mobilizations in recent Mexican history.

To the acknowledged anarchism of activists like Rodríguez should be added unacknowledged traces in party stalwarts like Campa. Until recently, the study of Mexican anarchism has focused on the fortunes of specifically anarchist organizations. However, it would be a mistake to conclude from their suppression and disappearance that Mexican anarchism has become an obsolete ideology.

Anarchist organizations were stamped out during the first two decades of the Revolution or otherwise fizzled from lack of popular resonance. Former members who tried to be consequential had two main options: they could line up with the PCM, or they could pursue a strategy independent of the party.

In Mexico the political realists cast their lot with the party. While the fundamentalists prepared for a final confrontation with capitalism, the realists proposed to reach a republic of equals by stages. To get rid of the lingering traces of feudalism in the countryside, they would act independently of the democratic bourgeoisie and the official party of the Revolution. Later, when conditions were ripe, they would turn the tables on both through a proletarian explosion. Such was the strategy adopted not without some confusion by Rodríguez and Jaramillo when they joined the Communist party in 1938.

Is there not something paradoxical about self-proclaimed anarchists supporting the PCM during its years of Stalinist ascendancy? Could they reasonably regard themselves as anarchists in an organization on speaking terms with the ruling party?

The term "anarchism" usually stands for an uncompromising defense of freedom in opposition to government coercion and cultural constraints. But it also targets a third enemy associated with economic despotism, exploitation, and material privilege. Mexican anarchists look on capitalism as their fundamental enemy. Ricardo Flores Magón, the progenitor of Mexico's indigenous anarchism, believed that capital is a form of theft and considered government and religion to be the allies of capital. Like Marx, he advocated the political organization of the proletariat and a policy of coalitions with both liberals and socialists. In this way, anarchists might unite with liberals to overthrow a tyrannical government, and then with socialists to abolish capitalism. So it is understandable that, after Flores Magón's party was suppressed, some of his followers turned to the Communist party.

In the effort to be consequential, Mexico's indigenous anarchists compromised their libertarian principles. But while many who joined the Communist party became cogs in a political machine, others injected an anarchist content into the party's bureaucratic mold. This accounts for the unique character of Mexicommunism, its periodic lapses into an independent policy of electoral abstentionism, and its intermittent support for armed struggle. It also explains the PCM's turnabout in the sixties, when it nominally opted for a new revolution to replace the Revolution of 1910.

In this long view of Mexican anarchism, Rodríguez's principal allies in the party consisted of militants like Campa who stood up against the Stalinist and neo-Stalinist leadership. The principled defense of the independent class interests of Mexico's workers had first drawn them together during the great railroad strike of 1958 and would again do so in the pastoral setting of Chiconcuac some two decades later.

But this confluence of Marxism and Mexican anarchism is only half of our story. Independent of the PCM and Rodríguez's activism inside and outside of the party, I hope to show that Mexican anarchism has acquired another lease on life. Rather than a time-worn ideology tied to the declining fortunes of the labor movement, Mexican anarchism has reappeared in different clothing under other names. A new generation of anarchists without connections to a professedly anarchist organization or ties to the

PCM has enriched anarchist theory and practice with a spectrum of new concerns.

Jaramillo rather than Rodríguez is the link between the old doctrinaire anarchism and the new style of anarchist critique adopted by other sectors of society besides organized labor. While his armed struggle of the 1940s and the 1950s inspired a resurgence of rural guerrillas in the 1960s, it did so in conjunction with the anarchist undercurrent of the Cuban Revolution. The student rebellion of 1968 and its aftermath became the embodiment of this New Left nourished by the Cuban Revolution and by the Maoist and Guevarist heresies within Marxism. Jaramillo was not only an ardent follower of Flores Magón, but also a Methodist preacher with a liberation theology that carried an anarchist message of redemption for the poor and powerless. In this role, too, he became a herald of a new revolution.

Thus Mexican anarchism in the 1970s and the 1980s dispensed with its former ties to the Communists. Its critique of the political bureaucracy in power and of the role of a "new class" in ripping off the Mexican Revolution soon replaced both Flores Magón's and the PCM's critique of the original bourgeois character of the Revolution. Meanwhile, liberation theology and ecology came to the fore with trenchant exposures of the economic causes of social inequality and the deteriorating conditions of life in Mexican society.

Nothing has been spared by this critique of the bureaucratization of everyday life, not schools, or hospitals, or automobiles, or computers, or the latest supposedly labor-saving devices in the home. The new anarchism targets the unforeseen consequences of the Marxist project: the endless multiplication of humanity combined with a reckless devastation of natural resources, addictive consumption, global pollution, and a panglossian reverence for technological progress and modernization with little attention to the social costs. To the Marxist theory of capitalist exploitation it adds a novel theory of bureaucratic exploitation and a critique of twentieth-century socialism. Besides showing how the possessors of education reap what they do not sow, it admonishes the working class for accepting the patriarchal values and hierarchical ordering of society in place of a final solution to the social question.

The political significance of Mexican anarchism before the Revolution is now well established. But was it a significant social force after the Revolution? Recent scholarship holds that it continued to be a vital force from 1917 to 1931. The turning point came with the organization of a state-supported party of the revolution in 1929 intent on controlling and co-opting organized labor, and the passage of the Federal Labor Code in

1931, which effectively curtailed the existence of an independent labor movement. But did this turnabout signify the eclipse of Mexican anarchism or was it able to survive and recover influence independently of the anarchist label? That question has yet to be answered. What follows are the first halting steps toward an answer.

THE POLITICAL SUCCESSORS OF RICARDO FLORES MAGÓN

R icardo Flores Magón (1874–1922), the so-called "intellectual author of the Mexican Revolution,"[1] supposedly left few political heirs and none who were influential. The program he sketched of a communist society without classes and without hierarchies has yet to be realized. His Partido Liberal Mexicano (Mexican Liberal party, PLM) disintegrated when its weekly *Regeneración* ceased to appear after March 1918. When his freedom from a U.S. prison seemed imminent at the end of 1921, plans were made to purchase a new printing press and to renew publication in Mexico City.[2] But these hopes were forever dashed when Flores Magón died under suspicious circumstances in November 1922. His intellectual heirs were reduced to the Grupo Cultural "Ricardo Flores Magón," which in 1924–1925 edited the principal collections of his articles, speeches, letters, and literary works, along with other documents and a biography by Spanish anarchist Diego Abad de Santillán. With this effort completed, says Armando Bartra, "the political trajectory of the Magonist current initiated with the first number of *Regeneración* . . . came to an end."[3]

Does this mean that the Magonist current was finished along with its political trajectory? An uncharitable reading would suggest so. But as Bartra indicates, the current persisted but lost its original force and either spread out in rivulets or became channeled underground.[4]

Emiliano Zapata (1879–1919) did more than anyone to implement Flores Magón's program. If one could establish the continuing influence of *zapatismo* (Zapata's radical agrarian current), therefore, one could conclude that Flores Magón's anarchism is not dead. Surely, anyone interested in Flores Magón's political philosophy should have a similar interest in the outcome of Zapata's agrarianism. Bartra is a case in point. Within a few years of compiling his Magonist anthology, he published a book on Zapata's political heirs.[5]

The topic still excites controversy. Flores Magón's sectarian and utopian schemes isolated him from the masses on a national and even local level, writes Arnaldo Córdova. The PLM belonged to the camp of the marginalized and defeated, had no political future, and was destined to disappear because its "Manichaean vision" had little resonance among the illiterate and ignorant masses, and because it closed its eyes to the mundane, everyday problems that could not wait for a final solution to the social question.[6]

On the eve of the presidential elections in 1911, the publication of the PLM's September 23 Manifesto wrecked its chances of becoming the second electoral party in the nation. Its failure to reach an understanding with the liberal mainstream was deplorable for the future of the Revolution, writes José C. Valadés, for "the PLM would lose its voice and support within the country . . . [and] Flores Magón would cease being the popular guide [he had once been]."[7]

In contrast to this dour appraisal, says Communist party dissident José Revueltas, Flores Magón bequeathed an authentic proletarian current of transcendental significance for Mexican workers. It was "the only one moving them to great independent actions and, therefore, the only one capable of guiding them toward the proletarian ideology [which], . . . after the disappearance of the House of the World Worker issued in a great mass movement in the [anarcho-syndicalist] General Confederation of Workers."[8]

Flores Magón's March 1918 Manifesto to anarchists everywhere and to workers in general called for a widespread insurrection against the belligerents in World War I. It gave to his political philosophy an international significance, says Gonzalo Aguirre Beltrán, that "to this day continues to move the conscience of our affluent and conformist society . . . [against] the rationalizations used to justify the parochial and intransigent nationalisms of a social system based on human inequality."[9] The international dimension of his thought is further evident in the influence his strategy had on Augusto César Sandino, who "hid his subversive intentions under the cover of the Nicaraguan Liberal party," just as Flores Magón concealed his intentions behind the PLM's liberal façade.[10]

Who to believe? According to James Cockcroft, PLM radicals after 1911 failed to play a direct role in shaping the outcome of the Revolution, but did so indirectly "through their influence on organized labor, ideological controversy, and occasional fighting units among Zapatistas and Villistas . . . [and] as especially influential figures in the 1930s under Lázaro Cárdenas."[11] He further suggests that they were by no means uninfluential during the early 1970s.[12] However, his research covers only the period from 1900 to 1917, so he fails to document his controversial thesis.

Today, hardly anyone disputes that anarchism has lost its political clout, that the "active reformism of the Obregón, Calles, and Lázaro Cárdenas regimes has relegated Mexican anarchism to a historical legacy."[13] But was Ricardo Flores Magón an "anarchist" in the conventional sense? Revueltas distinguishes "the doctrinal anarchist that was Flores Magón . . . [from] the proletarian ideologue *that he also was*."[14] He concludes that, as a proletarian ideologue, Flores Magón still has relevance for Mexico.

His heirs may be found almost anywhere on the Mexican Left. By "heir" I mean someone who acquires a particular trait or set of traits from a predecessor and carries on in a similar vein. One may become an heir in whole to a political tradition without ever belonging to it, and in part without ever knowing it. In determining who were Flores Magón's heirs, notwithstanding their indebtedness to other legacies, one should single out what each directly or indirectly acquired from him. Some were heirs to his 1906 program, which was considered "liberal"; others to his 1911 program, which qualifies as both "socialist" and "communist"; still others to the mystique of the martyred and stainless hero whose millenarian fervor, intransigent and inflammatory style, and poetic language made him revered by Mexicans of different political persuasions.

There were *magonistas* (Magonists) who joined similar or kindred organizations after their own collapsed, and others who invoked Flores Magón's name for quite dissimilar projects. Some made their peace with the revolutionary generals and official party of the Revolution and carried on the PLM's "liberal" legacy under a different name. Those who became the Communist party's allies in founding the Agrarian Leagues in 1923, as well as those who passed over into the Communist party, retained the PLM's socialist and in some instances its communist legacy. Its most spectacular heirs, who led the armed struggles, land invasions, and student demonstrations of the 1960s and the 1970s, resurrected features of the PLM's different programs while raising Flores Magón to a cult figure of the Left. Even the official party of the Revolution honored him as a precursor. Thus Flores Magón bequeathed a contradictory legacy through the PLM's dismembered parts.

As testimony to his continuing presence, his 23 September 1911 Manifesto still has symbolic value. The manifesto's call for a "new revolution" was revived in its original form by Rubén Jaramillo during his armed struggles in the state of Morelos in the 1940s and the 1950s, and subsequently in adulterated form by the Communist party in the 1960s and the 1970s. September 23 was the date chosen in 1941 for the first demonstration by organized labor in defense of workers' self-management in nationalized industries, in 1964 for the assault by rural guerrillas on a military barracks, in 1970 as the name of the armed nucleus of the Communist party's youth section reorganized as the September 23 Movement, and in 1973 as the name of the umbrella organization of the surviving political-military vanguards, the September 23 Communist League. As we shall see, the Magonist legacy did not exhaust itself during the Revolution of 1910 to 1917, but continued to have an impact on the Mexican Left.

FIRST CALL FOR A "NEW REVOLUTION"

The popular resistance to presidential despotism since 1940 was launched with an earlier resistance as a model. The prototype was the struggle of Flores Magón's PLM against the despotic presidentialism of Porfirio Díaz, who succeeded himself in office for most of the thirty-five years from 1876 to 1911. The struggle against the *porfiriato* (the popular name for the Díaz dictatorship) became the model for the resistance to the so-called *neoporfiriato* (the revived despotism of Mexico's presidents after 1940), likewise against conditions of widespread electoral fraud and a monopoly of power by the ruling party.

After the PLM adopted a new program for revolution in 1911, Flores Magón made common cause with Emiliano Zapata's armed struggle and attempted to influence it ideologically.[15] According to Cockcroft, Mexico had more than one political-military vanguard, "first in the PLM (until 1911) and then in the Zapatista 'army of the south.' "[16] What he does not tell us is how they inspired a second generation of revolutionaries who revived the armed struggle in the 1940s, and again in the 1960s, as part of the Magonist legacy of a "new revolution." Nor does he spell out the content of this "new revolution."

The PLM's original program of July 1906 called not only for armed struggle against the "elected" dictator Porfirio Díaz, but also for an agrarian and labor reform directed at smashing the *hacendados'* (big land-owners') economic and political power. This was to be the first step toward an anticapitalist and antibureaucratic revolution, whose agenda was kept secret until the PLM adopted a second and patently communist program in September 1911.

Although the PLM's armed struggle contributed to Díaz's forced resignation in May 1911 and his replacement by Francisco Madero, the PLM rejected Madero's program of "Effective Suffrage, No Re-election."[17] What Mexicans needed was not a new president, argued Flores Magón, but bread, housing, and land of their own.[18] More important than political liberty is economic liberty, he added, to be had only by the forcible expropriation of landlords and the vindication of the rights of workers.

On 31 December 1910, Flores Magón spelled out the strategy of his "new revolution." In an imaginary conversation, the protagonist of a new revolution asks a disillusioned old-style revolutionary what he fought for. The replacement of bad rulers by good, of an oppressive tyranny by a democratically elected government, was the answer. "But after our triumph, we continued working just as before, like mules instead of men . . . [so don't] risk your life for a new master." [19] To this the new revolutionary replied that a revolution should do more than substitute one ruling minority for another. It should abolish the "right to property." [20]

It did not suffice, Flores Magón explained in a follow-up article, to fight against Díaz's tyranny and then to hold elections in the hope the PLM's program might prevail. "The people is the eternal child: credulous, innocent, candid, and therefore always cheated in its aspirations." [21] Even supposing a miracle, that proletarians got themselves elected to Congress and their program approved, a second miracle would be required to enforce it. Rather than consent to their lands being expropriated, landlords would stage an armed counterrevolution against any government with the audacity to challenge their privileges.

The question therefore arises: "What is the point of postponing the expropriation of the land until a new government is established?" It will be much easier to expropriate when the people are under arms and the fever of insurrection has gripped them than when the tyrant falls and they return to their jobs. Benito Juárez was pressured not to expropriate the clergy until the war of reform was over, but he replied that if he waited until peace were declared, the clergy would lead the country into a second bloody struggle. "He chose to save blood and said: 'It is better to do in one revolution what would otherwise require two.' " [22] The lesson was clear. Once mobilized, workers and peasants should fight for their own program, should make a combined revolution that would topple not only the landlords, but also the bourgeoisie struggling to succeed them and the functionaries aiming to replace the bourgeoisie. It would be at once a bourgeois-democratic revolution and a socialist and communist revolution rolled into one.

In no uncertain terms the PLM's September 1911 program called for a war to the death against private property, political authority, and the established church. Not only lands would be expropriated, but also agricultural implements and urban industries—even private houses. [23] This program was not just a socialist one. As the manifesto spelled out the "egalitarian principles" of its final, or communist, solution to the social question:

Only those who are not willing to work will die of hunger, excepting the aged, the incapacitated, and children, who have a right to enjoy all. Everything produced will be dispatched to the community's general store, from which all will have the right to take WHATEVER THEY NEED THAT IS NECESSARY, without any other requisite than proof they are working in this or that industry.[24]

Said Flores Magón only two weeks before launching this new program, "nobody denies that in Mexico the revolution marches with giant strides toward communism."[25]

A conspiratorial strategy was designed to implement the program. The workers would be led by an "intransigent, resolute, activating minority" instigating the masses into taking possession of the land and factories.[26] At the same time, the PLM's intentions would be masked in order to confuse and divide the enemy. The fields and factories would be socialized, but in the name of liberal reform.

Everything reduces to a mere question of tactics. If from the start we had called ourselves anarchists [communists, or even socialists], only a few would have listened to us. . . . No liberal party in the world has our anticapitalist tendencies, which are about to launch a revolution. . . . In order not to have everybody against us, we will continue to . . . call ourselves liberals.[27]

The PLM adapted its strategy to historical conditions and the immediate objectives of the proletariat. But it refused to wait for all the objective conditions of revolution to be present before launching one. Long before Che Guevara became identified with the slogan "The duty of the revolutionary is to make the revolution," Flores Magón spelled out its intent in an article entitled "The Duty of the Revolutionary" (13 June 1914):

We are not satisfied to wait for the Mexican revolution to begin. Instead, we force, we precipitate, the revolution in order to have the opportunity to channel it through words and deeds toward communism. . . . We did everything we could to shake up the people, to make them rebel, and initiated the insurrectional movements of September 1906 and June 1908, preparatory to the tremendous movement that began on 20 November 1910 and that still is not over.[28]

The conspiratorial origins of the Magonist movement go back to 1903, when Flores Magón and his principal associates were jailed for propaganda against the Díaz regime. Even before their release in October and their voluntary exile in the United States, they had resolved on a conspiratorial plan. Their plan was to reorganize the Liberal movement by founding a nominal Liberal party aimed, first, at finding a pretext for arming the Mexican people against Díaz, and second, at transforming the Liberal revolution into a revolutionary war. "This was the plan that we later followed, that we revealed to nobody . . . , that we jealously guarded in our brains, waiting for the opportune moment." [29] The PLM, founded in Saint Louis, Missouri, in September 1905, was a conspiracy from the beginning. Concealment of their political intentions became a definitive mark of *magonistas*, first as avowed Liberals and later as nominal Bolsheviks when they teamed up with the PCM.

While sharing the concerns of modern socialists, the PLM was not an electoral party. For Marx and Engels, communist strategy aimed to win the battle of democracy by establishing universal suffrage for men. They advised their followers to seek allies among the petty bourgeois democrats in France, and to line up with the radical bourgeoisie against the conservative bourgeoisie in Germany and Switzerland.[30] Once the armed struggle was unleashed, the PLM vigorously repudiated this strategy, which made the struggle for democracy a precondition of the struggle for communism.[31]

Self-defined as communist, the PLM's "new revolution" was also perceived as communist by its enemies.[32] But it was a communism noticeably different from that of Marx and Engels. The communist society they envisioned was not a society of equals.[33] In its lower, or socialist, stage each worker would continue to own the capacity to labor, which would become public property only in the event of a fully developed communist society. Meanwhile, incentives for economic growth and training in specialized skills required a system of distribution based on merit.[34] The PLM rejected this temporizing strategy by insisting on distribution according to need and by refusing to recognize the acquisition of higher skills as deserving of higher pay.

Unlike the Communist parties that emerged on the heels of the Bolshevik Revolution, the PLM anticipated the freedoms of action and belief asserted by dissident communists in Eastern Europe beginning with the "Prague Spring" of 1968, the freedoms defended by marching students in Berlin, Paris, and Mexico City that same year. Besides social and political equality, Flores Magón insisted on a free choice of lifestyles consistent with freedom of belief, expression, and association. In a tribute to this liberal legacy that converged on anarchism and that distinguishes anarchism from bolshevism, he wrote: "The French Revolution gave us the right to think [as we please]; but it did not give us the right to live . . . [which] does not mean to vegetate. To live means to be free and happy . . . [to which] we all have a right." [35]

In summary, the PLM set its sights on a communist revolution with freedom and equality as its goal, socialism as a halfway solution, and a liberal program of agrarian and labor reforms as its immediate objective. A conspiratorial and insurrectionary strategy of direct action would be the means of implementing each. Such is the legacy, in whole or part, that Flores Magón bequeathed to an unlikely assortment of heirs that included communists and socialists as well as liberals, along with the Mexican government and the official party of the Revolution.

THE MAGONIST IMPACT ON THE REFORMIST LEFT

From the beginning, the PLM represented a coalition of socialist and communist currents. Cockcroft describes their partisans as "moderates" and "radicals," although the communist current also contained a moderate wing. In any case, the struggle between them came to a head in 1905, when the first split occurred. Failing to persuade Flores Magón to tone down his articles for *Regeneración*, Camilo Arriaga and Santiago De la Vega left Saint Louis and returned to San Antonio to write for the rival socialist weekly *Humanidad*. [36]

In its main outlines, this split followed the contours of Lenin's struggle within the Social Democratic party of Russia. At the second party congress in July 1903, Lenin's faction won a majority. Two years later Flores Magón's communist faction triumphed over the PLM's socialist wing. Because of the repression in their respective countries, both parties had to convene in exile, the former in Brussels and the latter in Saint Louis.

A second split occurred during the interlude between the forced resignation of Díaz as president in May 1911 and the election of Madero as his successor in October. This, unlike the first split, was sparked by PLM communists who agreed with Flores Magón in principle but diverged over matters of strategy. [37] Led by Juan Sarabia and Antonio Villarreal, this second wave of PLM reformists collaborated with the mainstream of the Revolution by endorsing Madero's bid for the presidency. Hoping to push the Revolution to a communist outcome gradually by peaceful means, they repudiated Flores Magón's strategy of permanent revolution as unpractical and premature. Alarmed by his public espousal of communism in 1911, they launched a rival *Regeneración* in August, published in Mexico City.

About the same time they formalized their split through the Junta for the Reorganization of the Liberal Party, subsequently known as the Liberal party to distinguish it from the PLM.

Liberal party reformists were active in founding the Casa del Obrero Mundial (House of the World Worker) on 22 September 1912. Both Sarabia and Villarreal, leaders of the 1911 split, were among its organizers. They were joined by De la Vega and Antonio Díaz Soto y Gama, leaders of the 1906 split.[38] Although the Casa included PLM revolutionaries as well as reformists, it was effectively captured by the reformists when sixty-seven of its members resolved in secret session on 10 February 1915 to support Gen. Alvaro Obregón and the Constitutionalist Army against the combined forces of Pancho Villa's Division of the North and Zapata's Army of the South.[39]

The Casa's left wing supported Zapata. The official motto of Zapata's army was "Justice and Law," as in his Plan of Ayala (28 November 1911). By July 1912, he had combined it with the PLM's 1906 motto, "Reform, Liberty, and Justice," so that it became "Reform, Liberty, Justice, and Law."[40] But in touch with both the revolutionary and the reformist sectors of the Magonist movement, Zapata also adopted the PLM's inflammatory slogan, "Land and Liberty,"[41] which failed to elicit support from the Casa's reformists.

The pact with Obregón boomeranged when the head of the Constitutionalist cause, Venustiano Carranza, suppressed the Casa in a presidential decree dated 1 August 1916. So in May 1918, its former leaders founded a new labor central, the predominantly reformist Confederación Regional Obrera Mexicana (Mexican Labor Regional Confederation). Thanks to its efforts, on 6 August 1919 another secret pact was signed with Obregón that nominally "gave to the Mexican labor movement the strength, dignity, recognition, and qualifications to take its first steps toward its ultimate goal of emancipation."[42] Nine of its eleven labor signatories had been former activists of the Casa.[43] A repudiation of the PLM's revolutionary legacy, this new pact reaffirmed the political strategy of the reformists.

PLM reformists not only led a minor side current of the Mexican Revolution, but also played a prominent role in the reforms institutionalized in the 1917 Constitution. In particular, they won a lasting victory for socioeconomic change in the two articles of the Constitution bearing on agrarian and labor reform: Article 27, declaring the nation's ownership of all minerals and oil deposits in the subsoil and providing for the division of large landed estates conformable to the principle of "land to the tiller"; and Article 123, ensuring the right to organize and to strike within the law, with state arbitration boards composed of equal numbers of representatives from workers and employers, and protective legislation on and off the job.[44]

For Ricardo's younger brother Enrique Flores Magón (1877–1954), the Constitution was a deceptive document used by Carranza and his lackeys to "hoodwink and attract the unaware laboring majority and, once they were captivated, to deny workers the tokens conceded to them by the article on labor."[45] But this was not the interpretation that prevailed among the reformists. Years later, in a change of face, even Enrique acknowledged that the PLM's objectives had been given a legal foundation by the Constitution. Although the Revolution was not over, he believed that further armed uprisings would be unnecessary.[46]

The 1917 Constitution contained major concessions to the Mexican Left in line with the PLM's 1906 program. But the long-run outcome of a Center-Left strategy was for the reformist Liberal party to dissolve and for its members to become swallowed up in the parties supporting the mainstream of the Mexican Revolution. Thus, after the coalition of parties that became the backbone of Obregón's presidency (1920–1924) and that of his successor Plutarco Elías Calles (1924–1928), most of the PLM's reformists ended by joining the official party of the Revolution or, like Enrique, supporting it from the sidelines.

THE CONVERGENCE ON MEXICO'S COMMUNIST PARTY

These were not the only major splits in the PLM. A third split occurred over how to respond to the Bolshevik Revolution of October 1917 and to the organization of Mexico's nascent Communist party two years later, in November 1919. Unlike earlier deserters from the PLM, this time the splitters were tempted to join forces with a worldwide communist movement ostensibly converging with their own. The most outstanding difference was the Bolsheviks' reliance on repression to maintain themselves in power. But the Bolsheviks had succeeded whereas the PLM had not, which lent credibility to their authoritarian measures.

In the last issue of *Regeneración*, in March 1918, Ricardo Flores Magón likened Lenin to the greatest revolutionary figure produced by World War I, "because he is at the front of a movement bound to provoke . . . the *Great World Revolution*."[47] During the next three years, he came to swallow those words. In a letter from Fort Leavenworth, Kansas, dated 8 February 1921, he protested the changed course of the Russian Revolution following the turbulent debates over the role of the trade unions during the critical year 1920, when Lenin and Trotsky saved the Bolsheviks at the expense of workers' self-management.[48] In a follow-up letter dated 22 February, he acknowledged with sadness the large number of PLMers who continued to defend the dictatorship of Lenin and Trotsky.[49] He urged his followers to join with Mexico's anarcho-syndicalists in the newly organized Confederación General de Trabajadores (General Confederation of Workers, CGT), founded in 1921, rather than joining the Mexican Communist party.

At the same time, he cautioned workers against fighting among themselves. Although they should steer clear of legal Marxists, it was advisable to cooperate with "revolutionary Marxists who do not travel the electoral road"—a message reaffirmed in Flores Magón's last letter before he died.[50] Addressed to Nicolás Bernal and dated 19 November 1922, the letter acknowledges his gratitude to the PCM and the Communist Youth for their efforts to secure his freedom.[51] For the PCM, this was Flores Magón's political testament, "his mandate to the Mexican proletariat and to its essential organizations to struggle together, to abandon sectarian differences."[52] But the party did not share his conception of the revolution at hand:

> The essential task of our revolution could not be the subversion of the existing system of property in the midst of an imperialist world as yet undemolished by war . . . the complex situation of our country required, as the central task, the organization of a vast anti-imperialist and antifeudal national front, within which the proletariat might create and consolidate its organizations . . . and in the course of its struggle gain hegemony over the revolution.[53]

Rafael Carrillo, secretary-general of the party from 1925 to 1929, who wrote these lines in 1945, says this is the course that Flores Magón should have followed. Evidently, the communism of the PLM's extremists placed them outside the impetuous torrent of the Revolution that enabled PLM reformists Heriberto Jara and Esteban Baca Calderón, and fellow-traveler Francisco Múgica, to occupy influential positions in the government.[54] Like the reformists who broke with Flores Magón in 1911, Carrillo concludes that the extremists should have stuck to their 1906 liberal program.

Although we shall never know how many Communists during the 1920s shared common ground with the PLMers, "features of the libertarian heritage are visible in the practices of the party right through the 1920s and 1930s."[55] Libertarian communists who chose the PCM, even belatedly, as did former Casa leader Rosendo Salazar in the 1930s, did so because it was the local mouthpiece of the Bolshevik Revolution and the only party in Mexico even nominally committed to communism. What initially attracted them to the Communist party may also account for their acceptance of its later reformist line. Thus Enrique Flores Magón eventually came to believe that his brother's most enduring contribution was not the PLM's 1911 program but its 1906 program, which supposedly opened the door to a continuing revolution within the framework of the Mexican state.[56] Although he never joined the Communist party, Enrique traveled the same road as the party from 1935 until his death in October 1954.

Unlike its socialist rivals, the PCM was not a mass party anybody could join, but a vanguard or elite of disciplined revolutionaries. In this respect, during its early years and until roughly 1935, it could claim to be following in the PLM's footsteps. Although the PCM's "left turn" in July 1929 responded to a worldwide phenomenon linked to developments within the Soviet Union and the Communist International, it simultaneously revived hopes for a "new revolution," a socialist revolution purportedly preparing the ground for a communist one.[57]

Instrumental to this convergence of PLMers on the Communist party was Nikolai Bukharin and Eugeny Preobrazhensky's *The ABC of Communism*, a popular exposition of the program of the Russian Communist party adopted at its 8th Congress in March 1919. This work achieved international renown, making it holy writ for Communist party members outside the Soviet Union during the 1920s and the 1930s, while its Spanish translation served as a major document for PCM recruits. Echoing Lenin's 1917 revision of Marx's scenario for the lower stage of communism, the *ABC* bluntly declared that "the aim of communism is to secure equal pay for all . . . to work for a system of equal pay."[58] By adopting Lenin's program qualified only by the obstacles to its immediate realization, the PCM became an heir to the PLM's 1911 legacy.

Among the Magonists who joined or became fellow-travelers of the PCM were radical agrarians dismayed by the slow pace of land reform under the dual control of Generals Obregón and Calles. According to one estimate, "as late as 1923, fewer than 2,700 families still held more than one-half the national property, and a mere 114 owned one-quarter of the total."[59] As the leader of an agrarian revolt in the vicinity of Lake Pátzcuaro in Michoacán, Primo Tapia de la Cruz was catapulted into the national leadership of the League of Agrarian Communities. Elected secretary-general at its founding convention in December 1923, he became a close collaborator of Ursulo Galván, the foremost Mexican agrarian who, like Primo, joined the PCM after coming under anarchist influence.[60] The ideology that inspired him to become a militant in the anarcho-syndicalist Industrial Workers of the World (IWW), and then a Communist, was not *zapatismo* but *floresmagonismo* (the anarchism of Ricardo Flores Magón).[61]

José Romero Gómez was another *agrarista* (agrarian) who began his political life as a Magonist and later joined the PCM. A carpenter in the Lagos de Moreno municipality of Jalisco, he became secretary-general of the Regional Peasant League Magdaleno Cedillo between 1932 and 1938, while continuing to be active in both the PCM and the CGT.[62] He described how he became a Communist in the 1920s: "We were . . . following upon the communist movement in Russia. Initially I steeped myself in the libertarian ideas of Ricardo Flores Magón."[63]

In his memoirs, Valentín Campa recalls the continuing vitality of *floresmagonismo*. Flores Magón's initial declaration of support for the Bolshevik Revolution had an enormous influence that contributed to the decision to form the PCM.[64] "Magonism had made strong gains not only among artisans and the petty bourgeoisie, but also among wage laborers and wage earners in general . . . pressures that explain the deviations and confusions in the PCM during its entire initial period."[65]

While Magonists converged on the Communist party during the 1920s, the party also came under their influence. Manuel Díaz Ramírez, who began his political career as a Magonist and became an IWW "Wobbly," served as the party's secretary-general from 1921 to 1924. Despite the Communist International's ban on political abstentionism, he was instrumental in getting Lenin to accept the party's antielectoral and antiparliamentary line.[66] So strong were the Magonist and anarcho-syndicalist pressures within the PCM that Alberto Araoz de León, head of the party's local in Mexico City and general secretary of the Federación Comunista del Proletariado Mexicano (Communist Federation of the Mexican Proletariat), sided with the anarchists when the rupture occurred between Communists and anarchists at the CGT's first Congress in September 1921.[67]

José Valadés, head of the Communist Youth from 1920 to 1922, is another case in point. A member of the PCM's three-man secretariat headed by Ramírez, he was expelled from the party for insubordination in November 1922.[68] At the same time, a split occurred in the Communist Youth over the issue of autonomy or subordination to the PCM and resulted in the creation of the independent Anarchic Communist Youth.[69]

DIVERGENT PATHS

Valadés mirrored the cultural as well as the political upheavals unleashed within the PCM. A vegetarian and theosophist in 1919, he believed in the universal brotherhood of humanity predicated on a supposed "divine spark" latent in every human being. That same year he attended the lectures of Manabendra Nath Roy, the Hindu firebrand in Mexico City, whose discourses on theosophy aimed at propagating communism.[70] A founder of the Mexican Communist party, Roy instilled in his listeners an admiration for Russian literature and the Russian Revolution.

Influenced by a reading of Kropotkin's works and inspired by Lenin and the Bolshevik Revolution, in January 1920 Valadés and his friends founded the Egalitarian Youth.[71] Committed to spreading the egalitarian ideals of Communists as well as anarchists, the Egalitarian Youth became the youth section of the Mexican Communist party under a new name, the Federation of Communist Youth.

As Valadés recalls in his memoirs, from its founding in 1919 to roughly 1924, "the Mexican Communist party was under the influence of anarchism and vice versa."[72] This accounts for its initial toleration of Kropotkin's libertarian brand of communism alongside Lenin's authoritarian brand.[73] With his followers in the Communist Youth, Valadés occupied neutral ground in the increasingly frequent disputes between these divergent tendencies.

After his expulsion from the Communist party, Valadés continued to champion libertarian communism and government by the trade unions.[74] Basically, this was Flores Magón's amalgam of anarcho-communism and anarcho-syndicalism expounded in his two-volume *Semilla libertaria* (Libertarian Seed). So when Flores Magón's name reverberated through the streets of Mexico City during his funeral in January 1923, Valadés and his friends acknowledged him as their mentor.[75]

In August 1924, the CGT sent Valadés, its delegate in charge of organizing refinery workers, to Tampico, where the CGT boasted some twelve thousand members steeped in anarcho-syndicalism.[76] In the Tampico area, the Magonist current held sway over the local branch of the House of the World Worker, which, unlike the original Casa in Mexico City, had rejected the 1915 pact with the Constitutionalists headed by Carranza. True to Flores Magón's credo, none of its members had volunteered to join the ranks of the red battalions against the combined forces of Francisco (Pancho) Villa and Emiliano Zapata.[77] Moreover, in August 1916, when the Casa's headquarters in Mexico City were shut down and its leaders arrested, its Tampico branch had continued strong in alliance with a new arrival, the Industrial Workers of the World.[78] Because the center of the Casa's organizing activities had shifted to the petroleum industry—Tampico at that time was the world's greatest oil-producing region—Valadés turned to the Casa's local branch for help in his organizing work.

Valadés was supported by the local IWW. The IWW's Marine Transport Workers Union had spearheaded the organization of not only Tampico's maritime, dock, and construction workers, but also its petroleum workers.[79] Simultaneously, it had disseminated the credo of revolutionary syndicalism championed by the local Casa. Committed to a "final solution of the labor problem," the IWW's amalgam of industrial unionism, Marxism, and anarchism represented an ideological mix that included the role of a revolutionary vanguard to catalyze worker discontent.[80] The anarchist classics provided theoretical support for the IWW's "final solution" and for its strategy of direct action leading to a general strike and the establishment of rule by trade unions in a "Workers Co-operative Republic."[81]

In Tampico, both the Casa and the IWW had their offices in the same building. "They conducted meetings together and did propaganda work which eventually resulted in the participation of thousands of workers . . . [and] jointly staged strikes around demands for higher wages, better conditions, and union recognition."[82] The Petroleum Workers Local No. 230 and the Construction Workers Local No. 310, both IWW unions, grew to over one thousand members.[83] Besides holding weekly meetings in the industrial suburb of Villa Cecilia (today's Ciudad Madero), they cooperated with the Red Brothers of Villa Cecilia, an offshoot of the Tampico Casa, and with the Equals, an anarchist group dedicated to organizational work for the local CGT.

In September 1924, on a return trip to the capital via San Luis Potosí, Valadés persuaded Librado Rivera (1864–1932), Flores Magón's trusted collaborator, to join him in Tampico. There they agitated among the refinery workers at Mexican Gulf, the Huasteca Petroleum Company, and El Aguila. Supporting themselves by selling copies of Flores Magón's books and other anarchist classics, their success was immediate. The number of local groups grew, as did the "interest in anarchist literature and especially that of Flores Magón."[84] As a result, a majority of workers at the Huasteca joined the CGT.[85]

Following his release from prison in the United States in October 1923, Rivera returned to his home ground in San Luis Potosí. But persuaded by Valadés, in September 1924 he chose Tampico as the seat for his propaganda. Assisted by the Red Brothers of Villa Cecilia, who published the tiny but weighty journal *El Pequeño Grande* (Big Little One), he set up his printing press. The five thousand copies of his monthly *Sagitario*, named after a mythological centaur with bow and quiver, disseminated Magonism among Tampico's refinery workers.[86] He also arranged for the sale of Flores Magón's works in a cheap edition subsidized by the Ministry of Culture. Thus in Tampico, *floresmagonismo* and anarcho-syndicalism were going concerns.[87]

If anybody was worthy of being Ricardo Flores Magón's successor, it was Rivera. The four signatories of the PLM's 23 September 1911 Manifesto had been Ricardo Flores Magón, Librado Rivera, Anselmo Figueroa, and Enrique Flores Magón—in that order. As the editors of *Regeneración*, they had cosigned earlier articles in April, May, and June. Since their names were not listed alphabetically, the ordering tells us that Ricardo was the PLM's top leader followed by Rivera, his close companion and collaborator.

For reasons that are unknown, Enrique never enjoyed his brother's full confidence. In June 1917, Enrique had temporarily disassociated himself from the editorial board of *Regeneración*—again for reasons that are unclear.[88] Later, after Enrique and Librado returned to Mexico from prison in the United States, the first in March and the second in October 1923, Librado would refer to Enrique as the Magonist movement's "last deserter."[89]

This explains why Rivera did not join Enrique in a propaganda tour of Mexico in 1923–1924 and refused to collaborate with him on a common political project. Instead, they followed divergent paths, Rivera remaining faithful to Ricardo's legacy while Enrique charted a new course. Figueroa had died in June 1915, so that after Ricardo's death in November 1922 there were only two survivors of the 1911 Magonist leadership. Thus the movement became divided between Enrique's followers concentrated in Mexico City, Puebla, and Veracruz, and Rivera's allies in the Tampico area, Monterrey, and in the Grupo Cultural "Ricardo Flores Magón." The CGT included both currents.

In a rapid and extensive propaganda tour on his return, Enrique revived his contacts among Magonists by placing himself above their historical division into communists and socialists, extremists and moderates.[90] Calling for a united front of all sectors of the labor movement, he also appealed to the Communist party. Deserters from the Communist Youth were the first to respond, followed by Herón Proal's Sindicato Revolucionario de Inquilinos (Revolutionary Union of Renters), notorious for promoting IWW-type rent strikes and inciting to insurrection in the poor neighborhoods of Veracruz.[91] A member in 1919 of the same anarcho-communist group as Ramírez and Galván, Proal established close ties to the local PCM from January 1922 to May 1923, and then turned over to Enrique the editorship of his journal *Guillotina*. Although Proal's and Galván's communism may be traceable to more than one source, Flores Magón's *Regeneración* was one of them.

Later, other Magonists would follow Enrique's example. In January 1929, the PCM and its peasant organization, the Liga Nacional Campesina (National Peasant League), formed an electoral front with other political forces on the Left. Known as the Bloque Unido Obrero Campesino (Bloc of Worker-Peasant Unity), its candidate for president in the 1929 elections was the Magonist Pedro Rodríguez Triana, veteran of the June 1908 assault on Las Vacas in Coahuila. His program of government demanded the creation of workers' and peasants' soviets, the replacement of judicial power by people's courts, the arming of the peasants, a minimum wage, a ceiling on the salaries of public functionaries, and land and factories for the workers—a social revolution reminiscent of the PLM's 1911 program.[92]

In response to the military uprising against the interim government of Pres. Emilio Portes Gil in March, the bloc resolved on armed resistance against the coup mongers. On the eve of the rebellion's defeat, the bloc further resolved to keep its followers on a war footing. Government repression against the Communists and their Magonist allies, both inside and outside the Communist party, was immediate. The PCM was outlawed and the bloc practically eliminated as a result of government persecution and the arrest of its leaders.

This drove the PCM farther to the left. At the First Conference of Latin American Communist Parties in Buenos Aires on 12 June 1929, the leading Mexican delegate, David Alfaro Siqueiros, argued, to the consternation of the Comintern's representative, Jules Humbert-Droz, that Latin America was experiencing a prerevolutionary situation and that, if the Communists did not take the leading role in the coming insurrections, the bourgeoisie would.[93]

Evidently, the presence of Magonists in the PCM was still being felt, even after they left it or were expelled in May 1929, as in the case of Galván and other militants of the Peasant League.[94] Historians of the Mexican labor movement and of the Communist party have noted the influence of the Magonist legacy during the party's first ten years. This supposedly explains the party's theoretical and strategical mistakes or, depending on the type of criticism, its rupture with the Mexican government and its charting of an independent proletarian strategy.[95] Although the tension generated by the coexistence of Marxist and Magonist currents is perhaps clearest in the PCM's early opposition to becoming an electoral party and to working within the "yellow" trade unions, it resurfaced during the depression of the 1930s, and "there are echoes of this past as late as the 1960s and early 1970s in the PCM's policy of electoral abstentionism."[96]

THE MAGONIST REVIVAL
BY THE INSURGENT LEFT

Armed struggles launched independently of the PCM also played a part in reviving the Magonist legacy. Already in an article dated 6 October 1917, Enrique Flores Magón anticipated a renewal of the armed struggle.[97] Insurrectionary efforts by Ricardo's supporters continued to flare up until 1920, when Gen. Alvaro Obregón overthrew Carranza. But with the installation of a new regime with trade union bureaucrats sharing political power and an agrarian reform under way, the explosive situation of the preceding decades became defused. Not until 1929 would the social volcano again erupt.

It erupted again during World War II, beginning with the violent confrontation between organized workers and the postrevolutionary government of Manuel Avila Camacho (1940–1946), the last of the revolutionary generals to occupy the presidential seat. In the summer of 1941, the government-appointed director of the nationalized factories producing war matériel, Luis Bobadilla, imposed an onerous military discipline on the industry and refused to consult with union leaders on policy matters. After vainly petitioning him to abide by the norms in state enterprises, the Union of Workers in War Industry presented the matter to the secretary of defense, Gen. Macías Valenzuela. When this too failed to produce results, the workers resolved to take the matter directly to the president.

Assembling after work, they marched to the presidential mansion in Lomas de Chapultepec. An aide on the presidential general staff, Col. Maximiano Ochoa, took command of the situation and ordered them to withdraw. When they refused, he ordered soldiers from the presidential guard to fire on the demonstrators. Nine were killed, including the union's secretary, and eleven others wounded in a massacre that engraved on the memories of those who witnessed it the conviction that the government of the revolution had passed into the enemy camp.[98]

According to oral testimony by Valentín Campa, workers' resistance to the new system of presidential despotism—the *neoporfiriato* that installed itself after a lapse of three decades as the successor to the *porfiriato*—dates from this event.[99] But that is not its sole significance. The march to the presidential palace and the demonstration in front of it was not a random occurrence. The day was picked in advance and the action planned by the union's secretary in consultation with the workers. The date chosen for the demonstration might have been any day in September 1941, but in fact it was scheduled for 23 September—the anniversary of the PLM's September 23 Manifesto.

Six months later, on 9 April 1942, a strike by the independently organized workers at the Emiliano Zapata Refinery in Zacatepec, Morelos, was declared illegal.[100] This was the second instance during World War II of workers striking against a state-owned enterprise for defying the norms of workers' self-management. The strike's principal leaders, Mónico Rodríguez on the part of the refinery workers and Rubén Jaramillo representing the cane cutters, both acted under the influence of Flores Magón's *Semilla libertaria*.[101] While Rodríguez got the workers at the refinery to walk out, Jaramillo induced the peasants to stop cutting and delivering cane.

Rodríguez's interest in Flores Magón had been cultivated by his father, a mechanic in Torreón, Coahuila, where Mónico was born in 1919. His father later moved to Tampico and was there recruited into the PCM in 1928 by the charismatic Melquíades Tobías—an organizer of the petroleum workers in the Tampico area. In 1938 Mónico too joined the PCM along with Jaramillo, who dropped out in 1939 when the party began to favor government-management of nationalized industry.[102]

The April 1942 strike at the Zacatepec refinery was the prelude to armed struggle. Successive attempts on Jaramillo's life in February 1943 convinced him that not just the governor of Morelos but also the new president, Manuel Avila Camacho, had become enemies of the people. The counterrevolution, he concluded, had begun.[103]

In response, he revived the Magonist program for a new revolution. Known as the Plan of Cerro Prieto, the concluding seventeenth point acknowledged that, because the Mexican Revolution had been an exclusively agrarian one, a "new revolution should extend its scope of action so that, just as the landed estates were turned over to the peasants, the factories shall be turned over to the workers—no matter what." [104] Every means would be used to implement this peasant-worker program, including a new political party that Jaramillo founded in 1945, the Partido Agrario Obrero Morelense (Agrarian Labor Party of Morelos).

Within three months his uprising launched on behalf of this plan had enrolled in its ranks several thousand *jaramillistas* (Jaramillo's followers). Pursued by government forces throughout the state of Morelos, he continued to elude them for more than a year until his armed struggle ended with a peaceful settlement and government concessions in June 1944. A second armed uprising by Jaramillo in October 1953 also survived government persecution, until it too ended in a peaceful settlement in 1958.

In February 1961 Jaramillo again became a news item because of his systematic campaign of land seizures in the state of Morelos. By then Jaramillo's party had some fifteen thousand registered members.[105] Alarmed by Jaramillo's public support for Fidel Castro and invitation to visit Cuba, the authorities made another, successful, attempt on his life. In May 1962 he and four members of his family were kidnapped from their home and brutally executed. The political significance of his death was not lost on the PCM. It meant that the defense of the Mexican Revolution of 1910–1940 had become synonymous with counterrevolution and that the time was ripe for a "new revolution." [106]

Important as was Jaramillo's revival of the Magonist legacy, it was not the only model of insurrectionary politics within the Mexican Left. The *agrarista* heritage of armed struggle clearly owes more to Zapata and Villa than to Flores Magón. The schoolteacher connection—the tradition bequeathed by rural teachers whose revolutionary Jacobinism shows strong ties to the militant organization of peasant communities—is another important source of ultraradical discourse in Mexico. As red islands in a sea of bureaucratized politics in which the parties of the Left had become enmeshed, the *escuelas normales* (high schools for teachers) are famous for producing *luchadores sociales* (fighters for social justice). Besides the impact of these native traditions on insurrectionary politics, during the 1960s and the 1970s there was the influence of the Cuban Revolution, the cult of Che Guevara, the war in Vietnam, urban guerrilla warfare in the Southern Cone, and the Chinese Cultural Revolution.

There were other heirs to the PLM's legacy. From July 1959 through December 1963, local authorities in the township of Madera, Chihuahua, accused members of the wealthy Ibarra family of murdering two peasants and two schoolteachers and of wounding several others because of some eighteen thousand hectares of disputed property. It was in this climate of violence and intimidation that another schoolteacher, Arturo Gámiz, sought a peaceful solution to the conflict in negotiations with the governor. When these came to nought, he too turned to armed struggle as the sole remaining option.

The debut of Gámiz's guerrillas began in February 1964 with the dynamiting of a bridge on the Ibarra properties, followed in July with an assault on the judicial police who were on the trail of the guerrillas.[107] However, Gámiz is remembered not for these puny assaults, but for his effort to emulate Fidel Castro's July 1953 assault on the Moncada barracks in Santiago, Cuba. Gámiz's major feat in September 1965 was to attack the Madera garrison defended by some 120 soldiers. According to testimony by one of the survivors, the PCM was secretly behind the effort even though it publicly ridiculed the operation as childish.[108]

Gámiz was the local head of the Unión General de Obreros y Campesinos de México (General Union of Mexican Workers and Peasants) with direct links to the Partido Popular Socialista (Popular Socialist party). But his revolutionary creed had little in common with the ossified Marxism-Leninism of the party's caudillo, Vicente Lombardo Toledano. Gámiz separated himself from its leaders over the issue of armed struggle, as did

Oscar González Iriarte, who with five others survived the attack on the garrison and were able to hold out in the sierra between Chihuahua and Sonora until September 1968.[109]

Gámiz's political objectives had less in common with Marxism than with *floresmagonismo*. The immediate target of his indignation was not capitalism, or even imperialism, but "odious inequality."[110] Committed to a final solution to the social question, he looked forward to an imminent and total destruction of the existing social system and to its replacement by a society of equals that would "legally guarantee all the basic necessities and all social advantages, as just and indispensable compensation for the work each contributes in fulfilling the common task."[111] His younger brother Emilio shared his ideals. Pablo Gómez Ramírez, the coleader of the Madera guerrillas, may also have shared them. Noteworthy for his "love of social justice," Gómez had practiced medicine while simultaneously serving as a rural schoolteacher in Flores Magón, Chihuahua.[112]

The date of the assault may be significant. It was originally proposed for the night of 15 September, so that it would coincide with Independence Day and with the anniversary the next day of Father Hidalgo's "Grito de Dolores" (cry for independence from the town of Dolores) on 16 September 1810. But the proposal was rejected for evoking images of the past when the issue at stake was a new revolution.[113] Thus the date was set for 23 September.

By then the PCM had undergone another change of face by nominally reviving its earlier program of a new revolution, which from 1929 to 1935 shared common ground with the PLM's legacy. The party's change of line had been informally approved at its 13th Congress in May 1960. Thanks to it, Rubén Jaramillo rejoined the party in December 1961, after persuading some 220 *jaramillistas* to join the party with him.[114] Initially limited to a democratic revolution aimed at national liberation, the party's new program would later be redefined as socialist as well as democratic. In any case, it did not include a communist revolution.

By the time of the PCM's 14th Congress in December 1963, the Magonist legacy had received another boost with the publication of José Revueltas's *Ensayo sobre un proletariado sin cabeza*. Its author, an old-time Communist since 1930 but expelled in 1943, rejoined the party in 1956 in the expectation that it might be transformed from within. But his continued jibes at the leadership, exacerbated by his thesis of the historical inexistence of a communist party in Mexico, led to a second expulsion in 1960. Even so, the party was not impervious to Revueltas's criticism, so Flores Magón's independent strategy for the proletariat once again came under discussion.[115]

Unimpressed by the PCM's left turn, Revueltas characterized it as win-

dow dressing. The party had degenerated into a mafia of professional bureaucrats, he argued, for whom the existence of the party had become a
substitute for revolution. The essence of this degeneration he summarized
in a formula suggestive of Ignacio Loyola and the Jesuits: "I'd rather be
mistaken *with* the party than be right in *opposition to it*." [116] Despite all the
talk of a new revolution, he believed the 13th Congress had sealed the fate
of the last traces of a critical spirit within the PCM, its last hope of becoming a real communist party.[117] Such was the immediate background to the
organization of Gámiz's guerrillas.

The renewed interest in guerrilla warfare was not just a passing fancy
nor was the revival of interest in Flores Magón confined to the turbulent
1960s. During the 1970s his insurrectional legacy continued to be cited
approvingly by the PCM's new leadership.[118] Although this was mainly lip
service, it helped in recruiting new members who, under Revueltas's influence, had turned to Magonism during the student demonstrations of 1968
and 1971.[119]

Under the impact of the Cuban Revolution and the simultaneous revival of the Magonist legacy, it was not long before two other schoolteachers, acting independently of each other, would take to heart Gámiz's example. Following a massacre in the town of Atoyac, Guerrero, on 18 May
1967, Lucio Cabañas fled to the sierras where he organized his Armed
Commandos of Guerrero and the Peasant Brigade of Justice as the military and judicial arms of a new political party, the Party of the Poor. A
year later, after being liberated by armed supporters from the prison in
Iguala, Guerrero, Genaro Vázquez launched a second guerrilla attempt
under the auspices of an organization renamed in 1968 the Revolutionary
National Civic Association.

As in the case of Jaramillo's uprisings, the army was directed to intervene. It took fourteen campaigns from 1968 to 1974, involving at their
peak some ten thousand soldiers, to root out the followers of Cabañas and
Vázquez.[120] The first campaign placed platoons in most of the towns in
the sierras of Guerrero; the second, in 1968–1969, launched a veritable
witch-hunt with the help of paramilitary forces, arbitrary detentions, kidnappings, torture, and disappearances of civilians suspected of sympathiz-
ing with the guerrillas; the third, in 1970, led to the setting up of "strategic
hamlets" and the incursion into the sierras of whole regiments reinforced
by military and police helicopters, planes, and a network of secret agents
in search of the guerrillas.

Cabañas, inspired by the PCM's 1963 program for a new revolution,
had joined the party and was now in a position to implement the program.[121] But he also acknowledged a debt to a rival legacy. In a tribute
from the sierras on the occasion of Vázquez's death in February 1972,

Cabañas praised the leader of the Madera guerrillas.[122] Survivors of Gámiz's group had been among the first to incorporate themselves into Cabañas's party.[123] The cadres of various urban guerrillas also joined Cabañas. These included remnants of a movement influenced by the ideas of Mao and Kim Il Sung, along with others who took as their models Fidel Castro and Che Guevara.[124] These several legacies combined to shape Cabañas's program for a new revolution. Going beyond the PCM's new program, it was conceived as a *"revolución pobrista,"* a revolution of, by, and for the poor.[125]

Unlike Cabañas, Vázquez was a militant in the Popular Socialist party.[126] He was also interested in land reform. Shortly before Jaramillo was murdered in May 1962, Vázquez interviewed him at the offices of the Cuernavaca newspaper *¡Presente!* in an effort to establish an independent association of poor peasants.[127] Several years later, during a prison stint from 1966 to 1968, he began reading the Marxist classics.[128] By then he had become inspired by Guevara's example and by the writings of Régis Debray, as well as by Jaramillo's struggles in the state of Morelos.[129] About the same time, Revueltas's thesis of the historical inexistence of a proletarian vanguard and insistence on an independent strategy for the proletariat also made a deep impression on him.[130] Vázquez's socialist program stopped short of Cabañas's new revolution, but it was several steps ahead of the nominal revolution sponsored by the PCM.[131]

The controversial question is whether the guerrilla movements of Chihuahua and Guerrero came under the influence of Flores Magón. The line of descent is a tortuous one, but no less credible for its indirectness. According to Armando Bartra, the guerrilla movements of the 1960s "oscillated between the insurrectional style of the 1910 Revolution [*zapatismo*] and the new forms of struggle introduced by the Cuban experience." He adds that Jaramillo's successive uprisings in Morelos responded to Zapata's influence, and that "the insurrectionary groups of Chihuahua in 1965 and of Guerrero in 1967 were the heirs of *jaramillismo*, at the same time that they responded to the influence of the Cuban July 26 Movement."[132] But we have seen that Jaramillo was a professed Magonist, that he championed the interests of workers, not just peasants, and that Zapata too may be counted among Flores Magón's political heirs. Thus there is an indirect line of influence from Flores Magón through Zapata and Jaramillo to Gámiz, Cabañas, and Vázquez.

Flores Magón's influence also resurfaced in the September 23 Communist League, which succeeded in bringing together survivors of earlier armed organizations under a single roof. The origins of the League go back to the 3rd Congress of the Communist Youth in December 1970, when it resolved on a rupture with the PCM. A majority was won over to the position of Raúl Ramos Zavala. It was he who urged an independent proletarian strategy of active abstention in the electoral process, who "attacked the PCM as historically inexistent with arguments borrowed from the vulgar arsenal of a certain Trotskyist critique"—an allusion to José Revueltas.[133] Valentín Campa and Arnoldo Martínez Verdugo attended the congress in an effort to prevent a split. According to Campa's testimony, they argued four nights and four days against Ramos's faction, only to be defeated.[134]

The founders of the league ranked Ramos among the big three of the revived insurrectionary movement in Mexico, alongside Lucio Cabañas and Genaro Vázquez. Steeped in the writings of Trotsky and Mao as well as the classics of Marxism, he was influential in reviving the "old and new anarchism of Bakunin, Flores Magón, and Cohn-Bendit."[135] Under Revueltas's influence, he sought to "recover the real revolutionary theory buried for decades by . . . revisionism, opportunism, and Stalinist bureaucratism."[136] It was Ramos who established links with survivors of the assault on the Madera barracks—the September 23 Movement—from which the new organization took its name.[137] According to one survivor, he belonged to the nucleus of conspirators who planned the assault.[138]

Ramos organized the double-bank assault in Monterrey on 14 January 1972. It ended in disaster with the detention of some comrades, the death of others, and the dispersion of the remaining members. On 6 February, the police caught up with Ramos in Mexico City and killed him, but the guerrillas managed to regroup under the leadership of Ignacio Salas Obregón.[139]

It was Salas's insistence on organizational unity that led to the invitations to other groups to meet in Guadalajara on 15 March 1973, where the foundations of unity were laid in the new umbrella organization— the September 23 Communist League.[140] Efforts were made to recruit Cabañas, but when it became clear he would not be recognized as the league's political head he expelled the league's delegates from his Party of the Poor.[141]

The theoretical guidelines of the league were contained in three mimeographed documents, *Madera I, II*, and *III*, and in the *Manifesto to the Student Proletariat* by the Coordinating Commission of the Federation of University Students of Sinaloa. Holding that the university is a center for the production and reproduction of capital and that the student body is an exploited work force, the manifesto characterized the 1968 student revolt in Mexico City as an aborted proletarian uprising.[142] Because the manifesto added "University" to Flores Magón's somber trinity of "Capital, State, and Church," PCMers scathingly referred to the manifesto as the work of ultraleftists.

Such were the antecedents of an originally promising effort to recover the legacy of Flores Magón and to implement Revueltas's critique of the PCM by organizing an authentic communist league with an independent strategy for the working class. Unlike its predecessors, the league "counted on a large number of adherents distributed throughout most of the Republic, mainly in urban areas."[143] But the pressures of clandestine life and the presence of a militarist current, exacerbated by an apocalyptic messianism derived from Christian sources, transformed it into a gang of robbers, kidnappers, and ransomers.[144] Discredited by the rest of the Mexican Left and targeted by the intelligence services and the police, the league had no future and disappeared from the news by the end of the 1970s.

Did the guerrillas' revival of the Magonist September 23 legacy have any effect on the political mainstream and on the ruling party, the Partido Revolucionario Institucional (PRI)? Although there is no hard evidence, there are scattered suggestions that it did. The "democratic opening" proclaimed by Pres. Luis Echeverría (1970–1976) may be explained as an effort to defuse explosive sectors of the population responsive to the insurgents' propaganda. In part, it may be seen as a response to the guerrillas' symbolic challenge to the PRI's revolutionary rhetoric and failure to live up to it. And it may account for Echeverría's patronage of leaders of the reformist Left who might otherwise have used the armed struggle as political leverage against the government.

Before becoming president in 1970, Echeverría had distinguished himself for his hard line in suppressing workers' strikes and antigovernment demonstrations, and for his reputed complicity in the death of some three hundred protesting students in October 1968—the army massacre that undermined the legitimacy of the ruling PRI in ever-widening circles throughout the 1970s. Consequently, when he was tapped as the PRI's candidate in 1969, there was little to suggest that he would reverse himself in office by moving gradually to the left. Together with escalating student unrest, the emergence of militant labor organizations independent of government control, and a new wave of land invasions in the early 1970s, the armed struggle helps to explain Echeverría's about-turn.[145] The amount of resources earmarked by the president for the state of Guerrero, a hotbed of guerrilla activity and the focus of the government's "dirty war," was designed to neutralize the guerrillas' social base—another indication of possible guerrilla influence.[146]

The 1977 electoral reforms enacted by Echeverría's successor, José López Portillo (1976–1982), added one hundred seats to the Chamber of Deputies reserved for opposition parties and provided a national forum for the Communist party's watered-down program for a new revolution.

Although the PRI's ideological hegemony had been challenged before the guerrillas appeared on the scene, they may have contributed to the creation of a legitimate channel for opposition. Thus the actual defeat of the guerrillas must be weighed against their possible role in delegitimizing the government and compelling it to save face through concessions to the reformist Left—without which Cuauhtémoc Cárdenas's near victory in the 1988 presidential elections would have been unthinkable.

Among the various intellectual currents on the Left, responsibility for armed insurgence must also be laid at the door of José Revueltas's revival of the legacy of Ricardo Flores Magón. That Revueltas was an heir to Flores Magón's composite ideology is the testimony of his daughter Andrea. In a collectively authored prologue to his essay, she describes her father as "one of the first Mexican Marxists to recover and vindicate Ricardo Flores Magón, not as a simple precursor of the Mexican Revolution . . . , but rather as an authentic representative of the proletariat . . . [dedicated to] *preserving, above all, its independence as a class.*"[147] In line with anarcho-syndicalism, Flores Magón represented "the only labor movement in Mexico that gave to strikes the character of real class battles."[148]

Some of the guerrillas Revueltas influenced, however, were not always faithful to this legacy, and he became fully aware of their limitations when they began to exhibit the bureaucratic vices of the PCM. So he began wondering whether Lenin's theory of the vanguard might be at fault. This questioning eventually bore fruit. During the last years of his life he was confirmed in his doubts by a reading of the council communists who had disputed Lenin's conception of party organization—Anton Pannekoek and Karl Korsch, among others.[149]

Preoccupied with the bureaucratization of the Left, Revueltas declared himself in November 1971 in favor of a Magonist-type movement of transition, "functioning through local assemblies and . . . with a leadership that would be provisional and responsive to the principles of self-management."[150] This was the first major break with his Leninist past. As he noted in another revealing statement which fits in well with the new social movements of the 1970s, "A profound study of the events of 1968 would lead us to create a new movement on the margin of the political parties . . . that historically are already demonstrated to be obsolete."[151]

This was a far cry from his earlier view that "anarchism and anarcho-syndicalism had lost whatever influence they had in the labor movement of all countries and had in effect ceased to exist."[152] That may have been true in 1962, but it was no longer so after 1968. *Floresmagonismo* and its program for a new revolution, Revueltas discovered, had acquired a new lease on life.

TWO

THE CONSPIRACY AGAINST THE SUGAR COMPLEX AT ATENCINGO

Yes, I returned to Atencingo in 1938–39 to assist Porfirio, commissioned by Section 72 of the National Sugarworkers Union, to snatch Jenkins's 8,500 hectares and redistribute them among 2,043 peasants in nine villages, a struggle that ended in 1944 only after a prolonged and bloody war. I returned again in 1949 under instructions from the Communist party to recruit new members and to strengthen the existing nine cells in the region. To support myself I proposed to depict the history of the struggles at Atencingo in a great mural. This was my cover during my stay at the cooperative.[1]

There is an informal consensus among students of Mexican labor history that anarchism lost its centrality and that anarchist-oriented labor organizers ceased to play a prominent role after the victory of the revolutionary mainstream and the emergence of strong revolutionary governments.[2] By 1931, even the anarcho-syndicalist CGT had become little more than an organization on paper. However, its eclipse, following that of Mexico's House of the World Worker and of the PLM a decade earlier, tells us next to nothing about the fate of their individual survivors and of the anarchist legacy in general.

In *floresmagonismo* may be found not only an unlikely amalgam of the principal currents of European anarchism, but also a homegrown version of a conspiratorial political-military vanguard. The original version of this vanguard, the PLM, was effectively dissolved in March 1918 when its exiled leaders were sentenced to long prison terms in the United States and their journal *Regeneración* stopped being published. But PLM cadres made common cause with the Bolshevik Revolution in 1917, while in 1919 many of them joined the newly formed Mexican Communist party. For those whose anarcho-communism metamorphosed into anarcho-bolshevism, it was in the role of an informal vanguard that they continued as an underground of anarchist-oriented labor organizers in the postrevolutionary era.

My purpose is to show how this underground operated after 1931, when the CGT ceased being the principal seat of Magonist agitation. David Ronfeldt's *Atencingo: The Politics of Agrarian Struggle in a Mexican Ejido* (1973) is still the classic study of the political struggles in what was regarded as both the largest and the most productive sugar enterprise in all of Mexico from 1930 to 1970.[3] But there are admittedly missing pieces in his mosaic. Although Ronfeldt had direct contact with Atencingo's peasants, he had neither direct nor indirect knowledge of the Magonist efforts aimed at transforming the mill and the hacienda into self-managed bastions of a new revolution in Mexico. Our story focuses on the conspiracy and the conspirators. Based on a series of interviews and an exchange of correspondence with the conspiracy's sole survivor, at that time a militant in the PCM, the following account supplies some of the missing links in Atencingo's political history—one of the thorniest social struggles of the 1930s.

THE SETTING

The town of Atencingo, located in the fertile, river-laced valley of Matamoros in the state of Puebla, lies on a side road approximately halfway between the city of Cuautla, Morelos, and Izúcar de Matamoros. The valley extends in an arc some thirty miles long and four miles wide from the Morelos border to the town of Atlixco, forming part of Mexico's heartland of cane agriculture, sugar industry, and *zapatismo*. It is a fair estimate that between thirty thousand and forty thousand people lived in the valley during the 1930s and the 1940s. Their principal occupation was growing and harvesting cane for the leading industrial enterprise in the area, the privately owned sugar mill at Atencingo.

Ronfeldt's story of Atencingo's politics during the 1930s and the 1940s focuses on the struggle between the peasants and the mill owner, American-born William O. Jenkins. His empire in the valley dates from 1921, when he foreclosed on a loan to become the owner of the Atencingo mill and adjoining hacienda. Through a series of financial power plays, Jenkins forced the big landowners, threatened by expropriation and ruined by the Revolution of 1910–1920, to sell him their properties. Relying on his close relations to both the state and the national governments, he evaded the agrarian reform laws for more than a decade while resisting *zapatista* villagers mobilizing for new land invasions. Thanks to this strategy, by the mid-1920s he had appropriated and centralized under a single management the heart of the Matamoros Valley, embracing eleven haciendas spread over some 123,000 hectares.[4]

Jenkins's mammoth enterprise, the Civil and Industrial Company of Atencingo, comprised all but one of the sugar mills in the valley until, in the middle 1930s, he also acquired title to it. During the Revolution the *zapatistas* had burned the sugar mills to the ground, occupied the haciendas, and chased away the landowners. When cane cultivation was restored in 1921, Jenkins rebuilt the biggest mill at Atencingo and, as he acquired the others, stripped them of their equipment.

The story of the Atencingo sugar complex after 1920 is inextricably linked to Jenkins's financial manipulations and strong-arm methods. One reporter describes him as a "mysterious buccaneer-businessman," a virtual robber baron who by 1960 had amassed the largest personal fortune in Mexico for a foreigner, assessed at between $200 million and $300 million.[5] He hired *pistoleros* (gunslingers) to murder a half-dozen or more labor and peasant leaders who stood in his way. Besides violating Mexican law at will, he enhanced his fortune during Prohibition by illicit sales across the border of contraband alcohol produced at Atencingo as a by-product. After he was kidnapped by two *zapatista* generals in 1919, the U.S. government paid a sizable ransom that he supposedly shared with his captors.[6]

Jenkins was born in Tennessee in 1879. He arrived dead broke in Aguascalientes in 1901. There he "took a job as a railway mechanic for 50¢ a day . . . [until in] 1906, a U.S. missionary group staked him to enough capital to launch an itinerant haberdashery business . . . [after which his] wanderings took him to Puebla, where he went into small businesses [grain brokerage, real estate] and became the U.S. consular agent in the chaotic days following the 1910 revolution."[7] It was as U.S. consul that he profited from his abduction, after which he made a fortune in the sugar and alcohol business.

When Pres. Lázaro Cárdenas (1934–1940) threatened to expropriate his sugar holdings in 1937, Jenkins shrewdly gave the land to the government as a gift. By doing so, he was able to keep the refinery. So profitable was his Atencingo mill that in the mid-1940s he swallowed an entire five million dollars' of bonds issued by the Mexican government's holding corporation Nacional Financiera, after which he lent five million dollars to contractors of the projected four-lane highway from Mexico City to Querétaro, and then offered to lend another eighty million dollars to the government to help finance the superhighway from Mexico City to Puebla.[8]

By 1960 his reported holdings included the Bank of Commerce, finance companies, textile mills, cement plants, an automobile assembly factory, a soap factory, and the largest cinema chain in Mexico, assessed at twenty-six million dollars, not including the value of the buildings.

To this account should be added the image of Jenkins disseminated by his political enemies among the mill workers at Atencingo, who were chased from their jobs and were intent on expropriating him. According to Mónico Rodríguez, who became directly involved in the struggles at the mill, Jenkins raised himself from the lowly position of stoker on the Mexican railways to that of an independent businessman by stealing parts of engines and reassembling them to produce counterfeit money during the unpoliced turmoil created by the Revolution.[9] With the stolen machinery and counterfeit money, he allegedly put together his first textile factory in Puebla. He further enriched himself not only by sharing in the ransom raised by the U.S. government, but also by marrying a rich North American widow. With this booty he began lending money to the Spanish owners to restore the cultivation and harvesting of cane. Thus began the underhanded dealings of the financial tycoon who claimed to love Mexico enough to die for it. With bought-off allies among the state's political bosses, he made a habit of threatening and co-opting local peasant and trade union leaders into doing his will. The most hated man in Mexico in 1960, he had already acquired this reputation when our story begins in 1930.

THE CONSPIRATORS

By "conspiracy" I mean its common usage of planning and acting together secretly or the plan agreed on or the group taking part in a plot. Conspiracies need not be unlawful. Nor do conspiracies always involve deliberate trickery. For there to be a conspiracy, the plan need be neither clear nor carefully thought out. It may be confused, spontaneous, and willful. So the question arises: What kind of conspiracy, if any, depicts the reality of the harvest of hate at Atencingo where there was a long-drawn-out political movement by differently opinioned and rival tendencies, only one of which was Magonist-inspired?

The sole conspiracy was that involving the underground sugarworkers' union at Atencingo in conjunction with outside agitators from the mill in Zacatepec who in 1938 joined the PCM. Paradoxically, it reveals a peculiar blur of carefully planned and willful behavior, of political intransigence and ideological confusion. As late as 1938–1939, the Comintern's executive officers in Moscow complained of anarchist tendencies in the Mexican party, not about factionalism so much as lack of ideological clarity.

One should bear in mind Rodríguez's distinction between full-fledged Magonists, such as himself and Rubén Jaramillo, and Magonists in practice. Although the latter followed in Flores Magón's footsteps, they were mostly unaware of it. Unlike the former, they did not peruse his writings faithfully and repeatedly. They were not, as Rodríguez describes himself and Jaramillo, "LOVERS OF RICARDO FLORES MAGÓN."[10] But as he depicts his other companions, they were "Magonists in essence," which is to say that, "consciously or unconsciously, they always kept present in their practice the communism of Ricardo Flores Magón."[11]

Among the land-hungry *zapatista* villagers, Jenkins came up against Dolores Campos de Espinosa, the famed Doña Lola, born in the same year as Jenkins.[12] She and her husband, Celestino Espinosa Flores, and their son Rafael Espinosa Campos were the principal agitators for agrarian reform in the valley. After her husband died in 1924, their peasant followers chose Rafael to succeed him. But in 1929 Rafael was murdered by assassins on Jenkins's payroll, after which Doña Lola assumed the task of leadership.

Doña Lola and her socialist daughter "helped sympathetic mill workers (many of whom were villagers) organize an independent underground labor union, the Karl Marx Syndicate."[13] She also had sympathizers among the leaders of the workers, but "they went over to Jenkins's side, probably as a result of bribes."[14]

Because of Doña Lola's agitation and petitions for a government land grant, she succeeded in 1934 in divesting Jenkins of some 115,000 hectares representing more than 90 percent of his holdings.[15] Even so, he was left with the choice properties, the irrigated and cane-growing heartlands of nine haciendas plus the Atencingo mill. Not until 1938 did Doña Lola, in conjunction with conspirators at the mill, who had been chased from Atencingo but who had returned as outside agitators, succeed in divesting Jenkins of his remaining 8,000 or so hectares, but again minus the mill.[16]

Even without the cane fields, Jenkins turned the expropriation to his advantage by persuading the governor of Puebla to allow him to include loyal peons as *ejidatarios* and to exclude most of the *zapatista* villagers.[17] So, when Doña Lola became involved in further land invasions without the government's backing, she was imprisoned in Puebla. When released she was hounded by Jenkins and his cronies in the state government until she sought refuge with other exiles in the neighboring state of Morelos. Six years later, she prepared to return to Atencingo in company with other conspirators. But in May 1945, Jenkins's gunmen finally caught up with her.[18]

Seven conspirators were active at Atencingo, all of them Magonists and members of the Communist party.[19] Four of them—Porfirio Jaramillo, Prisco Sánchez, Adalberto García, and Agapito Vargas—belonged to the original conspiratorial cell at the sugar complex. Two outsiders, Rubén Jaramillo and Mónico Rodríguez, later became part of the team. Another outsider but a member of the original nucleus, Francisco Ruiz, recruited the Jaramillo brothers and Rodríguez into the PCM in 1938. Ruiz and Porfirio Jaramillo spearheaded the plot aimed at expropriating Jenkins and establishing an autonomous sugar cooperative. Although Rodríguez has little to say about the personal histories of Sánchez, García, and Vargas, except that they too were recruited into the party, he throws new light on the political careers of the others who plotted Jenkins's downfall.

Francisco Ruiz, the brains behind the conspiracy, was the first to become a Communist. He was already a party activist when Porfirio showed up at Atencingo in 1933. A barber by trade, Ruiz organized the first Karl Marx Syndicate at Atencingo from outside, by preaching Marxism to the mill hands who became his clients—a role he repeated by organizing a second Karl Marx Syndicate at the sugar refinery in Zacatepec in 1938. Rodríguez remembers him as the most politically prepared Communist among them, as moved inwardly by a Magonist essence, and as cultivating this essence in others. While encouraging the other conspirators to join the only political party even nominally committed to communism, he turned the meetings of their party cell into a study group focusing not only on the *Communist Manifesto*, but also on Flores Magón's *Semilla libertaria*.

Porfirio Jaramillo (1902–1955), Rubén's younger brother and Rodríguez's *compadre* (godfather), is singled out as the chief conspirator. He sought refuge at the Atencingo hacienda in 1933 after killing a local *cacique* (political boss) in his home town of Tlaquiltenango, Morelos. Wanted for murder, he changed his name from Salustio to Porfirio, the name he is generally known by.[20] After working as a day laborer on the hacienda, where peasants had yet to benefit from agrarian reform, he and Ruiz began organizing a group of adepts with whom they shared their radical convictions. Their purpose was to organize the first union of mill workers at Atencingo and, in collaboration with Doña Lola, to push simultaneously for the expropriation of Jenkins's lands.

When Jenkins got wind of their plans, his *pistoleros* prepared a series of ambushes that, once again, compelled Porfirio Jaramillo to flee for his life. Returning to his home state in 1936, he became employed at the sugar refinery under construction at Zacatepec. It was there that he joined the Communist party.[21] Although Porfirio was the principal labor agitator at

Atencingo both before and after he returned in 1938, Ronfeldt says nothing about his anarchist proclivities and secret links to the PCM.

Rubén Jaramillo (1900–1962) is best known for his role in organizing the independent cooperative of cane workers linked to the sugar refinery at Zacatepec, for his armed uprisings in Morelos in 1943 and 1953, and for his campaign for the governorship of the state in 1946 and 1952 at the head of his Agrarian Labor party. As already noted, he joined the Communist party in 1938, dropped out a year later, but rejoined it in 1961 with some 220 of his followers.[22]

Rubén Jaramillo was originally a *zapatista* and served as a captain in Zapata's Army of the South in 1917. At Zapata's headquarters in Tlaltizapán he came under Flores Magón's influence possibly through copies of *Regeneración* that circulated there, possibly through Flores Magón's representatives there, possibly through Antonio Díaz Soto y Gama, a former PLM moderate who broke with the reformist Liberal party in June 1912 and, after moving leftward, joined Zapata's forces in March 1914.[23] As a *zapatista* delegate to the 1914–1915 Aguascalientes Convention, Díaz Soto y Gama gave the following account of himself and the other anarchists who represented Zapata at the convention: "Those of us who led the delegation of the South . . . had become saturated with readings and impressions of the French Revolution and . . . the doctrines derived from the anarchist outlook of Kropotkin, Reclus, Malato, and the other theorists of anarchism," not to mention Ricardo Flores Magón.[24]

Rodríguez remembers Rubén Jaramillo carrying in his knapsack a copy of *Semilla libertaria*, both before and after he joined the Communist party. As he outlined his strategy to Rodríguez, it was a socialist and ultimately a communist strategy, but without calling itself "socialist" or "communist." Because he disputed the bureaucratic style and lack of principle of the PCM's leaders, he hesitated to become too closely identified with them. "You know," he later confided to Rodríguez, "in the party there are well-dressed people, like that Dionisio [Encina, the party's secretary-general during the 1940s and 1950s]. I've talked to him, and he already appears to be rich . . . and with more hope in politicians than in ordinary folk."[25]

Rather than the PCM, Rubén Jaramillo preferred an organization controlled exclusively by Magonists. His Agrarian Labor party was such an organization and so was the liberated zone in the Morelos plains of Michapa and El Guarín, following land invasions in February 1960 and again in February 1961. "It was a matter of choosing a region or secret place with some fifty people . . . , of cultivating the land in common and maintaining ourselves by our own efforts," he explained to Rodríguez. "We would begin with a socialism of our own making. . . . In this way, we would be creating an example for others to follow."[26]

Rodríguez was the youngest member of the conspiracy. What were his antecedents? His father, Samuel Rodríguez (1864–1937), was a mechanic in Torreón, Coahuila, and a member of a Magonist club before the Revolution of 1910. When the city was occupied by federal troops in 1913 during the post-Madero dictatorship of Gen. Victoriano Huerta, Samuel had to flee with his comrades to avoid arrest. In danger of being caught and executed for his Magonist ideas, he joined Villa's Division of the North. Mónico credits his father with having built the cannon used by Villa to take the city of Torreón in March 1914.[27]

Returning to his hometown after the disbanding of Villa's army in 1915, Samuel Rodríguez resumed his work as a mechanic on the railroads. In 1920, a year after Mónico was born, he moved to the outskirts of Tampico where he became a pipe fitter for a petroleum company. In 1928 he joined the Communist party but continued to recommend to other workers that they read *Semilla libertaria* and Flores Magón's *Tribuna roja*. He was unemployed during 1929. He then took a job at the El Mante sugar refinery in the state of Tamaulipas. There, in 1934, after being thoroughly versed in Magonism by his father, Mónico became an apprentice mechanic and an activist in El Mante's first union of sugarworkers.

In 1936 Mónico Rodríguez was contracted by the Emiliano Zapata sugar refinery being built in Zacatepec. After the refinery opened in 1938, he helped organize the first union there and simultaneously conspired to set up a producers' cooperative at Atencingo. When Porfirio Jaramillo returned briefly to Atencingo in 1938 and 1939, Rodríguez went with him. Their purpose was to enlist the cane cutters and mill hands in a concerted effort to expropriate Jenkins's remaining eight thousand or so hectares and to redistribute the land among some two thousand peasants in Atencingo and the neighboring villages. Rodríguez describes the struggle as a veritable war culminating in the final expropriation of Jenkins's land and the founding of an independent cooperative of peasants with Porfirio Jaramillo as the new manager.

In 1949 Rodríguez returned to Atencingo under instructions to develop the PCM's organization in each of the nine villages composing the sugar complex. After he became a party professional, he organized another twelve cells at factories in the city of Puebla and a Communist club at the state university, where he recruited faculty as well as students. In 1953 the party transferred him to Mexico City. However, in his effort to reconcile the party's communism with his reading of Ricardo Flores Magón, he increasingly fell afoul of its leadership.

Although the PCM got wind of his Magonism, it hesitated to discipline him because it needed his organizing talents and contacts with workers. Not until 1957 were efforts made to expel him. Determined to fight the charge that he and his close associates were factionalists, he argued that his work for the party had always taken a practical turn, that he interpreted his job with the party as serving the interests of workers directly, that he had kept his party affiliation secret in order to better mobilize them to stand up for themselves, that his disagreements with party policies were over interpretation rather than principle, and that he was not concerned with debating theoretical issues, which he left to the party's leaders. In the end he won his case. But disgusted by the treatment he had received and disillusioned by the PCM's high-handed disregard for mass work, he left the party in 1958.

A clue to Rodríguez's anarcho-bolshevism is contained in a work by Edelmiro Maldonado Leal, a leader of the party in the Federal District from 1950 to 1958, when Rodríguez was a party professional in the capital. In a photographic copy of chapter 8 in a letter Rodríguez sent me on 21 April 1992, he underscored the following passage: "The strategy followed by the unions under the influence of anarcho-syndicalism was called *direct action*, that is, the confrontation between workers and bosses without any intermediary."[28] Such was the strategy of the Magonist vanguard in control of the Communist cell at Zacatepec, which accounts for its flagrant violation of party policy when it led a strike against the government-managed sugar refinery in the middle of World War II.

During the late 1970s the party distributed a 45-RPM record that included on one side a ballad about Rubén Jaramillo followed by a second ballad in honor of Valentín Campa—the party's presidential candidate in 1976. But alongside these idols struggled countless unsung heroes whose names have been forgotten because they seldom if ever made the headlines. They organized workers behind the scenes, leaving the party's figureheads to reap the notoriety and the glory. They did the actual mobilizing and work of agitation, step by step, link by link, day after day, year after year. To ignore their role in the interpretation of Mexico's postrevolutionary history of social movements is to miss the muscles and the sinews. These energizing cadres of the PCM and its fellow-travelers deserve as much attention as its brains.[29]

THE SECRET HISTORY

Having determined that there was a conspiracy at Atencingo, the next question concerns its outcome. Although other forces made their presence felt, did the conspirators have a major role in the expropriation of Jenkins's holdings?

The plot against the Atencingo complex had two immediate aims: first, the organization of mill hands into an independent union that would begin by initiating collective contracts with the mill administration and end with direct action and pressure on the government to expropriate the mill and reorganize it as a workers' cooperative; second, agitation among the landless *zapatista* villagers, resident peons, and migrant laborers on Jenkins's hacienda for an agrarian reform that with government help would transform it into an ejido (peasant cooperative made possible by a government land grant). With the expropriation of Jenkins's properties, with the workers in control of the refinery and the peasants in control of the land, a giant step would have been taken toward implementing the new revolution that had inspired the conspiracy from its start. Although in 1936 the PCM shelved the strategy of making a new revolution in Mexico, the Magonist-oriented conspirators did not.[30] The conspirators were communists, but the communism they professed was not that of the PCM.

The conspiracy evolved through four principal stages.[31] During the first stage, from 1930 to 1935, the conspirators tried to establish an underground union at the mill with the support of Doña Lola while simultaneously aiding her struggle to expropriate Jenkins's immense holdings. The second act, from 1937 to 1939, saw a renewed effort to establish an independent union and to expropriate the properties Jenkins still retained after the agrarian reform of 1934. The third round, from 1945 to 1952, witnessed a further erosion of Jenkins's power in the form of a new government-recognized union at the mill and the restructuring of the peasant cooperative established in 1938 as a genuinely autonomous entity. The final round began with government intervention in the ejido's affairs and the forced resignation of its elected officers in March 1952, followed by renewed plotting by Porfirio Jaramillo to recover control, until the chief conspirators were kidnapped from a hotel in Mexico City and murdered by Jenkins's gunmen in February 1955.

From July 1929 to March 1935 the Communist party was illegal to the point of having to operate underground.[32] Valentín Campa devotes a chapter of his memoirs to the party's clandestine activities during the period when it pushed for a new revolution, a socialist one, premised on a revolutionary-democratic dictatorship of workers and peasants.[33] In order to operate effectively, party organizers had to keep their affiliation secret.[34] This explains the sparsity of the evidence linking the secret cell of communists with the underground labor union at Atencingo.

During the first stage there were some "serious disturbances within the local union," in part because of internal rivalries involving an organizer affiliated with the Confederación General de Obreros y Campesinos de México (General Confederation of Mexican Workers and Peasants) who was eventually murdered, and in part because of "agitation by allies of Doña Lola."[35] Union rivalries played an important role at Atencingo. However, the thorny question concerns the nature and objectives of Doña Lola's allies.

As Rodríguez recalls, Doña Lola and her "socialist" daughter were both secret members of the Communist party.[36] That explains the close relationship between "la compañera Lola comunista" and Porfirio Jaramillo who, incensed by the semislave system weighing on the backs of his companions, struggled to awaken in them a consciousness of their predicament. In this way he gained a group of adepts—Doña Lola's "allies"—who succeeded in establishing the first sugarworkers' union at the mill and its first collective contract. With his adepts, he conspired with Doña Lola to mobilize the peasants into making land invasions and galvanizing the government into granting an ejido.

Manuel Pérez, Jenkins's Cuban-born manager of the sugar complex, however, behaved like a conquistador. Having organized a loyal core of informers among the peasants to spy on Jaramillo, he succeeded in infiltrating Porfirio's group. With the help of another informer he hired an Indian herbalist known as "the Witch" to poison a Jaramillo supporter. About the same time, after he had his accomplices threaten to kill Porfirio and the struggle between the Karl Marx Syndicate and the mill administration reached an impasse, he hired two gunmen to carry out his threats. On his way to work one day, Porfirio noticed that he was being watched by strangers. Fearing an ambush, he mobilized his companions in self-defense and caught Pérez with the hired gunmen by surprise. But the political authorities had been bought by Jenkins, so Jaramillo had to seek recourse elsewhere.

Like Doña Lola, who had been threatened by Pérez, Jaramillo sought to elude his persecutors. But his enemies got wind of his refuge on her adjoining land. Since there was only one way to stop him, Pérez's gunmen continued to lay ambushes. They also succeeded in terrorizing his group at the mill and in undermining the independence of the newly formed union. So, in view of the hopelessness of the situation, Porfirio decided to try his luck elsewhere, among the workers installing the new refinery at Zacatepec. But he was not about to give up the struggle at Atencingo and planned to return.

The second stage began with Porfirio Jaramillo calling on his comrades at Atencingo to join him in constructing the new refinery in Morelos. As they arrived and became employed in the mill's construction, they reorganized their conspiratorial cell and enlarged it with new recruits. After organizing a construction workers' union at the plant, they made plans to liberate those they had left behind at Atencingo. For this purpose, they called a general assembly and petitioned the workers at Zacatepec to assist them in their efforts.

An agreement was reached with the mill's cooperative—at that time self-managed by the workers with Rubén Jaramillo in charge—to send a team of organizers led by Porfirio to assist their brothers in Atencingo. A leave of absence was granted and funds were requisitioned to cover their expenses. At the same time, they obtained the support of Local 72 of the National Sugarworkers Union at Zacatepec and through it the support of the country's largest labor central, the newly founded Confederación de Trabajadores de México (Confederation of Mexican Workers, CTM).

As a by-product of their efforts, Porfirio's comrades succeeded in establishing an independent union at Atencingo, Local 76 of the Sugarworkers Union. More important, they succeeded in pressuring the government to expropriate Jenkins's remaining eight thousand or so hectares, leaving little more than the mill to the owner. Thanks to a presidential decree similar to the one covering Zacatepec, Jenkins's former haciendas were reorganized to become the Ejidal Cooperative Society of Atencingo and Annexes. So, having completed their task, in 1939 Porfirio Jaramillo and the rest of his group returned to their jobs at Zacatepec.

The background to the expropriation is an intriguing one. On 9 September 1937 representatives of the workers and peasants of the Atencingo complex filed an official petition sponsored by the National Committee of the CTM. Socialist-inspired and using the wording of a letter by the CTM's Marxist leader, Vicente Lombardo Toledano, it proposed that "the whole enterprise, that is, the fields, the means of transport, and the factory, be delivered to the workers, who will manage it in a cooperative form, for which the government will set the most adequate procedures."[37] That the prospect of expropriating the mill, not just the fields, won the approval of President Cárdenas is suggested by the government's subsequent expropriation in February 1939 of both the lands and the refinery at the sugar complex of El Mante.[38]

The CTM in 1937 had a vested interest in these expropriations. By then Lombardo Toledano had become a fellow-traveler of the Communist International while the Communist party became "for a while the dominant force in the most important state federations of the newly formed national workers' federation."[39] This inside knowledge adds weight to the testimony of Mónico Rodríguez, the sole survivor of the struggle at Atencingo, that the PCM was behind the conspiracy and that he and the other conspirators kept their party affiliation secret, despite the fact that the party no longer operated underground after 1934.[40]

Porfirio Jaramillo kept abreast of events at Atencingo and in 1939 his brother Rubén visited the complex on behalf of the conspirators. But in a letter to President Cárdenas, Rubén reported that the cooperative existed in name only.[41] His conclusion was based on interviews with members of the ejido. Besides technical questions concerning credit, yield per hectare, and the cost of cutting the cane and hauling it to the mill, he asked about the benefits to the cooperative:

> How much did the *ejidatarios* receive in profit dividends? How many kilograms of sugar did one ton of cane produce, and at what price was the sugar sold by the mill? How much did the *ejidatarios* pay in taxes to the state government? Did they have documents showing they were associates of the cooperative? How many members of the cooperative's administrative council were mill workers? Did the ejido have an efficient medical service, and schools for the children?

The answers, he discovered, showed that the ejido's associates knew virtually nothing about the cooperative. "They only know that they receive their salary [wages], which they earn as peons [not associates] . . . and that their work day is up to twelve hours."[42]

Rubén Jaramillo concluded that the land redistribution at Atencingo had yet to change anything fundamental. In effect, "'neither is there any cooperative or anything that looks like one.'" On the contrary, "'so long as a land distribution such as that in Morelos is not made in Atencingo, it cannot be said that those of Atencingo have a satisfactory life economically . . . [but only] that in Atencingo one man [Jenkins] exploits the rest.'"[43] When his plea to the president fell on deaf ears, the conspirators in Zacatepec once more began to take matters into their own hands.

But there was an inevitable delay. The workers and peasants at the Zacatepec complex began facing problems of their own. Until then elected by the associates, Rubén Jaramillo was replaced by a government-appointed administrator of the cooperative. A major strike by the mill hands in support of the cane cutters in 1942, followed by Jaramillo's armed uprising in Morelos in 1943–1944, interfered with the conspirators' returning to Atencingo until the end of World War II.

Then, in late 1945, the restless and cheated *ejidatarios* at Atencingo organized a commission that consulted with representatives of the Sugar-workers Union at Zacatepec. In line with the strategy of the mill workers at Atencingo, the commission was asked "to invite certain men then active in the Zacatepec region of Morelos—especially Porfirio Jaramillo, the brother of Rubén—to organize and lead them."[44] So Porfirio with his band of exiles from Atencingo returned in 1946 to set matters right. Thus began the third stage of the conspiracy aimed at undermining Jenkins's control of the sugar complex once and for all.

During the 1946–1947 struggle, the government supported Porfirio Jaramillo's efforts to free the cooperative from Jenkins's control. With Porfirio as the newly elected manager in February 1947, his followers finally came to power. But when he installed his cronies in the ejido's appointed offices, he again aroused Jenkins's bitter opposition.[45]

Under Porfirio Jaramillo's leadership from 1947 to 1952, the *ejidatarios* gained legal possession of the lands they had occupied and refused to relinquish since the last land invasion in 1939.[46] Jaramillo initiated a series of reforms that included the purchase of tractors, the building of schools for campesino children, cooperative stores, a casino with pool tables, a machine shop, and a new office building. The mural on an interior wall of the new office headquarters—painted by Rodríguez's team of muralists—depicted Pérez handing a pistol and a purse to the peasants' ejidal representative and Jenkins whispering conspiratorially behind Pérez's back.[47]

Jaramillo's progress in achieving reforms was not matched by the ejido's technical performance, however. On the heels of some initial success in 1948–1949, cane production dropped to unacceptably low levels during the remainder of his administration. This sudden failure resulted less from agricultural and financial mismanagement than from the implacable feud between the cooperative and the mill administration brought on by Jaramillo's reforms at Jenkins's expense.[48] On the one hand, Jenkins's strategy was to make the cooperative fail financially. On the other hand, in reprisal against his obstructionist methods, the *ejidatarios* deliberately reduced the production of cane for the mill while seeking new buyers elsewhere. So Jenkins complained to the government that the ejido was being managed by incompetents, thereby inducing the government to intervene.[49] The upshot was that, physically threatened and forced to resign, "Jaramillo stepped down without attempting to incite the assembled ejidatarios."[50]

The fourth and last stage of the conspiracy dates from Porfirio's resignation in March 1952 to his assassination in February 1955. "Although they had been ousted from office, the jaramillistas [Porfirio's followers at Atencingo] did not give up; instead, they . . . began to engage in vocal opposition and agitation during early 1953, and by mid-1955 they had secured majority support in the ejido."[51] Their overriding objective was the return of the cooperative to the *ejidatarios* through revocation of the 1952 decree replacing self-management with a state-appointed manager.

Meanwhile, Porfirio left Atencingo to lobby in Mexico City against the government's takeover, believing that it violated the 1937 Law of Cooperative Societies. So the struggle continued on two fronts, with Jaramillo pressuring his allies in the government while his top aides filled in for him during his absence.[52] But when the conspirators toughened their opposition and agitated to arouse the *ejidatarios,* Jenkins's *pistoleros* reappeared on the scene. In early 1954 a member of the conspiracy and a Communist party militant, Teodoro Sánchez (not to be confused with Prisco Sánchez) disappeared.[53] His brutally mangled corpse was discovered in June. Then in February 1955, Porfirio's lobbying efforts came to a halt when he and another conspirator, Fortunato Calixto, were abducted from their hotel and cruelly assassinated.[54] Their followers in Atencingo were not disheartened, but the heart of the conspiracy had stopped beating.

Although there are discrepancies in Rodríguez's and Ronfeldt's accounts of the struggle at Atencingo, they may be explained by the fact that Ronfeldt had no idea of the conspiracy afoot since 1930. Despite some faulty recollections, Rodríguez's story adds several missing pieces that draw attention to inaccuracies in Ronfeldt's account. While the famed Doña Lola helped sympathetic mill workers to organize their underground union, she was not their leader. Nor did the impetus for the unionization effort come from the aging Mexican Labor Regional Confederation or from the younger, more radical CTM.[55] It came from a conspiratorial cell of Magonists within the Communist party. By donning the CTM's outer garments and the PCM's underwear, the conspirators fooled the mill hands and the mill administrator at both sugar complexes into believing they were simple labor agitators. As might be expected in what became a protracted political movement, there were other actors not secretly bound together, among them Section 72 of the Sugarworkers Union and the peasants who participated in the mobilizations. Even so, the conspirators played a key role not only in initiating and leading the struggle to expropriate Jenkins's land, but also in determining the outcome.

THE JARAMILLISTAS

Was the conspiracy against the sugar complex at Atencingo an isolated occurrence or does it have some broader significance for a reading and interpretation of Mexican anarchism after the Revolution? I have already noted that the conspiracy was closely linked to the workers at the Emiliano Zapata refinery in Morelos. As part of the legacy of Enrique Flores Magón and the PCM, the conspirators' strategy aimed at implementing the social revolution of 1910–1917 within the framework of the Constitution. However, this first conspiracy contained the germs of a second conspiracy beginning with Rubén Jaramillo's armed uprising in 1943.

As the undertaking of a small minority, conspiracies are sometimes contrasted to popular uprisings. But as Trotsky observed, an element of conspiracy enters to some degree into all insurrections, which are never purely spontaneous and can be foreseen and prepared in advance.[56] Unlike a conspiratorial coup that merely replaces one ruling clique by another, Jaramillo's armed struggle fits Trotsky's description of a conspiracy subordinated to the interests of a mass movement.

Rubén Jaramillo's armed conspiracy had for its goal a new revolution rather than a revival of the old one. Because "the result of the so-called revolution of 1910 is not, not anything like, the triumph of the social revolution . . . there is a need to guide this new struggle to conquer the public power and to establish a government of 'genuine workers on the land and in the factories.' "[57] If we are to believe Rodríguez, the conspirators behind the Karl Marx Syndicate, the land invasions, and organization of a sugar cooperative at Atencingo were inspired by Rubén's high ideals, but disagreed with Rubén about the effectiveness of armed struggle and the need for a new revolution. There were thus two branches of the *jaramillista* movement.

The social movement fathered by Rubén Jaramillo was a by-product of the conspiracy. His followers organized a political party in the state of Morelos modeled on the PLM. Rubén's movement, according to Rodríguez, was Magonist from its inception and remains so to this day.[58] It also effectively merged with survivors of the *zapatista* movement in Morelos.[59] As a synthesis of *magonismo* and *zapatismo*, it owed its conspiratorial strategy to the PLM and its strategy of rural guerrilla warfare to Zapata's Army of the South.

Ricardo Flores Magón had encouraged this convergence. In July 1914 and in a major article in October 1915, he had defended the *zapatistas* against the false charge of clericalism made by anarchists who supported Carranza in the struggle against Villa and Zapata. In 1916 he published in *Regeneración* two of Zapata's manifestos, the Manifesto of Milpa Alta and the Manifesto of Tlaltizapán, and in October 1917 a speech by Díaz Soto y Gama.[60] Said Flores Magón of the *zapatistas*, "we know that those revolutionaries are not anarchists but, if they are not, they do the work of anarchists."[61] By expropriating the lands and factories of Morelos owned by supporters of the ancient regime, they behaved like anarchists. To use Rodríguez's language, they were "Magonists in essence."

Although Zapata stopped short of both anarchism and communism, he did so for reasons of political expediency, as did Flores Magón prior to the PLM's September 1911 Manifesto. Díaz Soto y Gama relates the following story. Presented with a book on anarchist theory by a *zapatista* colonel, himself an anarchist, Zapata read it, after which he said to the colonel,

"Frankly, although I am not altogether displeased by the ideas put forth, I realize that many, many years must pass before they can be put into practice."[62] To the *zapatista* general, Serafín M. Robles, who presented him with several books on communism, he gave a similar reply: "Those ideas seem to me good and humane, but I must tell you that it is not up to us to put them into practice; that will be the task of new generations and must take who knows how many years."[63] So, rather than impose too many goals on his followers and be unable to realize them, he decided not to modify or add anything to his Plan of Ayala that might acknowledge those advanced ideas.

Despite such reservations, Zapata looked on *magonismo* as an ally in his struggle against Carranza. This is evident from his 1915 invitation to Flores Magón to publish *Regeneración* in the territory controlled by his army and from his offer to provide the paper for its publication from the San Rafael paper factory he had expropriated.[64] It is also evident from the traces of Magonism he had already incorporated into the Plan of Ayala.[65] As Enrique Flores Magón depicted the links between the PLM and Zapata's Army of the South, "it should not be surprising that other rebels under different banners are more or less inclined towards anarchism, amongst them the Agrarians [*zapatistas*] . . . who go after the rich, the authorities, and the priestcraft." Because of this ideological common denominator, "Liberals [PLM anarchists] and Agrarians work in conjunction . . . [so] that there are now several communities living practically in accordance with our theories. . . . The Agrarians, by their contact with the Liberals who are mixed up with them in their towns and their 'guerrillas,' forming but one army, must as a consequence become anarchocommunists."[66]

Along with the Communist party, Flores Magón's followers were committed to a strategy of boring from within. They began by infiltrating the liberal movement against the dictator Porfirio Díaz and succeeded in dominating and surreptitiously taking over the Mexican Liberal party. Later, they sent delegates to Zapata's headquarters in an effort to influence the *zapatista* movement. But they operated openly in the House of the World Worker in Mexico City and gained control of its branch in Tampico without any evidence of trickery.[67] In response to the Bolshevik Revolution, they sincerely joined the Mexican section of the Communist International and induced the CGT momentarily to become part of it in 1922. By 1930 all of these organizations had disappeared except the PCM and the CGT. But the CGT would be eclipsed by a succession of government-backed labor confederations, while the PCM had the support of a rapidly growing international Communist movement. So, except for the principled

Magonists in the Federación Anarquista Mexicana (Mexican Anarchist Federation), Magonists sought collective support for a social revolution by joining or making common cause with the Communist party.[68]

The rationale for this strategy was summarized by Ricardo Flores Magón in "The Duty of the Revolutionary," republished in volume 2 of *Semilla libertaria*. The duty of the revolutionary is to make the revolution by joining every revolutionary movement, whether or not it has an anarchist or communist program.[69] His brother Enrique justified this strategy of subterfuge in an article published in Buenos Aires in the anarchist journal *La Protesta* (30 March 1925) by claiming it was dictated by expediency:

> Taking into consideration the people's hostility toward (or, better said, their *fear of*) advanced ideas, we realized how imprudent it would be to reveal our anarchist postulates—imprudence that would have as its result our isolation and our work reduced to nothing. For this reason, our plan was to organize and strengthen the Mexican Liberal party, and then to give it some kind of program (as in July 1906) that would serve us as a pretext for raising the people in arms against Porfirio Díaz. Then, once they were in full armed rebellion, *when the consciousness of strength converts cowards into heroes* . . . , we would present ourselves openly as anarchists in order to direct the armed movement toward a libertarian goal. . . . It was a painful task for us to have to conceal our anarchist identity, to confine our writings to patriotic harangues that left us cold, and to pretend to be politicians when we abhorred politics.[70]

Four years passed under this strict self-censorship until in 1910, on the eve of the Revolution, they gave to their writings a definite anarchist content. But for the timid in their ranks who were already propounding anarchist ideas, they were careful to appear as liberals. This precaution even characterized the manifesto of 23 September 1911, in which their anarchist and communist objectives were openly presented without once using these fearsome words.[71] Not until 1914, when the Revolution was in full swing, the danger of becoming isolated had passed, and their ideas had struck roots, did they present themselves in their true light.

Although by 1925 it had become evident that the Mexican Revolution had not lived up to their expectations, Enrique Flores Magón believed that the social revolution was not over. It had only "taken a nap," so that the same strategy would have to be retraced from the beginning by a new generation.[72] Such was the strategy revived by the Jaramillo brothers a decade or so later.

To this conspiratorial strategy Rubén Jaramillo added preparations for armed struggle. A recourse to arms becomes justified, he believed, whenever repeated attempts on the lives of revolutionaries paralyze their efforts at reform through purely legal channels.[73] Rodríguez maintains that on this score, too, Jaramillo was indebted to Ricardo Flores Magón. As Flores Magón noted in commemoration of the judicial murder on 13 October 1909 of the Spanish anarchist Francisco Ferrer Guardia, "his bloodied corpse proclaims to the whole world that . . . the peaceful road leads assuredly to martyrdom."[74]

Wrote Flores Magón of the fate of the Chicago martyrs in Haymarket Square on 11 November 1887: "Apostles of pacifism, believers in the political action of the proletariat as the best means for achieving economic emancipation, turn your eyes toward Chicago . . . [where] the four graves of Spies, Engel, Fischer, and Parsons proclaim this truth: 'Reason must arm itself.' "[75] To the anarcho-syndicalists who placed their entire trust in the general strike he retorted: "A peaceful strike is like sticking out one's neck for the executioner's axe." Rather than kneel down, one should stand up and return injury for injury, blow for blow, death for death. "So, let blood run in torrents, since that is the price of liberty!"[76]

This was the strategy for mobilizing workers that Rodríguez linked to armed struggle both before and after he become a professional organizer for the Communist party. During the presidential campaign of 1951–1952, he tried to organize a clandestine vanguard within Rubén Jaramillo's movement in Morelos. While Jaramillo was campaigning for governor, Rodríguez warned him that his political allies could be depended on only in the short run. As soon as differences emerged, they might turn against him; his movement needed another organization to resist repression. Only a closed, secret organization, Rodríguez urged, could plan for an armed uprising against the government in the event of electoral fraud or the banning of Jaramillo's political party.[77]

In 1961, following the repression of the massive land invasions led by Jaramillo in the plains of Michapa and El Guarín, Rodríguez reminded Rubén of what happened to Porfirio in 1955. If he persisted in his agrarian reform, he too would be assassinated. Once again, he pressed Jaramillo to go into hiding and to rely on a conspiratorial organization to carry on the struggle. Said Rodríguez, "I have a small circle of friends, politically prepared, so, if I say to them we need to form a new organization led by workers and peasants, they will join it." In this way the idea of creating a really revolutionary organization among close friends arose. "Well, without being altogether convinced, Rubén agreed."[78]

Jaramillo agreed to create a secret political-military vanguard within the Agrarian Labor party. Rodríguez spelled out the details:

In each town we will pick five comrades. For every ten villages we will have a plenary meeting with one or two delegates from each. I will give the explanation and you can add the finishing touches. "Well, comrades, you know the history of *jaramillismo*. . . . We want you to prepare for an uprising, so that you can be as capable or more capable than we. Toward that end, we are going to review and discuss with you the whole history of our struggle. We need to stand up to the enemy. Each of you must acquaint the other comrades in your group with everything you are going to learn from the politically prepared comrades who will come here. It is a matter of having Rubén disappear, so that your only contact with him will be arranged at a given moment. It is a matter of preparing yourselves when we're not here. The plan is to find a cave in the hills to hide Rubén and the other comrades."[79]

Thus Jaramillo's party would become the nursery of a conspiratorial organization preparing for an armed uprising. It was a matter of creating many Rubéns and of raising the level of revolutionary consciousness.[80]

Months passed without Jaramillo's putting this plan into operation. But the subject came up again at his initiative. "'We are in agreement with what you [Rodríguez] earlier said to us about organizing a new clandestine party . . . but I don't have much faith in the members of your political group.' 'Well,' I [Rodríguez] replied, 'I will join up with you, and maybe the others can help us in some way.'"[81] So they began to work together, to travel throughout the state, attending meetings with ten or so peasants in each place, hoping to implement the plan. But before the plan materialized, the judicial police backed by army units surrounded Jaramillo's home in Tlaquiltenango and kidnapped him with his wife and children. The next day they were found dead, some thirty kilometers away.

His assassination in May 1962 was a major blow to the *jaramillista* movement. But he had always been convinced that the struggle for a new revolution would be taken up by others. "They [our enemies] are going to kill me, but you must carry on the struggle, the idea. The idea will not die."[82] On another occasion, he reiterated: "I know they will kill me, but behind me there are others who will take up my cause. There are villagers who know my history, what I and they have suffered and struggled for. This struggle is not over and will go on, generation after generation."[83]

Mónico Rodríguez became a living testimony to that legacy. In a personal tribute to Rodríguez, poet Isaías Alanís says that death did not concern him. What mattered was the resolve to fight with every means available, with books, talk, frenzy, red wine, the strength of centaurs, the gaze of Medusa, to clean the slate and start again.[84]

THREE

RUBÉN JARAMILLO'S PLAN
FOR A NEW REVOLUTION

We know there exists or existed a "Plan of Cerro Prieto" inspired by Jaramillo. . . . There are many accounts—among them those of his wife and of his daughter Rachel, who is still alive—that this document belonged among his papers until the day of his death. From what we know we can infer that this "Plan" followed the grand lines of Zapata's "Plan of Ayala." But we have not been able to unearth said document.[1]

Despite President Cárdenas's ambitious program of land redistribution during the 1930s, when he was succeeded by President Avila Camacho in December 1940 the Mexican countryside still had a sprinkling of large landed estates. "Some 800,000 people were still living on haciendas . . . , more than half the cultivable land consisted of estates of more than 5,000 hectares . . . [while] over 60 percent of the peasants eligible to receive lands had either inadequate parcels or no land at all."[2] In Zapata's state of Morelos the Mexican Revolution of 1910–1917 had been fought in the name of "Land and Liberty," but the structural causes of social discontent remained and traces of the old regime had re-emerged. The revolutionary generals and politicians had amassed huge tracts of land for themselves through the government controls they had imposed on communal lands and peasant organizations. Zapata's principal successor in Morelos responded to the outcome of Cárdenas's reforms in this way:

Is all this what we fought for? We went to the revolution like dogs, not knowing what we were fighting for. I'm a *zapatista*, but we are now discovering that after Zapata's revolution to defend a piece of land, it now seems that we are worse off than before. . . . Formerly, the landowner was an individual and now we are up against a gang of spongers.[3]

The "gang of spongers" refers to the beneficiaries of the new order organized in the ruling party, who were using their political offices to enrich themselves. Meanwhile, the peasants' dependence on government credit and state-financed technical assistance for their traditional Indian village lands, mostly divided into individual holdings, harnessed them to a network of controls that inhibited their capacity for independent political action.[4] Political control over the peasants had been ensured in August 1938 when Cárdenas launched the Confederación Nacional Campesina (National Peasant Confederation) as the sole government-authorized bargaining agent for representing their interests.[5] Its leaders were handpicked by the ruling party and, like the newly established Confederation of Mexican Workers, it became a branch of the ruling party manipulated by the "gang of spongers."

When Cárdenas campaigned for the presidency in 1934, the peasants of Morelos sought his support for a sugar cooperative that would free the cane growers from their dependence on merchants and other intermediaries. Owing to the initiative of local leaders, studies were made and plans laid for the construction of a refinery at Zacatepec. But from the moment that the cooperative began operating in 1938, the government intervened in its affairs, ignoring its democratic statutes and appointing the manager. Because of the huge sums at the manager's disposal, his job soon became political booty and a source of government corruption. So, after having appealed to the government to assist them, the peasants began to resist government encroachment.

As long as Cárdenas was at the helm, peasants in the state of Morelos supported the government and its initiatives. All this changed under his successor. But even before the succession took place, Cárdenas's actions were being questioned. The fact that he had defended Avila Camacho's revolutionary credentials smacked of duplicity. As Rubén Jaramillo, the principal spokesman for peasant interests in Morelos recalled, "while Cárdenas was still president I smelled a rat . . . and now [that] we have not just a stench but a real plague . . . the counterrevolution has begun."[6]

Although Cárdenas distributed more land during his six years in office than all his revolutionary predecessors combined, by 1939 his agrarian reform was in retreat in a shift to the right accentuated by his successor's resistance to the program of land redistribution and stiffer policy toward organized labor. The fact that Avila Camacho was neither the workers' nor the peasants' friend became evident with the crackdown on workers' administration of nationalized enterprises and the massacre of workers in front of the presidential mansion on 23 September 1941.[7] These events were followed by a similar crackdown on workers' and peasants' self-management at the sugar refinery in Zacatepec. The latter sparked a resurgence of armed struggle and the organization of an independent agrarian labor party, this time for the purpose not of reviving the Mexican Revolution and carrying it to completion, but in the name of a "new revolution."[8]

LAUNCHING THE "NEW REVOLUTION"

It was not the first time in twentieth-century Mexico that an attempt had been made at revolution in the Revolution. Was this new call from armed peasants and their worker allies in any way influenced by their predecessors? What triggered it and what forms did the new insurgence take?

From July 1929 until October 1935 the Communist party pushed for a new revolution, a socialist one, based on workers' and peasants' councils tantamount to a revolutionary democratic dictatorship of workers and peasants.[9] But the rise of European fascism prompted the party to adopt a policy of accommodation to the Mexican government and a new line of "putting the Mexican Revolution in motion again." Even so, talk of a new revolution persisted until the party plenum of June 1937.[10]

The call for a new revolution was part of the legacy of Ricardo Flores Magón's PLM, the Communist party's principal precursor as a source of communist ideology unrelated to Marxism and the Bolshevik Revolution. In an essay in *Regeneración* (31 December 1910), Flores Magón noted that Francisco Madero's constitutionalist revolution might put an end to political tyranny, but could not prevent its reappearance with democratic trappings.[11] A strike at its roots in the system of property would have to be the work of "new" as opposed to "old revolutionaries." This distinction became the basis of the PLM's new program in a manifesto issued on 23 September 1911, urging a revolution against capital as well as political and clerical despotism.[12] It was this program that prompted PLM members to support the Bolshevik Revolution during its early years and to call for a united front with the Communists, despite unresolvable differences with the "dictatorship of Lenin and Trotsky."[13]

The peasant-worker movement in Morelos did not appear in an ideological vacuum, but responded to the legacies of the PCM and the PLM. While Communist agitators influenced by Flores Magón's legacy took the lead in organizing the refinery workers at Zacatepec, his legacy also gained a foothold among the cane cutters. The outcome was a peasant movement linked to the interests of organized labor. Its goal was the "new revolution" set forth by Rubén Jaramillo in his Plan of Cerro Prieto.

Besides apolitical expressions of social discontent, state-sponsored land invasions, and spontaneous occupations, peasant movements in Mexico have in exceptional cases taken the form of independent class movements. Whether guided by a Marxist-Leninist party or by a charismatic peasant leader of the likes of Zapata, such movements have addressed the larger issues of social reform.[14] The peasant-worker movement in the state of Morelos from 1942 to 1962 is a classic example.

Rubén Jaramillo was a charismatic leader typical of such a movement, a movement that continued under its own momentum even after his death. In a watered-down version, his land-for-the-tiller movement, according to a somewhat exaggerated account, "came to encompass most of the nation."[15]

Why did workers and peasants follow Jaramillo and risk their lives in so doing? Was it, as he explained, because he always took "the side of the weak and poor against those who oppress and abuse them?"[16]

> People follow me because they have seen me struggle on behalf of the poor since I was fifteen years old, when I joined the forces of my general, Zapata. They follow me because my religion has not let me forget that I am a man and a peasant ... . [because] the more I think about Christ's ministry, the more I feel like a man and the prouder I am of the class into which I was born.[17]

They followed him as the "new Zapata" because his Plan of Cerro Prieto revived the radical agrarian ideology of Zapata's Plan of Ayala. They followed him because they knew he had nothing to gain from his struggle except the benefits it might provide for others, because as he put it, "I am a fanatic in my wish to serve my own kind, and because I have no desire to occupy some public office in order to enrich myself or to feel the joy of power ... because they know that together we are fighting for justice."[18] They followed him because of the self-effacing qualities that made him, according to one account, a precursor of Che Guevara and the Colombian guerrilla priest Camilo Torres.[19] That is why his movement, like theirs, became personified in a proper name.

JARAMILLO'S FIRST ARMED UPRISING

The trouble that sparked Jaramillo's first armed uprising dates to 1938–1939, when workers at the refinery attempted to organize a trade union free of government control. In 1938 Francisco Ruiz, the PCM militant who had helped to organize the first independent trade union at the sugar refinery in Atencingo, began to organize workers in Morelos.[20] Ruiz put together a political study group at the refinery and got it to read and discuss the *Communist Manifesto*. That same year he recruited Jaramillo into the party along with Mónico Rodríguez, a young machinist at the Zacatepec mill.

In April 1942 Jaramillo and Rodríguez joined forces to launch the first strike at the factory—despite the fact that it was formally a cooperative. While Rodríguez mobilized the workers and organized a walkout, Jaramillo incited the peasants to stop producing and delivering cane. But the strike was declared illegal, its leaders were cast in the role of conspirators, and Jaramillo was deprived of his status as a member of the cooperative.[21]

When he continued agitating, the government-appointed manager of the refinery tried first to buy and then to intimidate him. Having failed at both, he met with the governor of Morelos to plot the peasant leader's detention and possible elimination. On 12 February 1943 the state judicial police joined by the manager's hired gunmen lay siege to Jaramillo's house, in vain because he did not return home after being warned of his imminent arrest. Three days later they tried to catch him on the plot where he was cutting cane, but he escaped a second time. A third attempt occurred on 17 February at a bridge he had to cross on the way to work, but his friends alerted him in time.

Jaramillo gives an eyewitness account of his first armed struggle in his autobiography.[22] Fearful for his life and his patience exhausted, Jaramillo turned to armed struggle in self-defense and for lack of any other option. By the end of February he had assembled a sizable force including former-*zapatistas*, who were mounted and moved from place to place. Passing through the villages of Morelos and the border towns of Puebla, he organized popular juntas to distribute copies of his Plan of Cerro Prieto and to explain the reasons for his rebellion. The continual aggressions against the cane growers by the manager of the Zacatepec refinery in collusion with the governor were not the only causes for complaint. Jaramillo also became the rallying point for generalized resistance to military conscription during World War II. He did not oppose military service, but he wanted it to be voluntary and protested the hardships imposed on peasant families when breadwinners were taken from their homes and lodged in military barracks.

In March 1943 he and two hundred of his men began preparations for one of the most audacious assaults in the annals of Mexican guerrilla warfare, the simultaneous capture of the three most important towns in southern Morelos—Zacatepec, Jojutla, and Tlaquiltenango. With the forces under his immediate command he was able to take his home town of Tlaquiltenango, but the six thousand or so men disposed to join his guerrillas dispersed on reaching the other two cities. Nonetheless, he repeatedly eluded capture by the Mexican army and was able to continue roving the countryside and distributing his propaganda.

In May Lázaro Cárdenas, then secretary of national defense, tried to mediate the conflict but to no avail. In a personal message to the guerrilla leader he offered safe-conducts to all, but Jaramillo rejected them as only paper guarantees.

The armed struggle continued until the ambush by government troops at El Agua de la Peña near Alsaseca, Puebla, on 12 December 1943. Although Jaramillo's men escaped with only two wounded, their morale was broken and they had to disperse. This last action was followed by a respite in the armed struggle and an invitation by President Avila Camacho to visit him at the Government Palace for the purpose of ending the conflict.

The interview with the president took place on 13 June 1944 and resulted in Jaramillo's accepting the amnesties and safe-conducts for himself and his followers. Jaramillo asked that the peasants, workers, and employees at the Zacatepec refinery be exclusively charged with its administration. He also asked that the system of forcible conscription be modified to permit the youth to receive military instruction in their own states and municipalities on weekends, without interrupting their labors during the rest of the week. Although the government did not release its stranglehold on the refinery, it modified the system of military conscription. The president also offered to distribute lands in Baja California to Jaramillo's followers. But after visiting the area, Jaramillo concluded that to accept the land would amount to exile without guarantees.[23]

From then until his second armed uprising Jaramillo tried to work within the rules of the political game. With his companions in arms he founded the Agrarian Labor Party of Morelos and in October 1945 agreed to run as its candidate for governor. This party, which soon had close to fifteen thousand dues-paying members organized in twenty-nine municipalities, later established itself on a national scale as the Agrarian Labor Party of Mexico.

Jaramillo's followers who inspected the polls and watched over the final counting claim that he ran away with the election. In 1946 the newspapers momentarily recognized his victory, but subsequently retracted when the official party declared that it had won.

In the wake of the election, Jaramillo's followers were persecuted, kidnapped, tortured, and assassinated by the judicial police and gunmen hired by the manager of the refinery. Under those circumstances an armed clash with Jaramillo's supporters seemed inevitable. In August 1946, in an attempt on Jaramillo's life followed by a shoot-out in the village of Panchimalco just south of Jojutla, the army was called out and he again fled to the hills.[24] He had no intention of leading another armed uprising, but he sought to defend himself by disarming his enemies and replenishing his arms and ammunition.

After that, and until 1951 when Jaramillo again prepared to run for governor, the task of reorganizing the party from hiding was among his chief concerns. But his most important action during this period was the support he gave to the striking workers at the Zacatepec refinery.[25] In 1948, having succeeded in removing the old managerial clique and its hired killers, the workers called on Rubén for help when the new manager resisted their demands and confronted them with gunmen of his own. Jaramillo sent his agents to organize huge assemblies in which workers and peasants together protested the manager's actions. When a series of partial work stoppages failed to produce results, the workers struck and occupied the factory. With Jaramillo's backing they also armed themselves. Federal troops intervened, but bloodshed was averted when the workers surrendered and a compromise was reached.

JARAMILLO'S SECOND ARMED UPRISING

In preparation for the 1952 elections, Jaramillo's party joined the Federación de Partidos del Pueblo (Federation of People's Parties) organized by Gen. Miguel Henríquez Guzmán, who campaigned to wrest the presidency from the official party.[26] But the ruling Institutional Revolutionary party (PRI), founded in 1946 as the successor to Cárdenas's Party of the Mexican Revolution, assured its victory through the use of electoral fraud. Henríquez's supporters were then hounded and persecuted with the objective of breaking up his coalition of popular organizations.[27]

As in 1946, Jaramillo's followers believed he had won the race for governor of Morelos. Poll watchers reported that soldiers carried off the ballot boxes at polling centers where Jaramillo was leading. This accounts for the wave of official terrorism and repression in the wake of the elections and Jaramillo's resolve to take up arms a second time.

Under the new governor of Morelos a rash of political assassinations broke out in which the victims were dumped along the highways as a way of terrorizing the local population. The brunt of the repression centered on Jaramillo and his party. When his protests fell on deaf ears, his delegates met with Henríquez's delegations from the various states and together they resolved to confront the government's violence with a generalized insurrection. Their plan called for a simultaneous armed uprising in the states of Sonora, Chihuahua, Michoacán, Querétaro, Hidalgo, Veracruz, Oaxaca, Guerrero, and Morelos. Jaramillo was partner to the proceedings. The date set for the uprising was 4 October 1953.

Very little is known about Jaramillo's second uprising and its aftermath because he failed to leave an account. In an effort to reconstruct what happened, Juan Vargas and I asked Rodríguez to put us in touch with some of the participants. An interview was arranged with Víctor Trujillo González, a former captain in Zapata's Army of the South and a director of the Agrarian Labor party in the state of Morelos, and with Gorgonio Alonso, who participated in the attack on Cuernavaca in October 1953. Further details were provided by Arnulfo Cano, former chief of police in Jiutepec, Morelos, whose home served as Jaramillo's temporary headquarters, and by Rubén's blood relatives and their spouses, his brother Reyes Jaramillo and wife, María de Jesús Palma Sánchez, in Tlaquiltenango, Morelos, and Porfirio Jaramillo's widow, Aurora Herrera, at her home in Jiutepec. The following composite account of the main events is based on their testimony.[28]

Jaramillo began rousing his people to arms with a re-edition of his 1943 Plan of Cerro Prieto. With the backing of Henríquez's followers in Morelos, he planned to concentrate his forces on taking the capital city of Cuernavaca. A Jaramillo sympathizer with a contingent of 350 men from Guerrero promised to take Jojutla and Zacatepec. *Jaramillistas* from the outlying villages of Alpuyeca, Atlacholoaya, and adjacent towns planned to join him. Approximately a kilometer north of Zacatepec near the village of Tetelapa, some 40 of them waited for the signal to go into action. They waited in vain. Their man from Guerrero never arrived. Later they learned that the plan had been discovered and the uprising had been called off.

A similar situation transpired outside Cuernavaca. On the night of October 3, Gorgonio Alonso at the head of a band of some twenty *jaramillistas* seized the police station in his home town of Emiliano Zapata. From there they marched on Jiutepec, where they also captured the strategic centers.[29] After reaching the outskirts of Cuernavaca, near the town of Atlacomulco, they waited for other forces to arrive before assaulting the penitentiary. While Alonso's group assembled at the southern entrance to Atlacomulco, Jaramillo's men were assembling near the eastern end. The timing was perfect, but through a twist of fate they missed each other.

Meanwhile, other groups of *jaramillistas* had been directed to seize the Government Palace, the offices of the judicial police, the telephone and telegraph exchanges. These reinforcements never arrived. On entering Cuernavaca, Alonso's group ran into federal troops and had to disperse. For three days Alonso hid in a *barranca* (gorge) northeast of the city. Then he took refuge in the nation's capital and did not rejoin his family until five years later—when Jaramillo and his followers were amnestied through the efforts of the new president-designate, Adolfo López Mateos (1958–1964).

For several months Jaramillo remained in hiding. But he emerged at the head of thirty guerrillas to attack the village of Ticumán on 7 March 1954. After a quick trial in the central plaza they executed the town's mayor, the chief of police, and two merchants accused of slicing off the soles of a peasant's feet and railroading him out of town.

Jaramillo then marched south with the aim of taking to the hills near Zapata's former headquarters at Tlaltizapán. On the way his men expropriated the provisions they needed from a local merchant, but in their flight they carelessly abandoned the emptied cans of preserved food. Farther south in the vicinity of El Higuerón, a platoon of soldiers caught up with them but were ambushed before even alighting from their truck. The only survivors were a nephew of the previous governor and the platoon's captain, José Martínez, who was badly wounded. Jaramillo decided to spare their lives, an act of generosity he would afterward regret. The captain got his revenge in 1962 when, after kidnapping Jaramillo, his wife, and three children from their home in Tlaquiltenango, he had them brutally murdered beside the ruins of the ancient city of Xochicalco.

During this second armed uprising Jaramillo moved freely throughout the state of Morelos protected by his followers in the Agrarian Labor party—fifteen thousand of them. These served as his eyes and ears, alerting him to the presence and movements of the army and the judicial police. For a time his men hid out in the mountains of Tepoztlán and Amatlán, in the northern part of the state. Arnulfo Cano, former chief of police in nearby Jiutepec, hid Jaramillo with twenty other guerrillas in his house for almost two months. The quarters were cramped but they served Jaramillo as temporary headquarters. Delegations from different parts of Morelos came to visit him to formulate plans and to discuss strategies for carrying on the resistance against the government. He had another base of operations in Tetelcingo, a few miles east of Cuautla. He also sought to organize sympathizers in other states.

The government did not take Jaramillo's second uprising lightly, especially his kidnapping of Pablo Carrera, a counselor at the Zacatepec refinery, and the refinery's inspector, Angel Abundis, freed after a ransom of thirty thousand pesos. Pres. Adolfo Ruiz Cortines (1952–1958) deployed mechanized units and cavalry supported by artillery and the air force. Bent on exterminating the guerrillas, he offered neither amnesty nor safe-conducts until persuaded to do so by the 1958 president-designate, López Mateos. It was López Mateos who reversed the government's policy by granting an amnesty to Jaramillo and his men, by promising to resolve the problems of the cane growers in his state, and by nominally agreeing to support Jaramillo's project for colonizing the plains of Michapa and El Guarín with thousands of landless peasants.

During the political campaign that preceded his election in July 1958, López Mateos met with Jaramillo for the purpose of getting his support. Persuaded by López Mateos's declarations of solidarity with the peasants, Jaramillo agreed to campaign in his favor. For a brief moment in 1958, he found acceptance among members of the ruling party. But his friendship with the president-elect did not last and by the end of the year it had turned into animosity.

In his appointed role as a special delegate of the League of Agrarian Communities arranged by the president-elect, and in his new job as supervisor of the elections of delegates representing the communal villages (ejidos) in Morelos, Jaramillo again threatened the interests of the political bosses and the manager of the refinery. The ejido delegates could be decisive in ending the usurpation of powers and series of frauds that had transformed the factory's managers into autocrats and millionaires. So Jaramillo aimed his strategy at winning these positions for his followers.

The so-called election of members of the administrative council of the Emiliano Zapata Cooperative of Workers, Peasants, and Employees at Zacatepec violated the most elementary principles of democracy. Its members were not directly elected in general assemblies, but indirectly by the ejido delegates. On an appointed day the manager would invite the delegates to dinner at a hotel, such as the Riviera in nearby Tehuixtla, with plenty of drinks and women, and gifts of money. The next day the manager would ask them to confirm his list of candidates. In effect, the delegates were bribed and their corruption reinforced the manager's corruption—a vicious circle with no escape except through a change of representatives.

After Jaramillo succeeded in placing sixteen of his followers as delegates of the ejido, the manager of the refinery and the governor became alerted to the danger. The alert turned to alarm when Jaramillo publicly supported the peasants' demand for an increase in the price of cane. First, he helped to organize a committee of struggle to defend their rights, then he began preparing a massive assembly to present their demands. When López Mateos learned of these developments, he asked that Jaramillo cancel the proposed assembly. Jaramillo refused to comply.

Then the governor of Morelos sought an interview in which he offered, on the part of the management, a gift of 1.5 million pesos, a residence wherever Jaramillo wished, and the latest-model car—on condition that Jaramillo retire from the struggle. Jaramillo turned down the offer and the assembly convened on the same day, 2 November 1958. The manager was tried in absentia for a series of abuses and errors in administration, for mishandling funds, and for complicity in the assassination of members of the cooperative. Other demonstrations followed while the peasants refused to cut and deliver cane. López Mateos then broke off relations with Jaramillo, who had achieved at least one of his objectives: the old manager was replaced by a new one.

THE MICHAPA AND EL GUARÍN "LAND INVASIONS"

Next to his defense of the cane growers at the refinery, Jaramillo's most important action in support of the peasants of Morelos consisted of his settlement project in the plains of Michapa and El Guarín.[30] Situated at the extreme western end of the state, the rock-covered plains seemed unsuited to cultivation. But because they lay in the basin of the Amacuzac River with possibilities for irrigating them, a group of millionaires planned to convert them into residential farmland. Among the millionaires behind this project were Eugenio Prado, a former manager of the refinery, and former president Miguel Alemán (1946–1952). Cattle ranchers in the area held titles to some of the lands under the false pretext of constituting a half dozen or so communal villages and stood to profit from the project. The rest of the lands belonged to authentic ejidos. But because the cattle ranchers had taken de facto possession, they would not permit the peasants to cultivate them.

When the *ejidatarios* decided to parcel out and cultivate a portion of the lands, they ran into opposition from the ranchers and ejido delegates in the ranchers' pay. At that point, early in 1959, they turned to Jaramillo for help. He agreed after they promised to join a united front with landless peasants throughout Morelos with the aim of settling the entire valley. In this way the project received the backing of his Agrarian Labor party.

In conformity with the prevailing agrarian code, Jaramillo organized a group called the Unified Peasants of Morelos and began negotiations with the Department of Agrarian Affairs and Colonization for establishing a settlement of approximately six thousand families. The projected colony of Otilio Montaño would begin by cultivating twenty-four thousand hectares of virgin land to be parceled out in lots of four hectares per family. Some 80,000 pesos in contributions were raised to have those lands surveyed and their boundaries demarcated by the Department of Agrarian Affairs, and another 150,000 pesos to "persuade" González Lascano, a high functionary of this department, to do his job and to have the project legalized.

Afterward, two assemblies were convoked with the representatives of the local ejidos and the owners of the uncultivated lands according to the requirements of the law: one on 17 May and the other on 23 August 1959. The peasants supported the project but the cattle ranchers refused to participate in the proceedings, thus ceding to Jaramillo and his followers the legal right to occupy the lands.

In February 1960, the first occupation occurred involving some one thousand landless peasants, eight hundred of whom were armed. They began the work of clearing rocks and building houses. But the ranchers countered with a campaign of intimidation aimed at expelling them. Under pressure from the ranchers, the head of the Department of Agrarian Affairs appealed to Jaramillo to remove his people until the process of legalizing the settlement could be resolved. Jaramillo and his followers complied but when some of the peasants stayed on, the ranchers took over, burned down their houses, and drove the peasants out.

Shortly after Jaramillo withdrew his people, the Department of Agrarian Affairs, subsequently renamed the Secretariat of Agrarian Reform, reversed its earlier decision favoring the project. Jaramillo then attempted to interview President López Mateos (1958–1964), but the president refused to see him. A year passed and Jaramillo's followers became impatient with the legal obstacles and decided to reoccupy the lands. In February 1961, a second land "invasion" began led by six hundred of the three thousand peasants enlisted in the project. Others soon joined them. Gorgonio Alonso assembled a truckload of peasants from Emiliano Zapata, Arnulfo Cano, another truckload from Jiutepec. All across the state peasants belonging to the Agrarian Labor party descended on the plains of Michapa and El Guarín. This time the army intervened to eject them.

Jaramillo did not give up the struggle to found his colony and continued pressing in Mexico City for a legal resolution. But by then his project had become a threat not only to the big landowners in the area, but also to the federal government. Jaramillo and his peasants had succeeded in questioning the government's commitment to reform and the basis of its popular support. By choosing to operate within the legal system, he had exposed the government's hypocrisy and resistance to social change. That he had twice won the election for governor in Morelos might be disputed, because only the government had access to the final count, but nobody could deny the peasants' right to land under the Constitution and the provisions of the agrarian reform.

The objective circumstances that led to the *jaramillista* movement were not peculiar to Morelos. They included corruption in the public and private administrations of the sugar refineries, open robbery in weighing and paying for the peasants' cane and rice, cultivators without land and land without cultivators, political gangsterism on the part of state authorities, and systematic repression of the people's leaders by hired gunmen, the judicial police, and the army. But while these conditions were present elsewhere, the subjective conditions were not. This explains why Jaramillo's movement did not spread beyond the states immediately bordering on Morelos, and why only in his state a broad movement of peasant self-defense caught fire. What Morelos had, but the other states did not have, was a strong *zapatista* tradition for revolutionaries like Jaramillo to build on. Jaramillo had at his disposal what other agrarian leaders lacked: a people imbued with the collective experience and ideology of resistance to government repression. This legacy, of which the people of Morelos are the principal heirs, received a new infusion of blood from his Agrarian Labor party.

THE MASSACRE AT XOCHICALCO

Jaramillo is remembered not only as a second Zapata for championing the landless peasants of Morelos, but also for the brutal massacre that ended his life and the lives of other members of his family. He had long been a political nuisance to the government and by 1962 had become a major liability. So the political authorities plotted to "disappear" him.

Jaramillo had soiled the populist image of the left-of-center president. He had disobeyed López Mateos's orders not to intervene in the dispute at the Zacatepec refinery, and he had refused to wait for the president's authorization before settling the plains of Michapa and El Guarín. He also threatened to embarrass the government in connection with Pres. John Kennedy's proposed visit to Mexico in June 1962. He planned to ask for credits from the Alliance for Progress to promote the economic development of his settlement and had enlisted thousands of peasants in Zacatepec to petition the American president for aid on the day arranged for Kennedy to visit the refinery.

The political authorities also fretted over Jaramillo's projected trip to Cuba at the personal invitation of Fidel Castro. There they expected him to receive not only economic aid for his colony, but also military training for his supporters. On his return to Mexico he could become an even worse headache for the government. His charismatic personality and simple but fiery speech might mobilize the peasants to armed resistance. With his experience as a guerrilla leader, his intimate knowledge of the terrain in his native state of Morelos, and the unconditional backing he enjoyed from the peasants, he was in a position to lead a movement of national liberation.

At that time the international political conjuncture favored the emergence of guerrillas throughout all of Latin America. In January 1962, at the historic meeting in Punta del Este, Cuba was expelled from the Organization of American States. A week later, on 4 February, Fidel Castro replied with the *Second Declaration of Havana*, exhorting the Latin American people to armed resistance against U.S. imperialism. Under those circumstances, it should hardly cause surprise that Jaramillo stood out as a dangerous threat to Mexico's ruling party.

Jaramillo's increasing identification with the Cuban Revolution was cause for positive alarm. In April 1962, in a public meeting in Cuernavaca's *zócalo* (central plaza), he openly expressed his support for Fidel Castro and Cuban socialism. This was not an isolated act. Early in 1961, anticipating a Yankee invasion like the one that occurred at the Bay of Pigs, he and Mónico Rodríguez had organized several meetings to express solidarity with Cuba. We know that he was planning to visit the "Alligator Island," because Rodríguez's wife, Adalberta, had gone to Zacualpan in the state of Mexico to get the necessary documents for his passport. Later, in November of that year, she made a trip to Mexico City to solicit the return of Jaramillo and 220 of his men into the ranks of the Communist party. A month later they were accepted.

Evidently, the official party considered Jaramillo to be a far more dangerous man in 1962 then it had in 1943 and again in 1953, when he actually led movements of armed resistance. Since there were now reasons to believe that his troublemaking was directed mainly against the government, the government seriously questioned whether he had a right to live. The first attempts on his life had come from gunmen hired by the manager at the refinery at Zacatepec, with the help of the judicial police and the governor of Morelos. Only later had the army become involved in a supporting role. In the only attempt that would prove successful, the initiative would come from the federal government.

On 23 May 1962 Jaramillo's house in Tlaquiltenango was surrounded by a group of sixty soldiers and members of the judicial police who had arrived in two army trucks and accompanying jeeps. A machine gun was placed at the entrance and another in the rear. When Jaramillo resisted, the soldiers broke into the house and seized him. Because his wife and three sons insisted on going with him, they too were forced into a waiting car. Hours later their bullet-riddled corpses were discovered near the ruins of Xochicalco.

Who had given the order for his execution? Capt. José Martínez led the surprise attack supported by Heriberto Espinosa, head of the state's judicial police. An official investigation of the crime led to the temporary detention and questioning of Martínez, after which he received another promotion. (His first promotion had come in reward for earlier actions against the *jaramillistas*.) Months later, in the village of Telolopan, Guerrero, near the border of Morelos, the two of them were kidnapped and questioned by Jaramillo's supporters concerning the real perpetrators of the crime. Before being executed, they were tortured to the point of confessing. The orders for the assassination had come from the attorney general of the republic, Fernando López Arias, from the secretary of defense, Gen. Agustín Olachea, and from the president's private secretary, Humberto Romero.[31]

A confession extracted under duress lacks credibility, but Jaramillo's daughter Raquel had escaped from the house on that fatal day to seek the help of the town's mayor. He refused to intervene because, in his words: "We cannot do anything, it is an order from the district attorney's office in Mexico, and everything is according to the law."[32] Reporters from the newspaper *La Prensa* later discovered that ten agents of the federal police under orders from the district attorney had in fact gone to Tlaquiltenango for the purpose of arresting Jaramillo.[33] So the confession is more credible than it might otherwise appear.

The indiscriminate murder of members of Jaramillo's family was a massacre in miniature—like that in front of the presidential mansion in September 1940. It added to the pattern of police, paramilitary, and military ambushes that would continue through the 1960s and into the 1970s and nourish a revival of the armed struggle independent of the *jaramillista* movement. The local peasants have engraved it onto their collective memory. Says an anonymous ballad from Morelos:

> He was a simple man,
> A man without fault,
> He was Rubén Jaramillo,
> A second Zapata.
>
> People of Tlaquiltenango
> Witness to his murder,
> Will remember to tell it
> At the hour of vengeance.

THE PLAN OF CERRO PRIETO

Jaramillo's Plan of Cerro Prieto, which he began distributing in March 1943, became the program not only of his first and second armed uprisings, but also of his Agrarian Labor party. In testifying to its importance, it was revived in February 1960 and 1961 in connection with his land invasions in the plains of Michapa and El Guarín. However, none of the 1943 copies appear to have survived. Those members of his family and close associates whom I interviewed confessed that they had either burned their copies or buried them in long-forgotten places.[34] Virtually all of the plan's later editions have also disappeared. The one in my possession is dated 28 November, but the year is missing. Entrusted to me by Rodríguez's son-in-law Renato Ravelo, it provides the single most important clue to the ideology of the *jaramillista* movement.

THE PLAN OF CERRO PRIETO, TOWNSHIP OF TLAQUILTE-NANGO, STATE OF MORELOS.
TO THE PROGRESSIVE FORCES OF MEXICO:

Those who support and make up the REVOLUTIONARY NATIONAL JUNTA with its seat in Cerro Prieto, Township of Tlaquiltenango, Morelos, in the exercise of our class rights, make known to the citizens of this country the following PLAN, based on the considerations that are expressed herein:

FIRST: That the Mexican people, during their long revolutionary journey from 1810 to our own day, have declared themselves against tyranny.

SECOND: That the Constitution of 1917 legitimated the concern that inspired the revolutionaries of the PLAN OF AYALA, among others, who saw in it the fulfillment of their most cherished ideals.

THIRD: That this Constitution has been trampled on in recent years by men in public office who have used their power to commit the crime of high treason against the country, seeing that to maintain and enrich themselves in the government they have had to resort to violence that undermined the people's right to freely elect their rulers.

FOURTH: That the local and federal authorities, fruit of the corrupted political monopoly of the PRI, conspiring with the perverse leaders of the trade unions and peasant associations, are preparing again to make a mockery of democratic principles by imposing another president of the republic during the next six years.

FIFTH: That all monopoly is anticonstitutional and antipatriotic. Nonetheless, the milk, bread, flour, sugar, electrical, and metallurgical industries— all of them—are monopolized and, if by some strange quirk anything remains, brutal exploitation has not even left us any pigsties. Because the UNION OF SCAVENGERS is controlled by a monopoly, poor Mexicans do not have a right even to garbage.

SIXTH: That these monopolies are, in addition to being anticonstitutional, organized by foreigners who are only interested in amassing wealth in order to export it to their own countries, and that the government, in order to even the score, has decreed the devaluation of our currency. In this way, Mexico has been converted into a supplier of raw materials and into a consumer of industrial goods, giving rise to want and inflation that become worse every day.

SEVENTH: That the government is not absolute. Nonetheless, it behaves like a despot and totalitarian by imposing authorities, governors, deputies, senators, magistrates, etc., by increasing taxes in order to enrich itself and also to maintain a swarm of bureaucrats (parasites of money and of the public), sheltered by the Judicial Statute and Law of Immobility. It permits the exploitation of natural resources, as in the SAN RAFAEL AGREEMENT, but it does not allow the villages, even on their own properties, to cut down a single weed.

EIGHTH: That these proceedings take place with such ill will that, if we do not defend our rights, the government imposed on us now and in the future will go on treating the people as a real enemy. This government is a long way from protecting the people's rights precisely because it is not a government of the people.

NINTH: That the Revolution flaunted in this way has created a new class of rich people who are at the same time generals, governors, deputies, senators, men of influence, householders, monopolists; these people, in connivance with foreign companies sheltered by the "Good Neighbor Policy," exploit the worker in the city and the countryside to the utmost degree.

TENTH: That these abuses in the public domain are only a small reflection of the bourgeois and capitalist regime that has Mexico in its clutches but ought to disappear.

ELEVENTH: That there are revolutionary chiefs in this country who are trying to make a new revolution, but whose program, if they have any, we ignore. Therefore, we have to proclaim the present one.

TWELFTH: That the distribution of land in individual parcels has contributed to the exploitation of man by man, has added to the traffic in hunger, has provoked disorganization, and has caused the failure in part of the national agrarian program, which has not achieved its goals. Consequently, these parcels must be reorganized in a collective form, putting an end to the "protected zones" whose owners are chiefs of operation, military commanders, governors, senators, former presidents of the republic, and gentlemen farmers, so that they may be turned over to the villages whose ejidos are too small.

THIRTEENTH: That agriculture is a decisive factor in the life of the people and must be stimulated with machinery, fertilizers, etc., produced inside the country, which requires according to this plan the immediate establishment of a heavy industry that can manufacture all the machines the people need—locomotives, trucks, buses, planes, sewing machines, typewriters, tractors—and all that currently comes to us from foreign markets and naturally results in an economic bloodletting in our country of millions upon millions of pesos that we greatly need to spend here. In order to achieve this objective we shall proceed to the expropriation of the electrical industry.

FOURTEENTH: That the Constitution has not been observed for the following reasons: although Article 28 prohibits monopolies, Article 4 guarantees "free trade," so that a private merchant or purchasing agent for the government can appeal to it for protection, as do all monopolists and intermediaries; the same is true of the producers of alcoholic beverages, whose "industrial freedom" is inviolable. This leads to the conclusion that the first twenty-nine articles of the Constitution are only a dead letter, because in practice they have permitted the libertinism of the press, the clergy, the capitalist bourgeoisie, to the point of traffic in "justice," all to the disadvantage of the country and particularly of the peasantry, which in spite of everything that is said continues to live in the most frightful misery. Consequently, the Constitution should be immediately revised, so that it may become a practical law and not a bloody trick. For example, there should be a decree forbidding the production of alcoholic beverages, the result of which would be to end drunkenness and to free the country from all its dismal consequences.

FIFTEENTH: That the result of the so-called Revolution of 1910 is not, not anything like, the triumph of the social revolution—considering what we have seen from the preceding observations—so that there is a need to guide this new struggle to conquer public power and to establish a government of "genuine workers on the land and in the factories," a National Council of Workers that would be born from below, that would be the administrator of the public wealth, that would renew itself periodically, confiscating the riches and stately homes acquired in the shadow of the Revolution in order to turn them over to the poor or to benevolent societies, while new population centers are established in healthful surroundings.

SIXTEENTH: That foreign trade has been and continues to be unfavorable to Mexico, which makes it imperative that our money should be revalued, that the sale abroad of basic necessities and raw materials should be suspended, and, if there are surpluses after all internal needs are met, that these should be sold to or exchanged with the country that will pay most for them, which is to say that exchange should occur on the basis of reciprocity.

SEVENTEENTH: That the increase in the workers' wages has been illusory in practice and has even served as a pretext to raise the prices of basic necessities, bringing increased want so that the worker can never get along with what he earns and must always ask for a bigger increase in wages, hurting without intending to hurt the peasant on the ejido to the extent of betraying the peasant slogan "Land and Liberty." Consequently, this problem must be resolved immediately, so that the worker may see that the country's improvement does not rest on a nominal increase in wages but on the disappearance of entrepreneurs, monopolists, and intermediaries, big and small, who in their eagerness to become rich quickly make the articles of prime necessity pass from hand to hand before reaching the consumer, exploiting step by step the worker whether on the farm or in the factory, which explains why the peasant's product turns on his own misery. This is to say that the Mexican Revolution was exclusively an agrarian one, and that it is necessary that this new revolution should extend its scope of action so that, just as the landed estates were turned over to the peasants, the factories shall be turned over to the workers—no matter what.

BECAUSE OF WHAT HAS BEEN SHOWN AND ESTABLISHED, IT SHOULD BE RESOLVED AND IS RESOLVED:

FIRST: The disavowal of the present legislative, executive, and judicial powers, both federal and local, with the exception of those identified with this plan.

SECOND: The REVOLUTIONARY NATIONAL JUNTA declares before the nation and the entire world that it makes the PLAN OF AYALA its own plan with the additions mentioned in the following points of resolution for not having been fulfilled in their totality. Taking into consideration that the people are heeded only when they take up arms, it will struggle alongside them until it secures the victory of the present plan.

THIRD: As an additional part of the PLAN OF AYALA, we make the clarification that the lands, mountains, and waters that have been transferred or in the future shall be transferred to the villages will be governed by the collective system in conformity with the regulation that will be expedited for that purpose.

FOURTH: By virtue of the fact that the Mexican people are exploited with respect to articles of prime necessity—sugar, bread, milk, cloth, electricity, fertilizers, machinery, etc.—those industries will be nationalized and administered by the workers themselves, without losing sight of the need to establish a heavy industry for manufacturing tractors, trucks, and all the machinery required for the development and progress of a civilized people.

FIFTH: Once the revolution is victorious, the Junta of Revolutionary Chiefs, assembled in a Constituent Congress, will map out the new constitution of the republic according to this plan.

MEXICANS! Come join the ranks of the Revolutionary Movement of the People! Do not respond with indifference to the anguished call of the home-

land! The afflicted native land expects each one of its sons to do his duty!
Be on time for the historic encounter with destiny!

"MEXICO FOR THE MEXICANS"

Cerro Prieto, Tlaquiltenango, Morelos, 28 November 19——.

Signed: Rubén M. Jaramillo

DATING THE PLAN

Cerro Prieto (Dark Ridge) consists of a range of hills approximately two
kilometers south of Tlaquiltenango, Jaramillo's hometown, on the east
side of the road to Lagunillas. The plan took the name of the hills where
Jaramillo presumably formulated it. His autobiography, whose narrative
breaks off early in 1947, relates that he was hiding in the village of San
Rafael in June 1943 when a cavalry detachment arrived in search of him.
Failing to extract any information from the townspeople, the lieutenant in
command chided an assistant of the municipal government: "What? You
don't know what plan Jaramillo is fighting for?" The assistant replied:

> Look, Mister Lieutenant. . . . About four months ago Jaramillo passed
> through this village followed by eighty men and left some documents called
> the "Plan of Cerro Prieto," and the simple truth is that we have seen he is
> right, that the people are learning something, and that it is possible that his
> ideas will spread throughout the country.[35]

Considering that Jaramillo did not have an armed force at his disposal
until he was joined by a contingent of twenty-five men on 21 February
1943 in La Era, Morelos, followed by two other contingents on the same
day from Santa Cruz and San Rafael, we may date the original plan as
having been formalized during the last week of February or the beginning
of March 1943. Thus the 28 November plan cannot be the original one, if
only because its reference in Point 4 to the "corrupted political monopoly
of the PRI" dates it after the ruling party was reorganized and renamed
in 1946.

What, then, is the year of the 28 November plan? The further reference in Point 4 to the ruling *camarilla*, "preparing again to make a mockery of democratic principles by imposing another president of the republic
during the next six years," indicates that the country was near the end of
one presidential term and the beginning of another on 1 December.

Another clue is provided by the "devaluation of our currency" referred to in Point 6. Ruling out the first two devaluations by President Cárdenas in 1940, the next devaluation, by Pres. Miguel Alemán in 1949, resulted in a loss in value of the Mexican peso from 4.85 to the dollar to roughly 8 pesos. This was followed by Pres. Adolfo Ruiz Cortines's devaluation in 1954, which lowered the exchange rate to 12.50 pesos. Since there was no devaluation during President Avila Camacho's term of office, the options may be narrowed to the approaching end of Alemán's term in 1952 or of Ruiz Cortines's term in 1958.

Ruiz Cortines was elected in July 1952, but he did not assume office until 1 December. The reference in Point 11 of the Plan to "revolutionary chiefs . . . trying to make a new revolution, but whose program, if they have any, we ignore," is clearly to the leaders grouped around General Henríquez, who were preparing for an armed uprising because of the electoral fraud, the massacre by government troops of his followers in downtown Mexico City on the eve of the elections, and the systematic persecutions that ensued. Further references in the plan to the Revolutionary National Junta and to the Revolutionary Movement of the People are to Jaramillo's insurrectionary organization, which emerged as an integral part of Henríquez's conspiracy.

Although the insurrection was not launched until October 1953, it had been brewing since July of the previous year. In brief, the plan must be dated *after* the devaluation of 1949 and *before* the installation of the new president on 1 December 1952, with a view to the armed uprising of 1953. The date of this second and revised edition of the Plan of Cerro Prieto may be established accordingly as 28 November 1952.

COMPARISON WITH THE 1961 *IDEARIO*

The Plan of Cerro Prieto was Jaramillo's basic plan of action. Although the plan was updated in 1952, the new plan bears the same name and, like Jaramillo's original program, is an exhortation to "Revolution."[36] That the 1952 plan continued to guide his struggle is evident from his 1961 *Ideario*—a sketch of his political principles. The *Ideario* appears in an appendix to Froylán Manjarrez's *Matanza en Xochicalco*, published together with Jaramillo's autobiography. It consists of thirteen points based on an interview with Jaramillo in February 1961 on the occasion of his second land invasion in the plains of Michapa and El Guarín. While reproducing the substance of his 1952 plan, it consists only of the journalist's notes. Let us see how they compare.

POINT 1: To perform an extensive work of orientation, of open organization among the people that will be firm, courageous, and diligent, toward the end of duly preparing them, once and for all, so that they resolve to seize political and economic power from those who for so many years have kept it unlawfully for their own exclusive advantage or personal enrichment.

POINT 2: To follow up this work with the immediate and effective political, economic, social, and cultural liberation of the Mexican people, taking as a guideline an effectively democratic and popular system.

POINT 3: To proceed without delay to the total nationalization of all the sources of national wealth that are now in the hands of a few bad Mexicans and foreigners, exploiters, and usurers.

POINT 4: To turn over immediately, and without the crafty, antiquated, and corrupt bureaucratic system of paperwork, all the barren and empty lands, whether they be small holdings or uncultivated ejidos; to turn over water and mountains to peasants who ask to use them, furnishing them with indispensable credit.

POINT 5: The development of agriculture and the mechanization of farmwork, the development of industry, transport, domestic and foreign trade, the establishment of markets for agricultural and industrial products—but without the intervention of voracious intermediaries who make life costly and burdensome for the people—and the total abolition of monopolies of whatever type.

POINT 6: The equitable and effective distribution of the national wealth by means of which the people's welfare may improve in the shortest time possible.

POINT 7: The education of the people must be easy, quick, and beneficial in order to overcome the fatal ignorance that, despite the many schools, weighs on them because of the deceit and ill will of those who are better qualified.

POINT 8: That all the knowledge and progress of science be placed at the disposal of the people and not be used to exploit them.

POINT 9: That an active campaign of orientation and organization be launched among workers and peasants in order to achieve with these forces, and with greater revolutionary effectiveness, the quick and lasting triumph of our social longings and objectives.

POINT 10: To combat energetically and quickly all the centers of vice, extortion, and their sources of support—because these are a determining factor of the misery, disgrace, and immorality suffered by the people—and to convert each center of vice into an effective center of culture.

POINT 11: To struggle for a new constitution that will be easier to understand and to apply in view of our present conditions; at least to reform the one we currently have.

POINT 12: That the federal and local governments proceed to lower the taxes currently paid, that they suppress the tolls charged on the highways, and that they search for some other source of state and federal income in order not to burden the people's pocketbooks.

POINT 13: The complete disbanding of the present army as a professional force that has always opposed the people's longings for work, prosperity, and happiness, a mercenary force serving the big landowners, industrialists, local bosses, and politicians imposed on the people by those in the government who have represented only the plutocracy, and because this army has been charged with machine-gunning peasants, workers, and the people whenever they demand better conditions of life. And that arms must be placed in the people's hands for the purpose of organizing an effective national defense.[37]

The *Ideario* is unquestionably socialist in its demand for the complete nationalization of Mexican industry, the expropriation of all foreign-owned monopolies, and the collectivization of agriculture. But it also suggests a communist component in the determination to seize political and economic power from the political bureaucrats and technocrats in charge of the public sector "who for so many years have . . . [used it] for their own exclusive advantage." As an implicit demand for workers' self-management and peasant self-sufficiency, the *Ideario* supports the 1952 plan for promoting nationalized enterprises and cooperatives managed by ordinary workers and peasants instead of experts or professionals. Its principle of power for the people likewise coincides with that in the earlier plan aimed at replacing the federal government with "a National Council of Workers [genuine workers on the land and in the factories] that would be born from below" (Point 15 of the Plan of Cerro Prieto). Accordingly, the *Ideario* calls for the "complete disbanding of the present army as a professional force" and its replacement by the people in arms (Point 13).

Where, then, do they differ? Unlike the 1952 plan, the *Ideario* envisions a prior stage of peaceful and legal accumulation of forces in preparation for the forcible seizure of power. Because it puts off a final solution to the social question, it may strike the superficial reader as a program of reform rather than revolution. But implicit in its call for a new constitution is a violent confrontation with the old one. This suggests that Jaramillo was preparing a third armed uprising in response to an anticipated new wave of repression—a surmise confirmed by Rodríguez's testimony.

Two conclusions emerge from these comparisons. First, the fact that Jaramillo's 1943 and 1952 programs call for a new revolution and bear the same name suggests that the differences between them are negligible. Second, the fact that the 1961 *Ideario* reaffirms the objectives of the 1952 plan suggests that it too is an adaptation of the Plan of Cerro Prieto.

SIGNIFICANCE OF THE PLAN

That the 1952 plan bears the same day and month as Zapata's Plan of Ayala suggests that it was cast in the same mold. But was Zapata's plan its principal source of inspiration? Although Jaramillo's autobiography conveys this impression, his biographer believes otherwise. Recording among other things his interview with Jaramillo in 1958, Raúl Macín presents a composite picture of Jaramillo as a *zapatista* inspired by repeated readings of the Bible. But Rodríguez claims that Jaramillo's political principles were inspired mainly by Ricardo Flores Magón. If Rodríguez is right, his interpretation should serve as a corrective to the prevailing stereotypes of Jaramillo as a new Zapata and as an evangelical precursor of the guerrilla priest Camilo Torres.

That Jaramillo was a champion of Zapata's radical agrarianism is the image he gives of himself in his autobiography. While informing the reader that he became a Mason in 1931, he says next to nothing about the religious roots of his ideology and effectively conceals not only his role as a Methodist minister, but also his early membership in the Communist party. The only hint that his appeals to "land and liberty," "social justice," and "social liberation" might have transcended Zapata's peasant ideology is his reference to "our revolutionary ideology" in a context in which "our" clearly includes workers as well as peasants.[38] As an anonymous pamphlet on Jaramillo's life and struggles notes, "he had participated in the Revolution and knew that its failure was due in part to the division between workers and peasants achieved through the connivance of *carrancistas* and *obregonistas* [the political coteries headed, respectively, by Venustiano Carranza and Alvaro Obregón] . . . , and that without a worker-peasant alliance any attempt at social revolution was doomed."[39]

The only full-length biography, Macín's *Jaramillo: Un profeta olvidado* (1970), acknowledges that there was more to him than the popular image of a new Zapata purveyed by the peasants of Morelos. His voice was that of a biblical prophet for whom Christ's example was paramount.[40] But what about his communism? In January 1960 he is reported to have said at a meeting of his followers: "My entire political project is inspired by the Bible, so that if there is a similarity between it and some communist ideas, it is nothing more than that. . . . I have never been and will never become a communist."[41] But that was sheer cover-up. Unknown to Macín,

Jaramillo had been a card-carrying member of the PCM in 1938–1939, a long-guarded secret unknown even to some of his closest followers. Nor did Macín know that he had rejoined the party in 1961—this time with some 220 of his followers but again secretly—a fact that did not become public until the secret was "declassified" by the party in June 1962 on the heels of his assassination.[42]

The communist dimension to Jaramillo's ideology became further evident with the 1978 publication of Renato Ravelo's *Los jaramillistas*. As a collection of testimonials by survivors of Jaramillo's armed struggles, it makes uneven reading. The sources are anonymous, understandably so in view of government repression. Nonetheless, recalling the armed land invasions of 1961, one interviewee remembered Jaramillo as saying, "Here the system of governance will be of a socialist type, all for one and one for all; everybody will work and everybody will have rest."[43] What is this if not Flores Magón's principle of equal burdens and equal benefits, the principle underlying the PLM's communism?

At about the same time, Jaramillo cautioned, according to another testimonial, that "there is no need to say socialism or communism," that is, to describe his system of governance for the occupied lands in such frightening terms.[44] Was this another cover-up? If so, it suggests the influence of Flores Magón, who had planned to make his new revolution under the protective mantle of the Mexican Liberal party.[45] If we had been honest, wrote Flores Magón, who would have listened to us? So, instead of calling themselves anarchists, his followers continued to call themselves "liberals" during the course of the Revolution, "but in reality . . . [went] on propagating anarchy and carrying out anarchist deeds."[46] Rodríguez believes that this was also Jaramillo's strategy.[47]

Had it not been for my many interviews with Rodríguez and my familiarity with his speech patterns, I could not have spotted his testimonial in *Los jaramillistas*. The following is the crux of his account of the sources of Jaramillo's ideology.

It happened in those discussions of a political character [in 1938–1939] that Jaramillo carried under his armpit the books of Flores Magón, *Semilla libertaria* and other incendiary booklets he was studying. It was on those books that he founded, shall we say, his politics. He was a religious person . . . but he read Flores Magón, and we began to lend him Marxist books. At that time discussions began of greater profundity, shall we say, until gradually our group of workers began attaching itself to Rubén and he began understanding many things, but always with the prescience of not compromising himself too much, [since] he always tried to preserve his political independence.[48]

Historians of twentieth-century Mexico have only recently begun the complex task of assessing Flores Magón's influence on worker and peasant movements since the Revolution.[49] That there was a communist vanguard with a communist ideology that did not fit the Marxist-Leninist mold did not bode well for the ever-watchful PCM, which dismissed it as ultraleftist. Yet the party came under Magonist influence and converged on Magonist ideology during the period from 1929 to 1937, when the call for a new revolution was first taken seriously by the party's leaders. And in a toned-down version, the same call reverberated during the 1960s and the early 1970s, when it reappeared on the party's agenda.[50]

Those with a personal stake in the Mexican Left would do well to heed the comments of José Revueltas, a former Communist party militant and one of the few beacon lights on the Left to have assessed positively the current that resurfaced in Morelos from 1942 to 1962. If both the Mexican proletariat and the peasant movement are without a vanguard, it is because, in his words,

> the Communist party, reflecting the scholastic mold in which it was formed, . . . does not acknowledge the positive contribution made by the great anarcho-syndicalist mass movement to the theme of working class independence. . . . It formally recognizes the need of a worker-peasant alliance, but in fact separates the agrarian movement from the labor movement for two reasons: (a) it does not understand that what must be encouraged and developed is the independence of the labor movement; and (b) it does not understand the class content of the governments of the Revolution and leaves in their hands the hegemony of the entire process [of social change].[51]

In the Plan of Cerro Prieto one finds a corrective to these two costly and mistaken judgments that account for what Revueltas called the "historical inexistence of a party of the working class in Mexico."[52] It was the policy of "unity at any cost" with the self-perpetuating governments of the Revolution and the policy of endorsement of the ruling party's initiatives that were responsible for the party's loss of independence under Cárdenas and under the new system of presidential despotism that surfaced after 1940.[53] As early as 1938, those policies prompted the PCM to reverse itself on the issue of workers' self-management by welcoming government control of nationalized industries as preferable to the chaos of industrial democracy.[54] The party's policies also distanced it from the budding popular resistance to the government's veiled dictatorship and from Jaramillo's armed struggles in the state of Morelos. Indeed, uncritical acceptance of

Cárdenas's Party of the Mexican Revolution and then of the PRI's revolutionary nationalist credentials so discredited the Communist party by 1959 that, having lost some of its best cadres and being reduced to a mere rump, it could no longer make a reasonable claim to being a "real party of the working class." [55]

FOUR

THE RESURGENCE
OF GUERRILLA WARFARE

The year 1962 brought not only the death of Rubén Jaramillo and the eclipse of the *jaramillista* movement, but also a revival of the Magonist legacy. The revival began with the publication of José Revueltas's *Un proletariado sin cabeza*. Inspired by "the torch proudly held aloft by revolutionary and socialist Cuba" and disgusted with the Communist party for stifling internal criticism and expelling him as a disruptive influence in 1960, Revueltas set to work to unmask the party's claim to being a communist party.[1]

Shortly afterward, the party abandoned its defense of the Mexican Revolution for an independent strategy aimed at a new revolution. In 1963 it adopted a program nominally committed to socialism through a democratic revolution of national liberation, a turn to the left that would later open the door to armed struggle.

What made the difference was the challenge presented by the Cuban Revolution. From a liberal and a democratic revolution against the unconstitutional regime of Gen. Fulgencio Batista, Fidel Castro's July 26 Movement had evolved into a movement toward socialism under the auspices of its successor, the Integrated Revolutionary Organizations. Founded in July 1961, this broad front was replaced in February 1963 by the United Party of the Socialist Revolution, and subsequently by a new Communist party committed to the simultaneous construction of both socialism and communism.

Under the influence of this change of course sparked by the Bay of Pigs invasion in April 1961, the Communist party with other forces of the Mexican Left in August founded the short-lived Movimiento de Liberación Nacional (National Liberation Movement, MLN). Although the MLN did not have a socialist program and barely survived the 1964 presidential election, in spreading the ideology of Cuba's leftward turn it visibly transformed the Mexican Left.[2]

The MLN's importance lay in its efforts to unite the Left in solidarity with the Cuban Revolution. This meant solidarity with other Latin American revolutionaries attempting to replicate the Cuban experience. In diffusing *castrismo* and *guevarismo* (the ideologies of Fidel Castro and Che Guevara), the MLN simultaneously gave a boost to their domestic equivalent, the legacy of Ricardo Flores Magón. The upshot of this confluence of Mexican and Cuban communism was a resurgence of the armed struggle in Mexico. Initially modeled on Castro's July 26 Movement's struggle against Batista, it evolved along the lines of Che Guevara's guerrilla war in Bolivia and the urban guerrilla struggles in Uruguay and Argentina.

Initially, the armed struggles of the 1960s were grounded in peasant self-defense mobilizations led by rural school-teachers under Cuban influence via the Communist party and by the MLN. Afterward, they were shaped by the student movement, again influenced by Cuban ideology transmitted mainly by the Communist Youth, the MLN having disappeared from the scene.

Were the principal guerrilla leaders, Cabañas and Vázquez, Magonists in essence, as Rodríguez contends?[3] As we shall see, they were the bearers of a peasant legacy of direct action, insurrectionism, and agrarian radicalism. Guerrilla warfare is a form of direct action; it is an anarchist strategy. Launching an insurrection before all the legal channels of redress have been exhausted is an anarchist strategy. Reliance on grassroots organizations and peasant movements of self-defense to instigate agrarian reform is an anarchist strategy. So these diverse features of the Magonist legacy shared a common denominator with Castro's and Guevara's *modus operandi* and with the resurgence of guerrilla warfare in Mexico.

These were not the only features shared by Cuba's new revolutionaries and their Mexican counterparts. Like Flores Magón, both Castro and Guevara sought a shortcut to communism that would not have to wait until the construction of socialism. Rather than an expression of "petty bourgeois idealism," said Castro on 13 March 1968, the aspiration to equality is a sign of "real communism."[4] One of the salient features of Cuban communism has been the effort to overcome not only bourgeois exploitation, but also distinctions of wealth and poverty. Like the communism of the Atencingo conspirators, the communism that inspired Mexico's guerrillas was not that of the PCM.

THE COMMUNIST PARTY CHANGES COURSE

In response to Nikita Khrushchev's report on the crimes of Stalin at the 20th Congress of the Communist Party of the Soviet Union in February 1956, a profound discontent swept over the lower and intermediate cadres of the PCM. As the "Resolution of the Party Conference in the Federal District" (19 September 1957) explained the principal root of this disaffection, after thirty-eight years the party continued to lead a rickety existence on the margins of the political process, so that it "not even remotely corresponded to the influence of a real vanguard party of the working class."[5]

A personality cult of the party's general secretary, bureaucratic excesses, and the absence of internal democracy rounded out the series of complaints. Who was to blame? The answer given by the conference was that the party's leadership, including the Central Committee, was primarily responsible.

Because of the party's mistakes, many of its new members had chosen to abandon it or had ceased to be politically active, while those who criticized the leadership were personally censured and subjected to severe sanctions. Meanwhile, additional errors were being committed by those impatient to reform the party's structure. As the Conference Resolution noted in response to the leadership's repeated violations of the norms governing party conduct, "several comrades in the Federal District took the mistaken road [of organizing factions] . . . outside regular party channels."[6]

Mónico Rodríguez and Edmundo Raya headed the list of those who, because of their disruptive influence and headlong criticism, had reputedly threatened the party's unity. On 3 August 1957, after they were directed to desist from such activities or face the consequences, sanctions were applied against them by the Committee of the Federal District.[7] Their paychecks were withheld and they were suspended from their party posts. But neither one had the opportunity to defend himself, so the conference lifted the sanctions for having violated due process in matters of party discipline.

The party's internal critics wanted it to become a real vanguard. Pressured by them, the conference called on the leadership to acknowledge its mistakes and to forge a Democratic Front of National Liberation against the big bourgeoisie in league with foreign interests. Described as an electoral front, the proposed bloc of four classes consisting of workers, peasants, petty bourgeois, and bourgeois producing for the national market aimed at overcoming both the party's isolation and the government's political monopoly.

The party's change of line, however, failed to satisfy Rodríguez, Raya, the "Karl Marx" cell, and Revueltas's "Friedrich Engels" cell in the Federal District. The PCM began to move in opposite directions: one, under the leadership of the Central Committee; the other, under the sway of the Federal District Committee and the party's "young Turks." Two opposed strategies were at stake, that of the Central Committee, which believed in the defense and continuity of the Mexican Revolution as the most effective means of reaching socialism, and that of the District Committee, which called for direct action and a decisive rupture with the Mexican Revolution.[8] Thus, confronted by the teachers' strike in 1958 and by the government's confrontation with the striking railway workers, the Central Committee opted for a compromise while the District Committee upheld the workers' intransigence.

Although the party's 13th Congress (May 1960) ushered in a change of leadership and a victory for the renovators, by then Revueltas had lost faith in the PCM. It was not enough that the 13th Congress had reestablished the norms of internal democracy, vindicated the memory of Hernán Laborde (who had been expelled with Campa in 1940), and readmitted Campa and his followers into the party.[9] Though there was talk of a "new revolution," it had yet to be defined as a socialist one.

From 1957 to 1960, precisely when the party was opening itself to a renovating current, Revueltas criticized it for not going far enough. He thereby failed to recognize, wrote Campa in retrospect, that the PCM was still the most experienced political organization on the Left with the greatest possibility of benefiting from that experience.[10] Yet Campa credited him with making common cause with the party during the tumultuous days of the student rebellion in 1968. Despite their political differences, Campa always respected him as a person and as a revolutionary. The esteem was mutual. When his book appeared in June 1962, Revueltas sent Campa a copy dedicated to "the great fighter . . . whom, despite political differences, I will always consider to be an unquestionable hero of the working class in our country."[11]

In the years following the 13th Congress, the new leadership began to amend the party's strategy. In considering the lessons of the teachers' and railway workers' strikes of 1958–1959, the PCM arrived at some startling conclusions: first, that it was impossible to launch a struggle for union democracy against the entrenched labor bureaucrats without confronting the Mexican government; and second, that the party's work in the trade unions controlled by the state had to be carried out in secret.[12] Ironically, these were the theses put forth by Rodríguez and Raya on the eve of the party conference in August–September 1957, and by Revueltas on the eve of the 13th Congress in 1960.

The party's shift to direct action, which opened the door to armed struggle, was a belated victory for Rodríguez. Even as a PCM professional, he had consistently violated party practice by operating underground. During the teachers' strike in April–May 1958, he had concealed his Communist credentials under the guise of a simple *padre de familia* (family head). In that capacity he had brought the parents of schoolchildren and their striking teachers together in an umbrella parent-teachers association with a secret revolutionary objective. He had proposed and implemented a strategy of direct action rather than negotiation with the government and had mounted an iron guard in defense of the illegal takeover of the inner patios of the Secretariat of Public Education.[13]

During the railway workers' strike that began in June, he continued to operate secretly in violation of party directives. After taking a job as a mechanic in a railroad workshop, he organized party cells in secret and violated party directives by conspiring with Campa and other expelled comrades.[14] When the party got wind of his activities, it intervened directly in the strike in the person of the then general secretary, Dionisio Encina. It thereby lost its camouflage while bringing on the wrath of the railway union's boss, Luis Gómez Zepeda, and undoing most of Rodríguez's work.[15]

Not until the party's 14th Congress in December 1963 was its proposed new revolution defined as a democratic, agrarian, and anti-imperialist one. However, the PCM failed to break with its earlier reliance on a bloc of four classes in which the assigned role of the national bourgeoisie contradicted the latter's real role as an appendage of imperialism.[16] Only several years later, at the party's 15th Congress in June 1967—Campa places the date even later, at its 16th Congress in 1973—did the party acknowledge that the national bourgeoisie no longer had any revolutionary potential.[17] Thus, the party's 1963 reliance on a bloc of four classes gave way to a new strategy based on a worker-peasant alliance with the petty bourgeoisie against the entire bourgeoisie and implicitly against the prevailing capitalist system in Mexico.[18]

When the 16th Congress convened in October 1973, the PCM was ready for still another program, this time in response to the burgeoning student movement, the armed struggle, and the government's savage repression of both.[19] Instead of a democratic revolution against the vestiges of feudalism and the new imperialism, the first of a two-stage movement leading to socialism, the "new revolution" was redefined as an organically combined "democratic and socialist revolution."[20] It would begin as a political revolution aimed at the conquest of power by the proletariat and its allies. Following the establishment of a revolutionary state based on democratically elected councils and a unicameral popular assembly with executive and legislative powers, it would then expropriate the big capitalists and introduce workers' self-management in nationalized industries.[21]

Although the succession of new strategies from 1960 to 1973 avoided all direct and explicit calls to armed struggle, they implicitly justified such a struggle by their repeated exhortations to a "new revolution" modeled on the Cuban example. "After completing its democratic and anti-imperialist tasks, the Cuban Revolution became transformed into a socialist revolution," declares the 1963 program. "Its example exerts a powerful influence over the Latin American peoples and their revolutionary forces, it teaches that a united people can defeat imperialist oppression, defend their independence against all the attacks of the North American aggressors . . . and move toward more advanced stages of social development. This is precisely what the Cuban Revolution exemplifies for the Mexican people."[22]

The change in programs suggests a Mexican adaptation and assimilation of the armed strategy of Fidel Castro's February 1962 "Second Declaration of Havana." Says the declaration: "In the antifeudal and anti-imperialist struggle it is possible to bring the majority of the people resolutely behind goals of liberation which unite the spirit of the working class, the peasants, . . . the petty bourgeoisie, and the most progressive layers of the national bourgeoisie . . . [into] great social forces capable of sweeping out the imperialist and reactionary feudal rule."[23] The rhetoric and goals of the declaration anticipated those of the 1963 program: a democratic front of national liberation based on a bloc of four classes as the prelude to a democratic government of national liberation.[24]

The party's 1973 program marked another step toward armed struggle in calling for "permanent revolution."[25] No longer were "two revolutions required to reach socialism . . . in two separate stages," but only a single "uninterrupted revolution."[26] The earlier program was faulted for having exaggerated the vestiges of feudalism in the countryside and for having misconceived the role of the national bourgeoisie as a revolutionary force.[27] Contrary to previous depictions of the Mexican bourgeoisie as "democratic," the 1973 program characterized it as "despotic." Although the Mexican Revolution had begun as bourgeois and democratic, it had changed into a bourgeois, despotic revolution under Presidents Obregón and Calles.[28]

What accounts for the change in programs? The PCM's brief flirtation with a strategy of armed struggle was fed by the traditions of despotic presidentialism, peasant insurrectionism, and anarcho-syndicalism that silently and insidiously led the party to adopt a policy of active electoral abstention.[29] Its shift to the left responded to the violence and repression of the years from 1968 to 1973 and to the need to stem the flight of cadres to the underground armed struggle movements because of the party's premature abandonment of secret and clandestine work.[30]

Besides the government's repression of the 1968 student rebellion, the "international movement based on the experience and conquests of the world proletariat, . . . in particular those of the October Socialist Revolution in Russia, the Chinese Revolution, the Cuban Revolution," also accounts for the change. As the 1973 program indicated, Mexican revolutionaries should "gird themselves to make the highest contribution of which they are capable to the world revolutionary movement, by making the revolution in Mexico."[31] The leftward turn of the Cuban Revolution in the middle and late 1960s had struck a sympathetic chord among PCM militants. Socialism in a single Latin American country is possible, Castro had argued, adding that even communism is possible by building a sector of free goods that promised to include housing, clothing, food, medicine, education, and recreation beginning with children and the aged.[32]

In never losing sight of communism and always endeavoring to be guided by it, Castro influenced the PCM to do likewise. Declares the 1973 program:

> As its highest objective, the project [for a new revolution] holds forth the following: to end the division of society into social classes, and therefore all social and political inequalities that emanate from this division; to create a new society in which each person is able to fulfill his capacities, in which the organs of coercion are replaced by communist self-management, . . . and in which society is governed by the communist principle "from each according to his capacity, to each according to his needs."[33]

Thus the example of the Cuban Revolution contributed to reviving vestiges of Magonism latent in the party.

Even after the party reverted to an electoral solution in 1977, it did not give up its rhetoric of a new revolution.[34] The idea of a new revolution had struck a popular chord during the student rebellion of 1968 and, as part of the lingering heritage of *floresmagonismo*, would remain in vogue until the hotly contested presidential election of 1988.[35]

Chafing under Revueltas's criticism, the PCM endeavored to become an authentic proletarian vanguard. But its new leaders never understood the full import of his critique and mistakenly charged him with "liberalism" and with wanting to liquidate the party.

> From his first interventions in the August–September Conference, Revueltas set forth his liberal conception of democratic centralism, according to

which the party's leaders would be obliged to suspend their work during periods of discussion in order to coordinate the party's diverse tendencies. Then, after he was voted down, he intervened with his well-known "thesis" concerning the "historical inexistence of the PCM," which placed him in the camp of liquidationism.[36]

Although the PCM charted a new course bordering on armed struggle, the changes failed to satisfy Revueltas.

THE NATIONAL LIBERATION MOVEMENT

The PCM's 1963 program for a democratic revolution of national liberation recapitulated the August 1961 program of the broader-based National Liberation Movement (MLN). The MLN's overriding concern was the defense of Mexico's national sovereignty. By this it understood the defense of the people's sovereignty vis-à-vis their own government, not just foreign governments.[37] On the domestic scene it condemned the "electoral monopoly of the official party" and the existence of "political prisoners," and in matters of foreign policy it repudiated "anticommunism as an instrument of penetration and division at the service of North American imperialism."[38]

The MLN made a special point of solidarity with the Cuban Revolution. It was Mexico's historical and continental responsibility to resist direct or indirect intervention in Cuban affairs, to support Cuba's agrarian reform just as Mexicans supported their own agrarian reform, and to disseminate as widely as possible the "achievements and objectives of the Cuban Revolution."[39] Mexicans should know the trajectory of the Cuban Revolution and be prepared to defend its leftward turn. Although "socialism" received no mention in the program, in his May Day speech on the heels of the Bay of Pigs invasion Castro placed socialism on the Cuban agenda.[40]

The origins of the MLN can be traced to the July 1959 founding of the Comité Impulsor de la Paz (Committee to Promote Peace), a group started by former president Cárdenas to protest the political and economic effects of the Cold War against communism.[41] With the participation of the PCM, the Popular Socialist party, and independent left-wing intellectuals, the committee's work led in March 1961 to the convocation in Mexico City of the Latin American Conference on National Sovereignty, Economic Emancipation, and Peace. The Mexican participants in the conference numbered one thousand, not to mention the many delegates from other Latin American countries. Its most immediate and urgent tasks were to resist foreign political and economic penetration, to win respect for the sovereignty and territorial integrity of Cuba, which the United States threatened, and to unify the Mexican Left as a means of pressuring the government to return to the revolutionary nationalism abandoned by the post-Cardenist regimes. Its importance is revealed in the fact that the Cuban delegation was presided over by Vilma Espín de Castro, wife of Raúl Castro, commander-in-chief of the rebel army.

The 1961 conference responded to two sets of events related to the Cold War: domestic repression of the teachers' and railway workers' strikes in 1958–1959; and U.S. pressure on Latin American governments to condemn the new course taken by the Cuban Revolution. Support for the anti-imperialist struggle was understood to be necessary for internal reforms, because domestic repression was closely connected to the Cold War. The connection became evident after a radio and television message to the Mexican people on 29 March 1959, when the attorney general attacked the railway workers for obeying ideologies and interests foreign to those of Mexico.

As a result of the conference, a national assembly was convoked on 4 August 1961. The opening speech at the assembly was given by Gen. Heriberto Jara, a former Magonist. General Cárdenas also addressed the assembly. Consistent with the principles laid down in the Constitution, he defended the delegates' efforts to implement the postulates of the Mexican Revolution.[42] Besides the two left-wing parties represented at the assembly, it included delegations from the National Confederation of Peasants, trade union delegates from the CTM, delegations from various states, several *zapatista* delegations, and representatives of Revueltas's Spartacus Group.[43]

In calling for the country's and the people's economic emancipation, the MLN tied its economic demands to the directing role of the state. Its program postulated as a major aim the "acceleration of industrialization."[44] At the same time, state intervention was justified by the incapacity of private entrepreneurs to promote sustained and autonomous economic growth.

The MLN's program agreed with the revolutionary nationalist project known as *cardenismo* (the ideology of Lázaro Cárdenas), but it also catered to the concerns of the Marxist-Leninist parties in the coalition. Those parties insisted on a basic transformation of the electoral system. They called for trade union autonomy and a widening of political participation by the worker, peasant, and popular sectors. Rather than a new revolution to attain this democratization, they relied on a continuation of the old revolution within the framework of the 1917 Constitution. Only through the democratization of the political system, they argued, could the revolutionary nationalist project guarantee an independent foreign policy, control of foreign investment, preponderance of the public sector, completion of the land reform, and redistribution of income to meet basic needs.

Although the program spoke of achieving its objectives by intransigent but "pacific" means, its concluding paragraphs contained a veiled call to armed struggle. By invoking Mexico's tradition of "revolutionary insurgence" against Spanish colonialism, the French occupation, Benito Juárez's reform, and the "struggle to the death" during the Revolution of 1910–1917, it left no doubt in the minds of MLN militants that an armed struggle was at hand.[45]

But the MLN failed in its initial objective of unifying the Left. In the conferences and round tables, members of the Old and the New Left discussed their political and ideological differences *ad nauseam* without reaching agreement. Nothing could be achieved through discussion with the wizards of Marxism-Leninism, because each wizard had a different version of the correct line. The struggle for unity bore little relation to the concrete realities and needs of the nation, while the *cardenistas* (Cárdenas's followers) became bored with the discussions. The starting point had to be an agreement between the major parties of the Left, not the groupuscules.

So the MLN gradually disintegrated.[46] First the Popular Socialist party broke off, then the PCM. Cárdenas and his current in the official party moved away, leaving the MLN completely in the hands of intellectuals of the New Left. Most of these people lived in the capital and had no ties to the workers and peasants. Some made prestigious careers for themselves and later cast their lot with the PRI. Enrique González Pedrero and Víctor Flores Olea, the successive directors of the Faculty of Political and Social Sciences at the National University in the late 1960s and the early 1970s, are examples. Thus the movement became not a coordinating committee of the Mexican Left, but a quasi-party without a future.

The Socialist party split off because of disagreement with the MLN's organizational structure. It wanted the movement to be a coordinating committee, or popular front, of the principal mass organizations and leftist parties, so it demanded a form of organic and functional representation. But the structure adopted permitted individual affiliations with a centralized direction. In effect, the MLN constituted a new party of the Left rather than a representative front of existing left-wing parties.

The critical conjuncture for the movement was the presidential succession of 1964, when it decided to abstain from the elections. This decision was partly a protest against electoral fraud by the official party, and partly a maneuver aimed at containing the partisan differences within the movement. But it also bordered on a blanket rejection of the political system.

The PCM hoped to participate in the electoral game by means of the Frente Electoral del Pueblo (People's Electoral Front) announced in April 1963. The Electoral Front could count on the support of organizations that also backed the MLN: the Movimiento Revolucionario del Magisterio (Revolutionary Teachers' Movement), the Consejo Nacional Ferrocarrilero (National Railway Workers' Council), the Central Campesina Independiente (Independent Peasant Central), and Genaro Vázquez's Asociación Cívica Guerrerense (Guerreran Civic Association). But because the MLN refused to participate in the 1964 elections, a split resulted among the organizations that backed it.

The *cardenistas* broke away because of the MLN's policy of electoral abstentionism. Cárdenas publicly supported the PRI's official candidate, Gustavo Díaz Ordaz, thus depriving the movement of support from the official Left. When the *cardenistas* walked out, the MLN lost the mass support of Mexico's worker and peasant organizations. So the emergence of the Electoral Front marked the decline and decomposition of the MLN.

The MLN's program issued in a confrontation with both the government and the official party. By its solidarity with the Cuban Revolution alone it won thousands of sympathizers, bringing about an important mobilization. This worried the government, while the disagreement between Cárdenas and President López Mateos concerning the Cuban Revolution increased official pressure on the movement. To this dispute was added the question of political prisoners. The MLN called for a struggle to liberate Valentín Campa and Demetrio Vallejo, the chief leaders of the railway workers, but López Mateos insisted on keeping them in prison. Finally, the president denounced the MLN for succumbing to communist infiltration.

During Díaz Ordaz's term (1964–1970) the pressures on the MLN increased. When co-optation did not work, the government resorted to repression. The MLN slowly weakened until its support for the 1968 student mobilizations led to the jailing of its leaders. It did not survive this last disaster, but by then some of its militants had already turned to armed struggle.

The MLN's contribution was not to reshape Mexican electoral politics, but to serve as midwife to a resurgence of guerrilla warfare. It did so by disseminating knowledge of the comparable struggle against political repression in prerevolutionary Cuba and of the radicalization of the Cuban Revolution. The beneficiaries of this knowledge included workers, peasants, students, and intellectuals both within and beyond the reach of the Marxist-Leninist Left.

Despite the MLN's commitment to respect the framework of the 1917

Constitution, it was already alerting its partisans to the rationale for a new revolution. It tacitly questioned the wisdom of abiding by a constitution that the political authorities had made inoperative. As Castro noted in his May Day speech in 1961, constitutions become outdated when they are not carried out.[47]

By refusing to participate in the 1964 elections, the MLN opened the door to an armed alternative. Thus it was the MLN, not the PCM, that first questioned the continuity of the Mexican Revolution in deeds as well as words.

MLN militants agreed with Castro that revolutions in Latin America would be made with or without a communist party.[48] They agreed with his speech on 13 March 1967, distinguishing authentic communists from those merely sporting the label. "If in any country those who call themselves communists do not know how to fulfill their duty, we will support those who, without calling themselves communists, conduct themselves like real communists in action."[49] What defines a communist, Castro added, is not membership in a political party, but one's "attitude toward the armed revolutionary movements . . . the guerrilla movement in Guatemala, in Colombia, and in Venezuela."[50] MLN militants got the message and soon began applying it to Mexico.

The most important guerrilla movements of the 1960s were launched by MLN militants. Although the MLN did not officially advocate armed struggle, the contagion of the Cuban Revolution and the currents for change were so strong that MLN militants began to emulate Castro's example. Castro had the utmost contempt for "pseudo-revolutionaries," who favor indirect over direct action.[51] Declared Castro in a speech on 26 July 1966: "We would have been in a real pickle, if, in order to make a socialist revolution, we had to spend all our time catechizing everybody in socialism and Marxism and only then undertake the revolution. . . . The business of thinking that the awareness must come first and the struggle afterward is an error!"[52]

In making direct action the touchstone for distinguishing authentic revolutionaries from their impersonators, MLN militants testified to a strong dose of anarchism. For doing the same, Castro was faulted by the Venezuelan Communists for aiding and abetting anarchist adventures in their country.[53] On 10 August 1967, he responded to the charge.[54] Mockingly, he adopted the same rhetoric in referring to his followers as "anarcho-adventurers, anarcho-terrorists, anarcho-Castroites!"[55] However, the Venezuelan Communists were not misusing the label in discrediting Castro, a label also used to discredit Lenin in 1917 and Mexico's guerrillas in the 1960s.[56]

This anarchist undercurrent in MLN ideology made it the duty of the revolutionary to make the revolution. As Flores Magón noted in "The Duty of the Revolutionary," anarchists should join every revolutionary movement and turn it to their own account. He traced this strategy to the Italian anarcho-communist Errico Malatesta. "Naturally, as Malatesta with clear talent foresaw, the [Mexican] revolution did not begin with a precise communist or anarchist program. . . . [We] practiced what Malatesta wisely counseled: 'We must join all revolutionary movements or those that may lead to revolution, and work so that events do not take a course other than what we want.'" As Malatesta said, "the masses will become anarchist and communist during the revolution, after it has begun." [57]

Had MLN militants read Flores Magón's *Semilla libertaria*? Or were they repeating in different words the lesson of Guevara's 1960 notes on the ideology of the Cuban Revolution? Wrote Guevara: "The revolution can be made . . . if the forces involved are utilized correctly, even if the theory [ideology] is not known." [58] Guevara claims to have learned this from experience, not from books. [59] In the same vein, disillusionment with the course of the Mexican Revolution was the overriding experience that led MLN militants to learn from the Cuban example.

MLN militants also became disillusioned with the temporizing tactics of the PCM. "Those who do not possess a truly revolutionary spirit cannot be called communists," said Castro, since only a revolutionary spirit, or revolutionary vocation, makes communists feel their cause deeply. [60] This means that communists are defined not by a cerebral understanding and espousal of Marxism, but by what they feel and do, "not by what they say they are, but by what they prove they are." [61] Virtually the same measuring rod led Rodríguez to impute to members of the Karl Marx cells in Atencingo and Zacatepec a "Magonist essence." [62] So it was not necessary for MLN militants to read *Semilla libertaria* to tune in on the same anarchist wave length as Flores Magón.

THE MADERA GUERRILLAS

The first of the MLN-influenced rural guerrillas made their début in the former Magonist stronghold in the state of Chihuahua. Their leader, Arturo Gámiz, was a militant in the MLN. His assault on the barracks in Ciudad Madera on 23 September 1965 was modeled on Castro's assault on the Moncada barracks in Santiago de Cuba on 26 July 1953. [63] But what newspaper reports did not reveal and political commentators missed was the Cuban government's hand in the operations.

In a story behind the headlines in the genre made famous by Jan Valtin and Eudocio Ravines but so filled with indignation and venom at Communist duplicity that he stretches the facts, Prudencio Godines, Jr., claims that Raúl Castro, the PCM, and the MLN were secretly behind Gámiz's guerrillas.[64] Individual members of the party and MLN were apparently involved, which is reason enough to sift through this eyewitness account by one of the guerrillas' few survivors. A self-declared fan of Francisco Villa and of Zapata's struggle for "land and liberty," Godines castigates the party for having betrayed not only the Madera guerrillas, but also the libertarian and emancipatory principles of original communism dating from the Great French Revolution and the 1848 Communist Manifesto.[65]

Godines, a nephew of Diego Rivera, was sent to school in the Soviet Union in 1946. There he was trained in sabotage and the use of arms as an agent of Moscow's underground network initially in Eastern Europe and then in Venezuela, Colombia, and Central America.[66] In June 1965, he received orders to return to Mexico with the mission of organizing armed nuclei like the ones Cuba had financed and assisted in other Latin American countries.[67] As the appointed "political commissar" in Gámiz's guerrillas, he allegedly acted as both an emissary of Raúl Castro and an informal delegate of the PCM and the MLN.[68]

While the Cuban government surreptitiously violated its policy of non-intervention in Mexico's internal affairs, the PCM's leaders secretly approved the assault but then publicly repudiated it as "suicidal."[69] According to Godines, no less a figure than Arnoldo Martínez Verdugo, the party's general secretary, had participated in the deliberations preparatory to the assault.[70] If one is to believe Godines, leading members of the party also plotted a second armed operation aimed at a takeover of the government house in the capital city of Chihuahua on 26 October 1965—foiled by federal agents.[71]

Godines's story is one of provocation and betrayal by the political advisers to the guerrillas, for, when the moment of truth arrived, the plotters made themselves scarce instead of coming to Gámiz's assistance with armed backing and peasant mobilizations as promised. According to a story that reads like Castro's aborted attack on the Moncada garrison and Jaramillo's second armed uprising in October of the same year, Gámiz's allies either deserted outright or conveniently lost their way to the appointed rendezvous.[72]

The death toll from the assault on the barracks included six soldiers and eight guerrillas.[73] Three members of Gámiz's group awaited the outcome in a wooded area about five miles from the scene. According to Godines, seventeen guerrillas participated in the assault, so there may have been as many as nine survivors not counting the backup group.[74] Successful in eluding army and air force units in hot pursuit, the guerrillas regrouped in the sierras of Chihuahua. Known as the September 23 Movement, under the leadership of Oscar González, this second group of guer-rillas continued operating until 1968.[75] In 1966 several of the group's members transferred their base of operations to the mountains of Gue-rrero and made contact with Cabañas when he was still leading a legal existence.[76] After he fled to the hills, they became the first combat-tested guerrillas to join him.

THE PARTY OF THE POOR

The most spectacular and enduring actions by guerrillas were launched in the tropical jungles of Guerrero under the command of Lucio Cabañas Barrientos (1938–1974). Starting in 1967, his guerrilla struggle continued for some seven years. Besides Jaramillo, Cabañas was the only one to con-front the army directly. The ambushes he set in June and August 1972 and in August 1974 had not been equaled in seventy years. Like Jaramillo, he launched slogans and raised political banners that won the support of the local population. As a man of outstanding organizational and agitational talents, he succeeded in building a movement linked not only to the peas-ants of Guerrero, but also to the student movement in Guerrero, Sonora, Aguascalientes, Guanajuato, Tamaulipas, and the Federal District.

An important factor in Cabañas's political formation was his militancy in the Communist Youth and later in the PCM and the MLN. Cabañas became a student leader on a national scale in 1962 when he was elected general secretary of the Federación de Estudiantes Campesinos Socialistas (Federation of Socialist Peasant Students).[77] When he became a rural teacher in Atoyac in 1964 he joined the Revolutionary Teachers' Move-ment.[78] In Atoyac he helped to organize the People's Electoral Front and the Independent Peasant Central. He worked in these organizations as a militant of the MLN and as a member of the regional committee of the PCM in Guerrero. He also received cadre training in the party's school in Mexico City.[79]

Cabañas was not a typical PCM militant. The only biographical sketches by those who knew him intimately or fought alongside him raise questions about his orthodoxy.[80] Only an anarchist could believe that a massacre was sufficient cause to launch an armed struggle, that popular indignation sufficed to do so, that it did not matter that the objective conditions of revolution were lacking, and that revolutionaries should consider ordinary criminals as "brothers."[81] That Cabañas called his or-ganization the Partido de los Pobres (Party of the Poor, PDLP) was a definite departure from Marxist theory, as was his interpretation of the Communist party's new revolution as a revolution in which "the poor will govern through a proletarian regime."[82] His focus on the poor suggests an anarchist derivation going back to Ricardo Flores Magón. It may also account for his asceticism. He did not take part in social events, he did not dance, he showed no interest in women, nor did he drink or smoke.[83] In these respects, he reminds one of Jaramillo.

He claimed that his steps were guided by "Francisco Villa, Ricardo Flores Magón, and Emiliano Zapata."[84] As Cabañas described his political formation, he became a revolutionary first, and a PCM militant afterward. "We were born in Ayotzinapa," he said of his fellow schoolteachers in the Escuela Normal Rural (teachers' training school in Guerrero), where Magonist ideas still circulated.[85] It is not by studying Marxism-Leninism that one becomes a revolutionary, he preached, but by uniting with the people, by living among the poor and demanding no privileges for oneself.[86] Besides "saints of the revolution," he paid tribute to "Christian saints" dedicated to the same noble ideal. Thus "the equality of the Apostles is also proclaimed by this socialist revolution . . . that the rich deprived of their riches shall not earn more than the worker."[87]

Cabañas's egalitarianism may explain his infatuation with the image of Che Guevara and his romanticizing of the Cuban Revolution as a "revolution of the poor." Castro and Guevara too figured as "saints" in his revolutionary calendar.[88] The influence of the Cuban Revolution on the Party of the Poor did not stop there. Carmelo Cortés, its principal theoretician, was a "Guevarist par excellence."[89] Testifying to Guevara's influence, Cortés became Cabañas's successor as leader of the party after the latter's death in 1974. As was the case with Gámiz's group, the ideology of the Cuban Revolution helped to sustain the guerrillas.

Barely a year after Cabañas returned to his hometown of Atoyac as a rural schoolteacher, the state government branded him a communist agitator and he was charged with the crime of social dissolution. On 21 November 1965 he and another rural schoolteacher, Serafín Núñez, organized in Atoyac an assembly under the auspices of the People's Electoral Front. A few days later an order arrived from the governor transferring them to the state of Durango, supposedly to render services in the line of duty but in fact to stop their agitation.

In Durango, Cabañas continued his agitation until the governor demanded that his salary be stopped. So he returned to Atoyac and organized a group of parents to demand the resignation of the school's principal and his own reinstatement, on the grounds that he had been dismissed arbitrarily. On 13 May 1967 there was a strike; the principal was forced down and Cabañas reinstated. But two days later the government intervened to cancel the arrangement. Then on 18 May, the federal police opened fire on a demonstration of three thousand, killing seven and wounding twenty. Two police were killed and the rest had to flee. Popular wrath was so great that peasants armed themselves and went in search of the attackers. The army occupied the town. Cabañas was declared responsible for the massacre, and fled to the mountains.

Representatives of the PCM and the Revolutionary Teachers' Movement searched for him and finally made contact. They discussed the political situation and tried to dissuade him from a guerrilla war. But as a fugitive from the law, Cabañas chose to defend himself by the only means he considered feasible. After arming himself and his comrades from the town of Atoyac and its environs who had accompanied him to the mountains, he broke with the PCM.

In a communiqué that appeared in the PCM's magazine *Oposición* (15 July 1970), Cabañas listed his party's major exploits beginning in 1969. These included the execution of two army officers and of two political bosses whose gunmen were killing peasants, an attack on the federal police as a reprisal for its crimes, armed pressure on a big owner to make him pay the wages of fifteen peons he was trying to cheat, and an armed protest over the political tour of Luis Echeverría that allowed him to visit only one of seven towns that form the Costa Grande region of Guerrero. Then, in April 1970 came the first kidnapping. The guerrillas demanded one hundred thousand pesos for the life of cattleman Juan Gallardo—and got the ransom. On 2 March 1971 they assaulted the Central Bank of Aguascalientes and got away with four hundred thousand pesos. On 16 April 1971 came another bank assault, this one in Empalme, Sonora, against a branch of the Commercial Bank. The second kidnapping took place on 7 January 1972: Jaime Farill, principal of Preparatory School Number 2 in Acapulco, fell into the hands of the guerrillas. They demanded a ransom of three million pesos. The action failed when the army rescued Farill on 13 April.[90]

As Cabañas recalled in his last recording a few days before his death, he began his struggle in the mountains with only six comrades.[91] The guerrilla band did not grow, and in despair three cadres dropped out. The struggle stagnated with only three combatants until 1969, when nine men joined up. Then they began the executions, shooting two of the main political bosses in Atoyac. The available arms hardly permitted more daring actions. Only after the first kidnapping in April 1970 did the guerrillas use the 100,000-peso ransom to buy powerful modern weapons. The bank assaults and the kidnappings between 1971 and 1972 allowed them to make a qualitative leap from a left-wing groupuscule of nine in 1970 to a force of thirty armed men carrying out the ambush of June 1972. In August 1972, forty guerrillas participated in the second ambush; and in August 1974, one hundred guerrillas took part in the third and fourth ambushes.

In Cabañas's first important political document published in the newspaper *Excélsior* (13 January 1972) he announced that the PDLP's Armed Commandos of Guerrero were responsible for the kidnapping of Jaime Farill. The name adopted by the guerrillas was at first an adaptation of the name used by the Armed Commandos of Chihuahua. But when Cabañas's guerrillas claimed national attention, this name disappeared and the guerrillas were referred to only as the Peasant Justice Brigade of the Party of the Poor.

Addressed to teachers, peasants, and other "working and downtrodden people" as well as to students at Farill's preparatory school, Cabañas's document explained the PDLP's shift to urban guerrilla warfare. The party had been "compelled to resort to kidnappings by the exigencies of a revolution in the making and . . . as a response to the chain of crimes and violence unleashed by the bourgeois class in power." To this account, Cabañas added in a follow-up communiqué on 3 February 1972 that,

> interned in the sierra, persecuted by thousands of soldiers, watched by dozens of helicopters that gun down every living thing, and victimized by indiscriminate bombings by military planes whose number increases from day to day . . . we continue nonetheless to have the backing of the peasant masses, while our struggle extends to . . . urban zones, transforming us into rural and urban guerrillas by the inclusion of peasants, students, professional workers, and citizens, all fed up with the brutal repression of the opulent classes and convinced that, with their laws and repressive apparatuses, these classes have closed every possible avenue of change based on an open, massive and popular struggle.[92]

Following the original influence of the Chihuahuan guerrillas, the PDLP met with representatives of other guerrilla groups. In May 1972, two representatives of the Revolutionary Action Movement arrived in the mountains to propose an alliance. In June they began to instruct Cabañas's followers in the tactics of guerrilla warfare they had learned as part of a group of fifty Mexicans trained in North Korea in 1969. There were four ambushes of the army by the Peasant Justice Brigade; Arnulfo Ariza, alias Mena-Mena, of the Revolutionary Action Movement directed two of them personally. In the middle of 1973 five militants from the new September 23 Communist League arrived. The new league, formed in March 1973, joined members of the old September 23 Movement and members of other armed movements in Mexico. But they drifted into ultraleftism and began a hidden struggle to change the political line and leadership of the brigade and the party. They were expelled in January 1974.

Fundamental to understanding Cabañas's politics are his "Guiding Principles of the Party of the Poor" (March 1973).[93] This document not only underscores the party's populist objectives, it also lays out its socialist and communist tasks. The "Guiding Principles" establish as the main targets of the armed struggle the conquest of political power, destruction of the exploiting bourgeois state, formation of a proletarian state, destruction of the capitalist system, the abolition of private property, the construction of a new society without exploiters and exploited, and the establishment of workers' self-management. The aim was to make not only a political and social revolution, but also a cultural revolution: "bourgeois culture, because it is counterrevolutionary and incompatible with the interests of the workers, must be destroyed—ordinary people will develop their own culture."[94]

In order to achieve these objectives, the document calls for extending the guerrilla war to the whole country until it turns into a general insurrection. Let the workers take over the factories, let the peasants seize the schools and universities, and let all the people mobilize to destroy the repressive police and military forces. This was not just a communist but an anarchist appeal adapted to the needs of guerrilla struggle, an answer to the massacre of Atoyac and to the massacres that followed on 2 October 1968 and 10 June 1971.[95]

On two occasions—on 17 March and again on 18 November 1972—the secretary of defense, General Cuenca Díaz, offered Cabañas an amnesty. But Cabañas remembered what had happened to Rubén Jaramillo, who, once disarmed, was murdered by the federal police and army elements. When Cabañas fled to the mountains in 1967, he resolved never to make peace with those responsible for the Atoyac massacre. The massacres on 2 October and 10 June only hardened his resolve.

Owing to the qualitative leap in both arms and number of combatants, the guerrillas' capacity for action grew while they prepared for their most spectacular exploits against the army. On 25 June 1972 came the first ambush, bringing down ten soldiers. The second, on 23 August 1972, resulted in eighteen soldiers killed, nine wounded, and twenty captured. On 9 August 1974 the third ambush occurred, with eleven soldiers dead, six wounded, and seventeen captured. On 21 August 1974 the fourth ambush was carried out: its toll was fourteen dead and fifteen wounded. There were also direct confrontations with the army, like that on 20 September 1974, which killed nine soldiers and wounded seven, and that on 11 October 1974, which left sixteen dead and fifteen wounded.

The bank assaults increased. On 22 December 1972 another expropriation involved a simultaneous attack by two commando groups, one against the offices of the Viking Construction Company in Coyuca de Benítez, Guerrero, with a booty of 42,000 pesos, and the other against the Mexican Bank of the South in Acapulco with a take of 230,000 pesos. On 13 April 1973 came another attack, this one on the Mexican Commercial Bank's branch in the Secretariat of Public Education, with a prize of 2,000,000 pesos.

Cabañas's most famous action was the kidnapping of senator and multimillionaire Rubén Figueroa, at that time the PRI's candidate for governor of Guerrero. On 30 May 1974 Figueroa went into the mountains to negotiate the end of violence in his state, but Cabañas refused to let him leave. The senator offered to sign an agreement by means of which fifty thousand pesos a month would go to organize and maintain the PDLP should it surface as a legal party. But Cabañas was interested in another matter: freedom for political prisoners, about three hundred throughout the nation. While these were in prison, the senator would remain under arrest.

In a communiqué dated 19 June 1974, Cabañas presented his terms in exchange for the liberation of the PRI's multimillionaire. The federal government should begin with a military withdrawal from the mountains. Once this was done, it would have to meet a series of demands, the most important of which were the liberation of political prisoners according to a list and a process that the PDLP would make known, the delivery of fifty million pesos, the provision of modern arms for the guerrillas, and the public diffusion of a recording of Cabañas and his comrades making speeches and singing guerrilla songs.

At the same time, Cabañas demanded from the state government the liberation not only of political prisoners, but of other delinquents as well.[96] Like the demand that arms be given to the guerrillas, this last demand was impossible to fulfill. Although Figueroa was ready to free political prisoners in his state, he could not free ordinary delinquents because the federal government refused to participate in such deals.

The senator's family and friends managed to raise the ransom money. Father Carlos Bonilla acted as intermediary, taking twenty-five million pesos to the mountains at the beginning of September 1974. The rest would be delivered after the senator's release. But on 8 September the army freed the millionaire and recovered fifteen million pesos of the ransom.

Figueroa's kidnapping was, nevertheless, the masterpiece and culminating work of the poor people's guerrilla war. The possibility of negotiating with a distinguished functionary of Echeverría's reformist government opened up. There was a chance of arriving at a political settlement concerning two key points: freedom for political prisoners, and legalization of the Party of the Poor as the civil arm of the Peasant Justice Brigade. The senator agreed to free all political prisoners in Guerrero. He was also ready to legalize and sustain the Party of the Poor, "because a pressure group in Guerrero with a revolutionary sentiment is highly useful for making, as Father Morelos knew, the rich less rich and the poor less poor." [97] So Cabañas could go on with the armed struggle in the mountains, while the PDLP was legalized on the plain. He might have had the best of both worlds, but when this opportunity presented itself he failed to take advantage of it. Instead, the army escalated its repression, the guerrillas' losses mounted, demoralization set in, their hideout was betrayed by an untested new recruit, and Cabañas was killed in a shoot-out on 2 December 1974.

The PDLP lingered on under the leadership of Carmelo Cortés. He had first won notoriety in 1966 as the leader of the student strike at the Autonomous University of Guerrero in Chilpancingo. According to one account, "Carmelo Cortés, an assiduous reader of Mao, Guevara, and the Marxist classics, had a theoretical preparation and a communist consciousness superior to that of Lucio." [98] In 1972, Cortés's faction in the PDLP broke away and began operating independently under the name of Fuerzas Armadas Revolucionarias (Revolutionary Armed Forces), but it maintained close ties to Cabañas and served in effect as the PDLP's urban armed fist. [99] Besides kidnappings and bank robberies in Acapulco, Chilpancingo, and Iguala, it carried out assaults in Cuernavaca and Mexico City between 1973 and 1975. In August 1975, in Cuernavaca in broad daylight, Cortés and his men assaulted the bank opposite the bus station at Casino de la Selva. Shortly after, on 1 September, he was killed in a shoot-out with the judicial police in Mexico City.

In 1985 the PDLP surfaced in connection with the 1 July kidnapping of Arnoldo Martínez Verdugo, a candidate of the newly formed Unified Socialist party of Mexico in the upcoming federal congressional elections. The former Communist general secretary was released after the payment of one hundred million pesos in ransom, which represented money plus interest that the PDLP claimed to have given the PCM for safekeeping after its abduction of Figueroa in 1974. The extensive press coverage of the incident—Martínez Verdugo was held captive for seventeen days— was a dramatic demonstration that Cabañas's guerrillas continued to have an impact on Mexican political life fully a decade after his death. [100]

THE REVOLUTIONARY NATIONAL
CIVIC ASSOCIATION

Next in importance to Cabañas's guerrillas, but with a broader base and significantly wider popular appeal, were the guerrillas organized by another rural schoolteacher and MLN militant from Guerrero, Genaro Vázquez Rojas (1933–1972). Unlike Cabañas, who joined the Communist Youth while still in school, Vázquez entered the PRI and only later gravitated toward the Marxist Left by joining the Popular Socialist party.[101] After teaching school in the slums of the Federal District and participating in the revolutionary teachers' strike and seizure of the Secretariat of Public Education in April 1958, he returned to his home state and in 1959 founded the Guerreran Civic Association. However, its campaign to democratize the state's government led to a massacre of his supporters in Chilpancingo on 30 December 1960, followed by a second massacre in Iguala on 31 December 1962, in which dozens were killed and dozens more wounded. The Civic Association was promptly outlawed and Vázquez was held responsible for the slaughter. Compelled to flee in order to avoid arrest, he remained in hiding for the next four years until federal agents caught up with him at the offices of the MLN in Mexico City on 9 November 1966.

From 1960 to 1966, when the PCM and Cabañas were propounding a "new revolution," Vázquez was defending the old revolution in an effort to implement an agrarian reform, to weed out corruption in government circles, and to push the country toward genuine democracy. Thus the seven-point program of his Civic Association, formulated in April 1966 while he was still in hiding, took for granted the "absolute respect for the Constitution of the republic" that undergirded his earlier 1960 program.[102]

Vázquez's 1966 program was followed by two new orientations, each more radical than its predecessor. After the Civic Association's first and only armed assault on 22 April 1968, which freed Vázquez from the Iguala jail for seven crimes that carried a term of life imprisonment, he renamed it the Guerreran National Civic Association.[103] Inspired by the MLN's August 1961 program and Fidel Castro's 1962 "Declaration of Havana," he prepared for a sustained guerrilla struggle in Guerrero aimed at extending the armed struggle to the rest of the country in coordination with other armed groups.

By the end of 1969 the new association had served its purpose and was reorganized as the Revolutionary National Civic Association (ACNR). Announced in December 1971, the ACNR's program reiterated Vázquez's earlier commitment to a "democratic, anti-imperialist, and antifeudal revolution."[104] To this it added an implicit commitment to socialism. Its four-point program called for the overthrow of the proimperialist PRI government of big capitalists and landlords; for a coalition government of workers, peasants, students, and progressive intellectuals; for the full political and economic independence of Mexico; and for a new social order that would benefit a majority of working people.[105]

But Vázquez's 1971 program was still a far cry from that of Cabañas. There was no direct hint of a communist or anarchist objective. While Vázquez acknowledged the historical inexistence of a proletarian vanguard, which accounts for his discrepancies with the PCM, he noted the impossibility of creating one in the absence of genuine democracy. The vanguard would have to be created during the armed struggle, not before. In that event, "and under the political direction of the proletariat, the revolution must lead to the *implementation of socialism*."[106]

In the communiqué outlining his four-point program, Vázquez reprimanded the Old Left for trying to build a mass political party under conditions of repression and for failing to underwrite the armed struggle. In retrospect, we can see that this amounted to a self-criticism since he had originally attempted to build such a party within the limits set by the Constitution.

Vázquez's armed struggle was modeled on Cuban sources. In particular, he exalted the "heroic and patriotic guerrilla movement in Latin America and the immaculate writer Régis Debray," whose writings had helped in spreading the guerrilla movement to Mexico.[107] After extolling the figure of Che Guevara, "the greatest of all contemporary fighters for Latin American freedom," his communiqué explained the reasons for his armed struggle: the memory of the assassinations of Emiliano Zapata, Francisco Villa, Rubén Jaramillo and his family; the repression against the teachers and railway workers; and the massacres in Guerrero since the early 1960s.[108]

In defense of their violated rights under the Constitution, Vázquez argued, workers and peasants had only one recourse. Against the "fascistoid" government of the "capitalist class in power," he urged that they arm themselves "to achieve national liberation and to construct a better society."[109] Force would be met with force: "to the repression and illegal deprivation of freedom [in reference to his jail sentence] . . . we consider it absolutely just to punish those characterized as enemies of the people."[110]

By then, Vázquez was depicting the PRI government as a "government of national treason" for having overturned the Constitution.[111] He had also arrived at a novel depiction of the Mexican state as a new edition of the old Porfirian dictatorship. Although the Revolution of 1910 was a bourgeois-democratic one, he claimed that its leadership had been taken over by the rich, who had imposed a new despotism of institutionalized lies and crimes.[112] Beginning with his first communiqué from the mountains of Guerrero (1 August 1968), he had urged students to join the "anti-feudal, anti-imperialist, and democratic revolution" and to prepare for armed struggle, since "to violence and repression one can only respond effectively and triumphantly with arms."[113]

Like Cabañas, Vázquez was influenced by the MLN, by "the speeches of Fidel Castro, the works of Che Guevara, the pamphlets, articles, and conceptions of Régis Debray."[114] But unlike the PDLP's, the ACNR's armed operations never went beyond bank robberies and kidnappings, and of these there were only a handful.[115] Considering the original civic nature of the ACNR, it seems likely that Vázquez's armed struggle aimed to achieve socialism by restoring the 1917 Constitution rather than by adopting a new constitution. Since he was not committed to smashing the bureaucratic apparatus of the state, the vagueness and ambiguity of his socialist program gives credence to the criticism that it was "ideologically and politically a populist program."[116]

Nonetheless, the ACNR qualifies as "anarcho-Castroite" because of its reliance on direct action and struggle for a new social order. Although there is no hard evidence indicating that Vázquez believed in either workers' self-management or communism, socialism is a stepping-stone to both. Vázquez continued to give lip service to the faith of most Mexicans in the Revolution of 1910–1917, but that may have been a strategical ploy like the camouflage adopted by the PLM in 1906.

After Vázquez died in an automobile accident on 2 February 1972, his band of guerrillas came under increasing repression and soon dissolved. Unlike Flores Magón, who spelled out his ultimate program before his flame was snuffed out, Vázquez lacked the opportunity to do so. But he left a trail of clues that adds up to something similar. I have mentioned his indebtedness to Fidel Castro, Che Guevara, and Régis Debray. Despite his differences with Gámiz and Cabañas, he followed in their footsteps. He was also strategically indebted to Jaramillo, whose advice he sought in 1962 in the offices of the Cuernavaca daily *¡Presente!*[117] So, if there is an anarchist component in the politics and strategy of Vázquez's mentors, then there should be traces of it in the ACNR.

IDEOLOGICAL GRIST
FOR THE ARMED STRUGGLE

The armed struggle of the 1960s and the 1970s did not spring forth from an ideological vacuum. In imperceptible ways it was nurtured in the bosom of the Communist party, whose political line moved steadily to the left. The Movement of National Liberation helped it along as did the speeches and writings of Fidel Castro, Che Guevara, and Régis Debray. The Madera guerrillas turned to Fidel Castro's Moncada strategy as a model of how to launch a revolution, while Cabañas and Vázquez looked to Che Guevara and Régis Debray for justification of their insurrectional strategy.

Since they lacked politically and theoretically trained cadres of their own, Mexico's guerrillas turned to foreign models for guidance. Their leaders were rural schoolteachers and university students, hardly the best equipped to develop a theory and practice of guerrilla warfare. Nobody in Mexico could boast of the theoretical background and political experience of Carlos Fonseca in Nicaragua, César Montes in Guatemala, Camilo Torres in Colombia, Douglas Bravo in Venezuela, Carlos Marighela in Brazil, Luis de la Puente Uceda and Héctor Béjar in Peru, and Raúl Sendic in Uruguay, not to mention the many gifted Argentines who joined the guerrillas.[118] Nor was there anyone with the military credentials of Turcios Lima in Guatemala, Ricardo Napurí in Peru, or Carlos Lamarca in Brazil to prepare them militarily.

But while they thought they were following foreign models, they were relying on native traditions. Mexico's guerrillas were unaware that they had revived Flores Magón's strategy of revolutionary war under a different name. Beginning with the PLM's desert revolution in Baja California in January 1911, Flores Magón and his magazine *Regeneración* tried to transform the constitutional war into a revolutionary war, into "an authentic 'social revolution'" through "direct expropriations [of fields and factories] carried out by the people in arms."[119] This strategy targeted two enemies, the defenders of a reactionary regime and the protagonists of a liberal political order that promised to leave the old social order intact. It was the strategy pursued with partial success by Emiliano Zapata and Rubén Jaramillo, and later successfully by Fidel Castro in Cuba. What appeared to be a Cuban strategy thus had a Mexican precursor.

The Cuban influence on the Mexican guerrillas has long been established and is today well known. But in reproducing both Castro's and Guevara's strategies, the Mexican guerrillas did so in the course of responding to a similar set of political circumstances. These shared a common denominator of intensified government and military repression. So to a similar predicament, Mexico's guerrillas gave a similar response that was not simply a matter of copying foreign models.

What has escaped attention is that the appearance of foreign influence did not match the reality. We have noted a discrepancy in the adaptation of Castroism to Mexico. It also happened that Guevara's strategy turned out to be something other than it appeared. In adopting Guevarism as their credo, Cabañas and Vázquez unknowingly committed themselves to a philosophy of guerrilla warfare with an anarchist dimension.

Guevara's political philosophy was heterodox by almost any standard. As early as March 1965, when he began concocting plans for making a permanent revolution on a continental scale in Africa and Latin America, charges of "Trotskyism" and of a "leftist-adventurist deviation" were leveled against him by veteran Cuban Communists.[120] Two years later a new charge was added. As he reported in his Bolivian diary, the Czech Communists began depicting him as a "new Bakunin."[121] Since Guevara had become the apostle of revolutionary war and in 1967 was attempting to extend it in the form of "one, two, many Vietnams," the Czech comrades were understandably concerned and quick to make the connection between the adventure-loving Argentine and the flaming Russian revolutionary who also aimed to turn the world upside down.

That Guevara was a "new Bakunin" was put forth in an article that appeared in the magazine *Reporter* (19 May 1967), organ of the Union of Czechoslovak Journalists. Stanislav Budin depicted Guevara as an "adventurer" and equated his belief that "socialism means war" with "anarchism."[122] I was in Prague when the article appeared and by chance had an opportunity to discuss it with Budin. Opposed in principle to everything Guevara stood for, he blamed Paul Sweezy's magazine *Monthly Review* for consistently defending Guevara's un-Marxist and anarchist propaganda of the deed.

What particularly distressed the Czech Communist was Guevara's strategy of making things worse as a condition of making them better. Wrote Guevara in a September 1963 essay: "We are passing through a stage in which the masses' pressure is very strong and is straining bourgeois legality, so that its own authors must violate it. . . . [Bourgeois democracy] tries to function without resorting to force. We must oblige it to resort to violence, thereby unmasking its true nature." But the immediate purpose of Budin's article was to warn against the incendiary effects of Guevara's message to the Tricontinental (23 April 1967), in which Guevara called for the creation of international proletarian armies aimed at provoking a succession of new Vietnams.[123]

Guevara summarized his strategy of guerrilla warfare under three leading principles. First, if the government is unconstitutional and people cannot defend their rights through legal channels, then guerrillas can win a war against the regular army. Second, it is unnecessary to wait for all the conditions of revolution to appear, because some of those conditions can be created by the insurrectional vanguard in the course of the armed struggle. Third, in underdeveloped Latin America the ideal terrain for waging guerrilla warfare is the countryside, in rugged mountain areas inaccessible to the army's motorized units.[124] Although Guevara may never have studied Bakunin's writings, his strategy was an anarchist one because it relied on direct action, because it called for an immediate revolution international in scope, and because it directly challenged the power of the state.

Guevara's strategy had not only an anarchist essence, but also an anarchist derivation. In Georges Sorel's 1906 *Reflections on Violence*, a bible of anarcho-syndicalism, one may discover the source of Guevara's reliance on the myth that guerrillas can defeat a regular army and that an "insurrectional foco," or vanguard, is the little motor for setting into motion the larger motor of the revolution.

Guevara's insurrectional myth may be traced to his reading of José Carlos Mariátegui, a convinced Sorelian.[125] His first wife, Hilda Gadea, recalled that they read and discussed several of Mariátegui's works together.[126] Guevara agreed with the substance of Sorel's and Mariátegui's claim that class warfare is not simply reducible to class interest, but requires a revolutionary myth to evoke enthusiasm and the determination and impulse to fight.[127]

In order to galvanize workers and peasants into making a revolution, Guevara relied on a saving minority. Through Mariátegui, he became inspired by Sorel's depiction of a charismatic vanguard of men of action rather than knowledge, whose sensitivity to the shifting moods of the masses enables it to transform feelings into deeds.[128] For Mariátequi, as for Sorel, the ideal revolutionary is an ascetic motivated by moral rather than material concerns.[129] In Guevara's words, the guerrilla is at once a "priest of reform," an "ascetic," and a "social reformer."[130]

What were the objectives of his anarchist strategy? Beginning with the duty of the revolutionary to overthrow Latin American dictators and to launch an agrarian reform, in a little more than two years Guevara had upgraded his project to include the replacement of constitutional regimes and the expropriation of native and foreign capitalists.[131] Rather than postponing communism until after the consolidation of socialism, he proposed to construct them simultaneously. By 1965 he was calling for the creation of a new communist man, not as an ultimate goal but as an end-in-view, based on the "education of the masses for communism."[132]

Such was the Marxist heresy proclaimed by the "new Bakunin." "Guerrilla struggle meant a kind of communism in microcosm—an environment that suppressed differences and acted as a midwife for . . . a community of fellowship in which all performed according to their abilities and shared alike." In Cuba, this "guerrilla communism" would become the microcosm of a new communist society.[133]

Guevara claimed to be a Marxist, but should one take his claim at face value? The only analysis of his Marxism worth mentioning is Michael Lowy's *El pensamiento del Che Guevara*, but as one astute commentator notes, "Lowy is blind to the anarchist spirit and content of Guevara's revolutionary theory."[134] As I have argued, his strategy qualifies as anarcho-Marxist: Marxist in theory and anarchist in deeds.

How did Guevara propose to implement his insurrectional strategy? Neither kidnapping for ransom nor bank expropriations figured in his arsenal of tactical objectives. One looks in vain through the pages of *La guerra de guerrillas* for even a hint of them. Guevara's manual repudiates "terrorism" that tends to victimize innocent persons while, in order to win over the local population, it admonishes guerrillas to demonstrate their "moral superiority" over the enemy.[135] It excludes the taking of hostages for the purpose of exchanging prisoners and their execution in the event the enemy does not comply with the guerrillas' terms. But in Mexico kidnapping became the guerrillas' favorite tactic.[136] So despite their paeans of praise to their favorite hero, Cabañas and Vázquez violated more than one of Guevara's tactical principles.

In order for guerrillas to be well received by the local population, Guevara advised them to become economically active, to establish small industries, to barter their products, and to pay for the provisions they might need, if not with money, then with promissory notes redeemable after victory.[137] This was not the practice of Cabañas's and Vázquez's guerrillas, who began by kidnapping rich cattle ranchers in the tropical state of Guerrero, but then shifted to bank robberies and abductions in Mexico's concrete jungles. So they came to have more in common with the urban guerrillas in Uruguay and Argentina than with Guevara's model, which had initially inspired them.[138]

Imperceptibly, Mexico's guerrillas had shifted from Guevara's strategy of rural guerrilla warfare to the strategy of urban guerrillas disseminated by a comparative unknown, the gray eminence behind the urban guerrillas in Uruguay and Argentina. Unlike Guevara, he was a self-declared anarchist and an admitted follower of Bakunin. His name was Abraham Guillén (1913–1993).

A member of Spain's anarcho-syndicalist National Confederation of Work and a militant in the Federation of Iberian Anarchists during the 1936–1939 Civil War, Guillén escaped from a maximum security prison after having his death sentence for anti-Franco activities commuted to ten years in jail. He fled to France in 1945, then made his way to Argentina. For his role as a military adviser to the Uturuncos ("tiger men" in Quechua), the first of the Guevarist-inspired guerrillas in Argentina's Northwest in 1959–1960, he was again imprisoned. On his release in 1962, he sought political asylum in Uruguay. It was through his political and military coaching of Uruguay's urban guerrillas, the notorious Tupamaros, that he indirectly made a contribution to the Mexican guerrillas who adopted their tactics.[139]

Guillén's impact on the Mexican Left dates from the first extracts of his writings by Fidel Miró in a book on anarchism and the student movement published in Mexico in 1969. Miró, a prominent Spanish anarchist, introduces the brief extracts with words from one of Guillén's youthful disciples: "The best way of brewing a stew among the revolutionary vexations in today's world is to mix the largest dose of anarchism with communism, and the largest dose of communism with anarchism." Disaffected student rebels in 1968 (anarchists, Trotskyists, Maoists, Guevarists), Miró observed, had already concocted such a brew, its basic ingredients being a mystique of violence, a myth of permanent revolution, and a mission of nihilism in relation to the values of present-day society.[140]

A more extensive discussion of Guillén's theories appeared in 1971 with the Mexican publication of Omar Costa's *Los Tupamaros*.[141] It was in the role of mentor to Uruguay's guerrillas, the author notes, that Guillén achieved international fame. They were the first to apply his dictum, "The time has come to reconcile Marx and Bakunin."[142] As the leading theoretician of urban guerrilla warfare, his 1966 *Estrategia de la guerrilla urbana*, republished in a revised edition in 1969, brought him more notoriety than any of his sixty or so other books, declared a Mexican Communist who interviewed him in 1981.[143]

For Guillén, as for Guevara, the objectives of a guerrilla war are both immediate and long-term. Although the immediate objective may be the overthrow of an unpopular and repressive regime, the next step is the abolition of capitalist exploitation and ownership of the means of production with the ultimate purpose of moving beyond socialism to communism. However, Guillén professed a different kind of socialism from Guevara's, a libertarian or self-managed socialism of freely associated workers' councils and cooperatives, opposed to state property and centralized planning.[144]

This explains Guillén's preference for the Chinese communes prefigured by the Spanish communes of 1936–1939. The Chinese communes do not have incomes "ten times higher for bureaucrats than for ordinary workers and peasants, and therefore have moved further toward communism than the great industrial enterprises, state farms and agricultural collectives in the Soviet Union." That is because the "popular communes have, and Soviet state enterprises have not, liberated themselves from commodity fetishism and the alienating effects of money."[145]

Guillén defined himself as an "anarcho-Marxist," a "synthesis of anarchism (direct action, participatory democracy, libertarian socialism . . .) and Marxism (dialectical method, materialist interpretation of history and the analysis of capitalist accumulation through surplus value)." [146] Depending on the mix, he detected several variants of Marxism wedded to anarchism in practice. Lenin and Trotsky were anarcho-Marxists, he argued, and so were Mao, Castro, Guevara, and the philosopher of the New Left, Herbert Marcuse. [147] The friends of equality, apostles of direct action who were neither Marxists nor anarchists, also figured in Guillén's revolutionary pantheon. [148]

Guillén's anarcho-Marxism is important for understanding the Mexican guerrillas because that is where their ideology led. As Guevara described a parallel phenomenon during the Cuban Revolution, the ideology of the guerrillas appeared in the course of the armed struggle, toward the end rather than at the beginning. So what they were fighting for was only dimly perceived by the guerrillas during the revolutionary war. [149]

How does Guillén's strategy for revolution differ from Guevara's? The differences are underscored in his only complete work by a Mexican publisher, his 1977 coauthored *Revaloración de la guerrilla urbana*. [150]

Against Guevara's first principle of guerrilla warfare, Guillén argues that the guerrillas can defeat a regular army only when a political coalition of all the disaffected elements in society can be mobilized to act independently. This may occur in response to a foreign invasion, an unconstitutional dictatorship, or a corrupt and anachronistic constitutional regime plagued by economic crisis from which there is no relief. Since guerrillas are not a substitute for the people in arms, their task is not to confront the regular army but to assist workers, peasants, students, and middle sectors to defend their own organizations.

Guillén objects to Guevara's second principle for presuming that the objective conditions of revolution are given in Latin America, that the guerrilla vanguard can create the missing subjective conditions, and that guerrillas must bunch together for their mutual protection. No matter how well-armed, well-disciplined, and well-trained they are, the guerrillas cannot create a revolutionary consciousness by directly challenging the repressive forces; they must do so indirectly by supporting mass mobilizations with firepower and by pushing people to acts of insurrection. In large cities where the forces of repression are concentrated, they must unite only for armed actions and disperse to escape detection.

Guevara's third principle applies only where the population can be mobilized so that the insurrectional energy is not lost in empty space. More important than a favorable terrain is a favorable population large enough when mobilized to make a difference. Guevara's mistake was to raise to a general principle the assumption that guerrillas should encircle the cities from the countryside. On the contrary, where the bulk of the population lives in large cities, urban warfare should take precedence over rural.

Guillén likens his strategy to the winning strategy of Fidel Castro, not the losing strategy of Che Guevara in Bolivia and of Guevara's followers throughout most of Latin America.[151] Castro believed that when popular violence breaks out, revolutionaries should defend the claims of peasants to the land (Zapata), provide peace and bread for a war-weary and hungry population (Lenin), protect people from arbitrary taxation (Mao), and defend the rights of ordinary citizens against violations of the constitution (Sandino). As a practical politician, he took people as they are rather than as they should be; he did not try to make heroes of them. He latched onto immediate grievances as a springboard to a more far-reaching goal, and revealed it only after his guerrillas became firmly entrenched in power.

Why did Guillén consider it necessary to re-evaluate the strategy of urban guerrilla warfare? The answer is that, like Guevara, Guillén led a pack of unfaithful imitators. Uruguay's Tupamaros fell victim to their errors, as did their Argentine counterparts. Those errors were less often technical or military than political. In the case of the Tupamaros, excessive centralization and the absence of internal democracy, a mystique of heroism combined with a cult of personality, dogmatic principles and sectarian objectives were their undoing.[152] To be effective, Guillén concludes, guerrillas must elicit trust and sympathy, not just respect for their political objectives and military capabilities.

From the dismal end of the Tupamaros and that of their Mexican counterparts, one cannot reasonably infer that a strategy of urban guerrilla warfare is bankrupt. "In view of the impatience and vanguardist proclivity characteristic of urban guerrillas in the two Americas, and their evident indifference to the model of the people in arms, the reverses suffered by them during the past decade should be attributed to their own mistakes, not to defects in Guillén's strategy."[153] As the essentials of his strategy are summarized in the "Introduction" to *Revaloración de la guerrilla urbana*, the guerrillas must increase in numbers and firepower through the support of popular causes, and the government's morale must be broken in a war of attrition, until the least damage inflicted on the enemy is more effective than making the enemy run.

FIVE

THE STUDENT REBELLION
AND ITS AFTERMATH

The CIA-sponsored invasion of the Bay of Pigs in Cuba took place on 17 April 1961. While the struggle on the Cuban beach was still in progress, some fifteen thousand Mexican students marched toward the central plaza in Mexico City to express their solidarity with the Cuban people. Suddenly, tear gas and police truncheons fell on the demonstrators. Repressive Mexico versus socialist Cuba—that image was engraved on the students' minds.

A year later Rubén Jaramillo was murdered with government complicity. Díaz Ordaz became president in 1964, but there was no amnesty for the political prisoners, Demetrio Vallejo and Valentín Campa, leaders of the great railway strike of 1958–1959. Its repression nearly destroyed Mexico's independent labor movement until the student rebellion set it in motion again.

In the decade of the sixties, political repression helped to raise the students' political consciousness. The law against "social dissolution," against "criminal association and sedition," hung like a sword of Damocles over those seeking social change. On the eve of the student rebellion of 1968 Vallejo began a hunger strike to demand his freedom. Some students at the National University also began a hunger strike in sympathy, while students of the Faculty of Political Science called on the whole university to strike in response to the slogan: "Freedom for Political Prisoners."

Already in 1968 an "*anarquisante*" (anarchizing) current committed to direct action had appeared from within the student movement, a current fed by Revueltas's critique of the PCM and by his revival of the legacy of Ricardo Flores Magón.[1] Direct action took three principal forms: student strikes, marches, and demonstrations against the government, followed by student-led urban guerrillas, and student participation in popular coalitions and neighborhood committees of self-defense.

As a by-product of the revival of the idea of a new revolution, the MLN contributed to the radicalization of Mexico's new generation and to the student mobilizations and days of rage in Mexico City. Although appearing on the heels of the French general uprising in May 1968, the student rebellion in Mexico was less influenced by French events than by the escalation of domestic repression. The students' number one demand was the release of political prisoners. At the top of the list were Demetrio Vallejo and Valentín Campa.

Students demonstrated against the PRI government for ideological reasons and in self-defense. The mobilizations responded to violence and the threat of violence from police, military, and paramilitary units and from campus hit squads in the pay of school authorities, business groups, and government agencies. Incensed by repeated violations of their constitutional rights, angered by feelings of political impotence, and impatient with the passivity of industrial workers and the reformist policies of the traditional Left, students began to arm themselves in preparation for a new revolution.

They took as a model the new tactics of armed struggle adopted by urban guerrillas in Argentina and Uruguay. Besides the capitalist system and the state bureaucracy, they targeted the universities as ideological partners in the system of repression. Fomented by dissidents of the Communist Youth, this anarchizing current called for the total negation of existing society, including the government-controlled trade unions and the aboveground parties of the Left. It aimed not only at destroying the Establishment, but also at the transformation of everyday life.

The 1968 student movement was a precursor of the new social movements that proliferated during the seventies and eighties. The students' reliance on self-governance through *coordinadoras* (coordinating committees) marked a watershed between the Old Left and the New. While the Old Left had concentrated on building a vanguard party, the New Left turned to community organizing and extraparliamentary activity on the margins of the political system. The defense committees that emerged during and after 1968 focused less on the economic conditions of the ejido, farm, and factory than on the need for collective action concerning neighborhood issues, such as potable water, access to electrical power, and improved housing, transportation, and health services. The mushrooming *coordinadoras* also spread to the established trade unions and peasant associations hitherto subservient to the ruling party. The Cuban Revolution served as an example through its grassroots organizations and self-defense committees.[2]

The struggle of Mexican students in 1968 was not fundamentally different from that of students and dissident intellectuals in Eastern Europe and the Soviet Union in 1989–1991. Like the former Soviet Leviathan, the Mexican state is a bureaucratic state, the organ of an administrative-professional class with a monopoly of political power. Although the private sector is ruled by a business class, the public sector belongs to the PRI. As in the former Soviet Union, efforts at social change turned into a struggle against the state.

THE STUDENT REBELLION OF 1968

The first student demonstrations began in April 1968. By July the barricades of burning buses, raids on Communist party offices, popular assemblies, and arrests of student and faculty leaders were old hat.[3] But it was then that matters got out of hand. On July 26 came the spark that set off the student explosion.

In the Juárez Semicircle the Communist Youth and other student organizations from the National University held a meeting to celebrate the anniversary of the Cuban Revolution. Meanwhile, in another part of the capital a demonstration of students from the Polytechnical Institute protested the *granaderos'* (riot-control troops') invasion of Vocational School Number Five. When a group of demonstrators from the Polytechnical Institute moved toward the central plaza, deviating from the route approved by the government, the *granaderos* attacked them. The students fled toward the Alameda Park and joined the demonstrators from the university in the Juárez Semicircle. But they did not escape the *granaderos*. Bleeding students, the wail of ambulances, hundreds of people beaten, barricades of overturned buses, smashed store windows, four hours of street fighting with the riot-control troops, the traffic police, the Federal Police, and the Secret Service was the outcome. Eight students lay dead, while others took refuge in the preparatory schools.

From July to October student unrest so plagued the political authorities that some feared a repetition in Mexico of the French student upheavals in May.[4] Rebellious students questioned not only the lack of democracy, but also the legitimacy of the PRI government and the ideology of the ruling party. Although the thrust of the rebellion called for upholding the 1917 Constitution, the movement contained a leftist side current that wanted a new revolution. The confluence of rival ideologies was vividly demonstrated by the banners and portraits the students carried. Pictures of Mao, Che Guevara, Ho Chi Minh, Lenin, and Trotsky appeared alongside those of José María Morelos, Emiliano Zapata, Francisco Villa, and Demetrio Vallejo, the popular leader of the great railway workers' strike of 1958–1959.[5]

As one student explained why he and his companions carried a picture of Che Guevara, "ideologically we identify ourselves with the revolutionary thinking of José María Morelos [the mestizo priest during the wars of independence who fought and died for agrarian reform] and the brothers Flores Magón . . . youth sees in him [Guevara] the prototype of the New Man who fought and gave . . . himself unconditionally to the cause of the people."[6] Guevara represented for these students a revival of the revolutionary current of Ricardo Flores Magón and the PLM at the beginning of the century. That there were anarchists among the demonstrators came as no surprise. The Mexico City police began searching for anarchists linked to the French "May Revolution," after several foreign students had already been jailed, including the daughter of American singer Pete Seeger.[7]

Student committees of struggle played a key role in the events of 1968 and in the genesis of the urban guerrillas and self-defense committees. The first committee of struggle came out of the Graduate School of Economics at the National Polytechnic Institute.[8] Following its lead, committees of struggle sprang up in nine other schools and departments that supported its call for a student general strike.

The strike on 30 July was organized to protest the government-backed repression of student demonstrators on 26 July and the government-subsidized student federation and the thugs used to intimidate student activities. The committee of struggle in the School of Economics put forth three principal demands: the abolition of the government-sponsored Federación Nacional de Estudiantes Técnicos (National Federation of Technical Students) and its hit squads; the expulsion of their members from the Polytechnic Institute; and the dissolution of the government's riot-control troops.[9] The National Federation's response was to denounce the "foreign agitators," the provocateurs of "Maoism and Trotskyism," and the "anarchists" and "anarchizing" elements responsible for the student mobilization.[10]

From the committees of struggle sprang the directing organ of the student movement, the Consejo Nacional de Huelga (National Strike Council, CNH). Officially constituted on 8 August 1968, the CNH consisted of 210 members, 3 elected from each of seventy schools and departments on strike in different states. Adopted by the CNH, the first major document of the rebellion demanded (1) freedom for all political prisoners; (2) dismissal of the police chiefs and a lieutenant-colonel; (3) abolition of the *granaderos*; (4) abrogation of the article in the penal code concerning the "crime of social dissolution," loosely interpreted as any immediate danger to law and order; (5) indemnization of the families of the student dead and wounded; and (6) determination of responsibility for the July repression.[11]

These demands did not imply an assault on the legitimacy of the Mexican Revolution, but aimed to reveal the disparity between the principles of the Constitution and the Mexican political system.

The most striking feature of the students' program was the priority assigned to freedom for political prisoners who were still serving out their sentences from the 1958 railway strike. They had originally demanded only the release of student detainees. But the Central Nacional de Estudiantes Democráticos (National Council of Democratic Students) had managed to broaden the appeal.[12] Founded in 1963 under the leadership of the Communist Youth, it had contributed to radicalizing the student movement. The Democratic Students' role in the student rebellion is indisputable: on 26 July in homage to the Cuban Revolution and Castro's July 26 Movement, they led the march on the central plaza that was violently repressed by the *granaderos*.[13]

The CNH's program was strikingly similar to the demands set forth by the Communist party at its 15th Congress in June 1967. Besides freedom for political prisoners, the congress called for the nullification of the crime of social dissolution. These were the two points of the CNH's program that had general political significance beyond the issues of the moment.[14] The Communist party also perceived the urgency of upholding the Constitution. Declared the political resolution at the Congress:

> Although from a strategic point of view we confront the . . . "continuation" of the Mexican Revolution with the thesis of a new revolution, from a tactical point of view . . . the country's democratic forces perceive the need to come out in defense of a Constitution that the ruling bourgeoisie violates as many times as it deems necessary to shore up its political monopoly and to put down by force the labor and peasant movement.[15]

The day after the army's first massive intervention, on 26 July, the PCM's headquarters were occupied by the army and its printing press destroyed on the grounds that it had promoted the disorder.[16] That the Communists had been influential behind the scenes was also the perception of students allied to the PRI, who had refused to take part in the 26 July student mobilization. In response to the attack, the PCM and the National Council of Democratic Students announced on 28 July the demands that would be adopted almost point for point by the students' directing organ on 4 August.[17]

The repression progressively escalated with lapses and interruptions until its climax on 2 October.[18] On 22 July the *granaderos* intervened to halt a fistfight between secondary students that had no political significance other than the brutality used to break it up. On 26 July they intervened again with more serious political consequences, including a toll of eight students dead and some five hundred wounded. A student strike was declared; classrooms were deserted. Students mobilized on an ever-increasing scale until almost half a million demonstrators occupied the central plaza on 27 August. But on 28 August, in a government effort to dislodge them, the toll was thirty-two dead. Then on 18 September the army violated the autonomy of the National University by occupying Ciudad Universitaria (University City), the central campus where over two hundred thousand students were enrolled. Two weeks later, at the Tlatelolco Plaza of Three Cultures, some fifteen thousand students demonstrated against the army's occupation. In what amounted to an ambush, the army responded with firepower, killing close to three hundred and arresting several hundred more.[19]

Protesting students responded in two radically different ways to the successive repressions. Those whose radicalism was kept in check by fears of prejudicing their careers and by the PCM and the Democratic Students leaders anxious to negotiate with the government adopted a "soft" line. The *brigadistas* (activists in the brigades of from five to ten students), who had taken to the streets and refused to make any concessions to the government, supported a "hard" line. Their model was the May Revolution in France with all its trappings: the absence of a continuing and centralized leadership, which frustrated efforts to capture the ringleaders; and the ban on special political interests, which denied the right to nominate representatives to the CNH.[20] These anarchist features of the movement kept it from falling under the control of the Democratic Students and the political parties of the Left.

The student brigades handed out leaflets and held lightning meetings at factories and public places to keep people abreast of the struggle against the government. Endorsed by most of the student activists, they accepted the justification for intransigence by ultraleftist groups of Trotskyists, Maoists, and Spartacists.[21] Dissidents among the Democratic Students also opted for intransigence. At a meeting of 150 young Communists on 14 September, a majority ignored the admonitions of the PCM leadership by agreeing to continue the strike.[22] Many broke with the party altogether, a portent of further splits in the wake of the 2 October massacre.[23]

The irony of the rebellion is that the soft line, or democratizing tendency, prevailed without initially achieving anything. The government refused to negotiate under any conditions, the Tlatelolco massacre was followed by the arrests of the remaining *brigadistas*, but within the next three years most of the CNH's six points were granted. Díaz Ordaz repealed the law against social dissolution. The leaders of the 1958–1959 strike, Vallejo and Campa, were freed. After the mini-Tlatelolco of 10 June 1971, the new president, Luis Echeverría, dismissed the chiefs of police. Other amnesties preceded as well as followed this event. There was a democratic opening, an electoral reform, and the legal registration of the principal unregistered parties on the Left. The student majority, representing the emergent middle sectors against the excesses of a fattened ruling class, eventually got its way. But could it have done so without the *brigadistas*, the intransigence, and violence of the ultra Left?

In broad outline, the student rebellion was inspired by disparate ideologies ranging from the liberal Center and democratic Left through the socialist and Marxist-Leninist Left to an anarchizing ultra Left.[24] Although the mainstream of the rebellion had liberal and democratic features, the socialist Left got a hearing through the student brigades, groupuscules of Marxist-Leninists, and dissidents from the Communist Youth.[25] The anarchizing Left also made its presence felt. Although it may be an exaggeration to say that "it gave the initial impulse, constituted the initial and effective basis of the mobilizations and the permanent revolutionary mechanism . . . [that] fired up the politicized sector of the students by its dynamism," it required "only four days and two frantic confrontations [before 26 July] to bring about massive intervention by the army."[26]

The direct-action current went beyond confrontation with the president, the PRI government, and the repressive forces by targeting the numberless hierarchies that were not directly political. Among them were parental authority, university pedigrees, and the bureaucratization of student life. Job-related professional concerns were not uppermost in the discontent expressed by this sector of relatively impoverished, younger students attending secondary and vocational schools. Although they lacked a global understanding of the political system, they were inspired by an apocalyptic vision. They combined conspiratorial methods with spontaneous insurrectional activity. They aimed at a complete negation of the system in favor of an "egalitarian society," but they also developed a program of concrete demands that included worker housing, popular education, and health care.[27]

Ultraleftist students engaged in fistfights with students loyal to the government, threw rocks and Molotov cocktails at the police and riot-control troops, traveled in requisitioned buses distributing mimeographed sheets full of denunciations, attended flash meetings in industrial zones and poor neighborhoods, took most of the beatings and suffered most of the casualties. They stoned the windows of the Secretariat of the Interior on 19 September, provoked and battled the *granaderos* on 20 and 21 September, erected barricades of overturned vehicles in a confrontation with the army on 22 September, and burned buses and engaged in a shoot-out with police that resulted in twenty dead and hundreds wounded on 23 September. Arrested by the hundreds, they were charged with robbery, damage to property, and homicide.

The actions of this sector became the pretext for the 2 October massacre in the Plaza of Three Cultures. After the massacre the secretary of defense, Gen. Marcelino García Barragán, announced to the press that the army had intervened upon request by the police to stop a shoot-out between rival groups of students—an allusion to ultraleftist extremists opposed by moderates loyal to the government.[28]

The combatants from the preparatory and vocational schools lacked a fully articulated ideology, but they knew what they wanted. The Mexican Revolution had been disgraced and betrayed, so another revolution was necessary. Such was the thrust of the press bulletin released by the National Union of Polytechnical Students on 13 September:

> Students at the Polytechnic Institute suffer terribly in their efforts to survive and study: 70 percent of them must have recourse to part-time work; their scholarships are insufficient; absenteeism is rampant among their teachers, failures and dropouts are increasing every year . . . young people in this institution want new political and social solutions; they reject the contemporary world as "unauthentic in its lifestyle."[29]

Having little prospect of completing their studies and obtaining employment commensurate to their skills, they had little to lose by going on a rampage and turning society upside down. So they were not intimidated by President Díaz Ordaz's State of the Union message on 1 September, when he threatened to use "all available legal methods" to ensure that the coming Olympics hosted by the government would not be disrupted.[30]

This was the sector for which Revueltas took intellectual responsibility, for which he was arrested in November 1968, and tried and sentenced to sixteen years in prison in September 1970.[31] The state charged him with having directed the student rebellion from behind the scenes. "Although this was a desperate fabrication on the part of the state," says one biographer, "perhaps no other leftist leader in Mexico could have been so honored."[32] He was amnestied by President Echeverría in May 1971.

That Revueltas had close ties to some of the student leaders is suggested by an article in the 10 November 1968 issue of *Novedades* by Julio Ernesto Teissier. "Who was the brains, the gray eminence, behind the CNH's Roberto Escudero and the followers of the Mao-Guevarist line? The best-informed circles in Mexico City claim to have irrefutable proof that this role was assumed, and is still played from hiding, by the writer José Revueltas . . . who launched the most committed of the youthful students into acts of provocation and terrorism."[33]

A police report of 20 August 1968 charged Revueltas with being co-author of a pamphlet for the First Congress in July of the Unión Nacional de Estudiantes Revolucionarios (National Union of Revolutionary Students). The pamphlet urged students "to ally with workers and peasants to attack the 'bourgeois dictatorship' and work toward the establishment of a proletarian government." [34] This was hardly a police fabrication.

On 21 August, Revueltas gave his assessment of the situation and an outline of the strategy and tasks of the Spartacus Communist League. Noting that student unrest had become the "detonator" of a popular resistance bound to lead to "armed struggle," he called for the "incorporation of the working class into the movement" and for the "overthrow of the bourgeois state." [35]

Revueltas claimed that the student rebellion had reached an impasse on 30 July and that the march of protest led by the chancellor of the National University on 1 August constituted a betrayal of the radical wing of the movement. By raising the banner of university autonomy and calling for negotiation with the government, the chancellor had effectively side-tracked the movement. In a move to recover the "revolutionary character of the democratic demands," Revueltas called for the symbolic takeover of the university and the immediate establishment of academic self-government with students in a leading role. At the same time, he urged the student vanguard to go underground as a precautionary measure against the anticipated "coup of extermination." [36]

The great merit of the student movement, according to Revueltas, is that it threatened to catalyze other sectors into making comparable demands. To this concerted challenge to the ruling party's political monopoly, the PRI could only respond by putting an end to university autonomy. "Under these circumstances, the movement's strategy seems very clear. One has to complement the movement's revolutionary and democratic autonomy with academic self-government, an authentic reform of higher education . . . that will represent the first step toward political self-determination of all the popular sectors with the working class at the helm." [37]

Mexico's student movement, Revueltas believed, was the catalyst of a "new revolution." "What is the significance," he asked, "of the banners of Che Guevara, Ho Chi Minh, Lenin, and Trotsky in the hands of the demonstrators . . . of the revolutionary themes and enlightened and novel slogans on the walls of the university's and Polytechnical Institute's buildings?" [38] They were signs of something more than a merely democratic movement. "Ho Chi Minh, Che, Mao, Trotsky. Why not other heroes, why not Mexican ones?" Were intellectuals on the Left and leaders of the two Marxist-Leninist parties responsible for injecting these symbols into the student rebellion? "Yes and no," answered Revueltas. Yes, insofar as the groupuscules to the left of those parties exercised some influence. No, insofar as the groupuscules operated only marginally.[39]

As Revueltas later acknowledged, the student rebellion was not a historically isolated phenomenon but had its roots in the repression of the great railway workers' strike, which put an end to massive workers' protests for a whole decade. "The students represented this proletarian current, which had been put off by the repression."[40] Although the brigades represented a small minority, the 1968 rebellion contained seeds of a "struggle that went beyond the CNH's six points."[41]

One can thank the student movement for the emergence of an "independent New Left," says Revueltas.[42] In 1958 the Marxist-Leninist parties did not understand that "the preservation of the railway workers' unions in independent hands was more important and represented a greater advantage from a class point of view than winning the strike."[43] As a result, the strike was lost and the union ceased being a bastion of the struggle for trade union independence.

The students exhibited the same spirit of intransigence as the railway workers. The campaign for the release of the strike's leaders, Vallejo and Campa, was a campaign for political freedom, "above all, freedom and independence for the proletariat," concludes Revueltas. Thus the struggle for democracy became transformed into a struggle for socialism by students and intellectuals "converted into natural and historical allies of the proletariat, which they were not prior to 1968 . . . into an independent New Left, which also did not exist before 1968."[44]

BLOODY THURSDAY, 10 JUNE 1971

Those who think that the student rebellion ended with the 2 October massacre fail to consider the events in its wake. The massacre made an indelible impression and the memory of it festered until student discontent again exploded, beginning with the strike in the Department of Philosophy and Literature at the Autonomous University of Nuevo León in September 1969.

Monterrey, the site of the university and the headquarters of the largest consortium of Mexican capitalists, the Monterrey Group, is a city in which the disparities between wealth and poverty immediately strike the eye. Understandably, it became the scene of a continuing student rebellion that helped to reactivate the student movement in the nation's capital.

The federal government's concessions to students in Mexico City had yet to spread out in comparable reforms at the state level. Meanwhile, the underlying economic causes of student unrest remained untouched. As the CNH explained in the "October 2 Manifesto to the Nation," issued two days before the CNH dissolved on 6 December: "This movement is an expression of the profound inequalities in the distribution of income, as a result of the concentration in a few hands of the wealth generated by the people, of the . . . lack of access to a dignified life by young peasants, workers, and students. . . . Society creates professionals and technicians to whom it offers no employment."[45]

The political authorities in Monterrey, the capital of Nuevo León, tried to pack the university's administration with people loyal to the governor and to the Monterrey Group of industrial millionaires who backed him. The governor, Eduardo Elizondo, overreached himself when he filled the administration with thirty-one representatives of private enterprise. In response, teachers and students declared a strike out of respect for the university's autonomy.[46]

In March 1970, faculty and students won a partial victory when the university's autonomy was upheld by the state government and the university council elected a new chancellor. But the state subsidy to the university was cut off when he catered to student demands. Pressured by the state government, he demanded the resignation of the university's administrative secretary, a man widely respected by the student body. This action undermined the chancellor's authority. He resigned in January 1971.

The university council elected a new chancellor in February, but the university's private patrons and the political authorities found him unacceptable. When he refused to resign, the state government intervened by changing the university's charter and the rules governing the chancellor's election. So in April another chancellor, a professed anticommunist, was "elected," with the result that there were two chancellors instead of one.

Meanwhile, the governor ordered the appointment of new heads of departments and schools who would comply with the changed rules. But the mass of students occupied the university's buildings and formed a solid front of resistance that prevented the appointees from taking office. In May the Monterrey police assisted by *porros* (slang for gangs of armed, lumpen youth subsidized by special interests) dislodged the students. But the students counterattacked by retaking the chancellery on 31 May. So the secretary of public education had to fly in from Mexico City to mediate the dispute. Víctor Bravo Ahuja called together seven former chancellors to draw up a new set of rules in collaboration with the university council. The next day, 5 June, both the anticommunist chancellor and Governor Elizondo resigned.

By then the student strike had elicited national attention. As early as 14 March, a number of schools and departments at the National University had declared their solidarity with the striking students in Monterrey. Although the CNH had dissolved, it was replaced by the Consejo Nacional de Lucha (National Council of Struggle), incorporating all the committees of struggle at both the National University and the Polytechnical Institute. On 15 April leaflets were handed out demanding the restoration of university autonomy. Other demands were added of national political significance: freedom for political prisoners and democratization of the trade unions. For the first time, student protestors in Mexico City acquired the active backing of a substantial sector of organized labor, the Revolutionary Teachers' Movement, the General Union of Mexican Workers and Peasants, the Communist rump of the Independent Peasant Central, the National Railway Council, and the Poor People's Organization of Nezahualcóyotl (the great shantytown east of the capital).

A huge march was planned for 10 June, the religious holiday of Corpus Christi. The march was to begin at Saint Thomas's Cap and proceed to the Monument of the Revolution. But in an ominous reminder of the events of September and October 1968, the Monterrey Group and its political allies in Mexico City made plans to stop it. Since the army was ordered to hold its fire, the supporters of repression turned to hired gangs to break up the demonstration.

Two groups of *porros* were summoned for this purpose. At the National University a professor in the Chemistry Department with connections to the Monterrey Group, Sergio Romero Ramírez, nicknamed "the Fish," instructed his hit men to intimidate the students' leaders. Meanwhile, in downtown Mexico City mid-level government officials ordered their groups of lumpen youth to break up the march. But there were differences over matters of tactics. The Fish's shock troops thirsted for blood, while the political authorities recalled the devastating effects of the army's repression in October 1968.

Four years after the events of 10 June a former student *porro*, Antonio Solís Mimendi, revealed details of the conspiracy in his *Jueves de Corpus Sangriento*.[47] The big money in Monterrey was scared of "communism" and hired the services of the Fish. On a secret trip to Monterrey he and an aide had a fateful meeting with the president of the Confederación Patronal de la República de México (Employers' Confederation of the Mexican Republic, COPARMEX), with the banker Eloy Ballina, and with others of the Monterrey Group. The go-between was a certain Garza Leal, known as "the Elbow," and the deal was made in an automobile moving through the streets of Monterrey—an old Mafia trick to avoid overhearing ears.

Solís was not privy to how much money changed hands, but it must have been a considerable sum considering the number of hit men who took orders from the Fish. Gerardo Medina Valdés, in his *Operación 10 de junio*, cites a report by Col. Alfonso Guerro that the public forces maintaining law and order numbered only nine hundred compared to fifteen hundred secretly employed gunslingers.[48] The Fish alone had at least six "Centurions," each with a hundred thugs under his direct orders. "We will no longer be despised *porros*," he was reported as saying, "but chiefs of a powerful political movement that will overturn the government."[49]

The Monterrey Group had been enraged by President Echeverría's intervention in the student conflict in Nuevo León. It also feared the government's revived populism and other threats to its business interests. So the Fish was instructed to discredit the government by provoking a bloodbath on 10 June.

In a re-edition of the Tlatelolco massacre, an ambush was prepared with the foreknowledge that the police would be cordoning off the marchers. While the police relied on tear gas to quell the students, the Fish's street gangs and sharpshooters did most of the victimizing. Official sources admitted to only eleven killed, but a single *porro* confessed to seeing more than thirty dead. The hospitals were filled with hundreds of wounded; hundreds more were mercilessly beaten.

The *porros* played a key role in these events, but have received only sparse attention in the literature on the student rebellion. Backed by school and university authorities with political connections to the ruling party, they controlled most of the student associations in Mexico during the 1960s and the 1970s. Instead of concentrating on their studies, they were busy with student affairs. But they almost always passed to the next grade, some with high marks, unless they chose to remain in the preparatory schools or university programs as "fossils" controlling students and being paid for their efforts. Although they initially appeared in the schools and universities of the capital, they subsequently became active in the various state universities and technical institutes. Because of their role in the genesis of student-backed guerrillas, a detailed description of them is in order.[50]

Their origins go back to the early Madero presidency. Strictly speaking, *porros* and *porras* are cheerleaders of both sexes during student reunions and sport events. But the term "*porro*" later acquired another and sinister meaning. In Mexican student life "cheerleaders" became the nickname for student gangsters and lumpen youth hired to terrorize and break up meetings of politically active students opposed to university and government policies. In this usage, *porros* translates as "torpedoes," gunslingers ready to shoot or attack without warning. Blackmail, threats, robbery, and violence became their way of life.

Torpedoes placed on a government payroll and organized into shock brigades that received military training were called *halcones* (hawks). Initially, they learned their military skills under the supervision of Col. Raúl Mendiola Cerecero, chief of special services of the Metropolitan Police during the administration of President López Mateos. After October 1968, Gen. Alfonso Corona del Rosal not only gave them military training, but also organized them militarily into special units under his command. The hawks were supported by subsidies from various government agencies.

Their origins may be traced to 1940, when Cárdenas's ruling party began recruiting children of Mexican workers for legally questionable political tasks. Fifteen-year-olds were selected and trained to break up political meetings and smash the election stands of the opposition presidential candidate, Gen. Juan Andrew Almazán. When Almazán's supporters defended themselves, special commandos, protected by police, went into action. The original organizer of these student shock brigades was the same Corona del Rosal.

Ruiz Cortines and López Mateos used the hawks to repress protests. In the Citadel of the Federal District they were known by their wrist bands of adhesive tape and their brush haircuts. During the railway strike in 1958, they carried I.D. cards with a three-colored band and a badge reading "PRI police." [51] Their leaders received money from López Mateos's private secretary.

In 1965 Jorge Eduardo Pascual, bodyguard for Alfonso Martínez Domínguez, the administrator of the Federal District, trained his pupils in the Venustiano Carranza Park in the capital. The capital's mayor entrusted him with the task of cleaning up the main streets, which were crawling with penny vendors. The vendors and beggars were a scandalous sight for the eyes of American tourists beginning to arrive in droves, and the government wanted to hide these ugly signs of poverty and lagging development. So Pascual's hawks went to work on the unfortunate Lazarus layers of society until, after bloody attacks and petty robberies, the marginalized poor disappeared from downtown Mexico City.

Different chancellors of the National University, directors of preparatory and vocational schools and higher educational centers throughout the nation have required the services of torpedoes as bodyguards and campus police.[52] During the 1968 student rebellion they were famous for beating their victims with truncheons on the university campus. In University City they got money from the chancellory and from the principals of every preparatory school dependent on the National University. They were invaluable in breaking up student demonstrations and quelling student agitators.

Other torpedoes were hired by the Special Services of the Central Department of the Federal District. They received two thousand pesos a month from the Central Department for guarding the subway installations. When this was not enough money, they assaulted and robbed citizens in the streets. Protected by the political authorities, they shot and stabbed people, machine-gunned schools like the Vocational Number Five in the Citadel, and on several occasions used dynamite or homemade bombs to disrupt assemblies.

Juan de Dios Vargas, a sociology student at the National University and a teacher at the Vocational School Number Five from 1969 to 1975, gives an eyewitness account of torpedo intimidation:

> I watched with clenched fists when torpedoes ripped out the eye of a student during an attack and blackjacked and kicked several others who stood up to them. Paralyzed with fear, I had to look on helplessly from the windows as they beat students with clubs in the quad below. On another occasion in the school's prefectory, they raped the female students who had remained after hours to work on problems with their classmates. I have been robbed by them in broad daylight and on several occasions compelled to give "donations to the needy" to quell their thirst for liquor. After a student at the Vocational had been shot and killed, I called on teachers and students to organize in self-defense. But I made no headway because the school's authorities relied on torpedoes to silence student protest. Confronted by these and other aggressions, how can one expect politically active students to continue to defend themselves by peaceful and legal means?[53]

The torpedoes were turned into hawks by their mental warps and material poverty after October 1968. The infamous General Corona del Rosal paid them off in various government offices: Petróleos, Banobras, and the Control Department of the Federal District. On the payroll, they were listed as "auxiliary services" under the codes R1, R8, and R10.

When they were not undergoing training or serving as shock forces, they were employed as bodyguards or busy hunting unidentified "terrorists." The hawks had different training camps: Ixtapalapa, San Juan de Aragón, and the Cuchilla del Tesoro. The best-equipped camps for commandos was in San Juan de Aragón: it had pits, tracks, hanging bars, wooden stairs, vehicles, a military academy. They practiced judo, karate, tae kwon do. But they stripped off the mysticism that often accompanies such disciplines and learned them only to kill. They studied the use of firearms, from the simplest to the M2. To conceal their training, their camps were surrounded by barbed wire and police guards kept bystanders away. Their second-in-command was Colonel Díaz Escobar, who supervised their exercises three times a week.

Like the famous Nazi assault troops of Heinrich Himmler, hawks had to be a certain height, in this case at least 1.70 meters (5 feet 6 inches). Their age ranged between eighteen and twenty-three years. They needed a graduation certificate from primary school and a military service card to qualify. Once recommended by a politician, a military man, or another hawk, they had to endure three successive runs around the obstacle track. No one was supposed to give his real name: each was known by a nickname. The hawks were recruited from criminal gangs, from the Fish's torpedoes at the National University, from "the mummies," "the Nazis," "the bad boys of Peralvillo," from peddlers of the Jamaica market, and from soldiers who had been court-martialed. The justice of the government promised all these lumpen elements impunity.

According to a member of the conservative National Action party, Gerardo Medina Valdés, the hawks were divided into "groups" at the base level, each with a minimum of 16 pupils. A "Spaniard" had 105 hawks under his command; a "professor" had even more.[54] Every day the password changed. The police knew it, and the hawks could resort to a secret telephone number if they required police aid. The parents of a young hawk had no idea what he was doing for a living. In 1968 the "professors" earned seventy pesos daily, not to mention the bribes they picked up. They received training from the FBI, and twelve of them went to Japan and South Korea for practice in the martial arts. In England they took courses in criminology.

The hawks went into action on 2 October 1969 to stop the commemoration of the Tlatelolco martyrs at the great cathedral and at Saint Thomas's Cap. In April 1970 they had a workout during the repression of the Deportivo de la Magdalena Mixhuca in Mexico City. On 4 November 1970 they rampaged in the towns of Celaya, Irapuato, and León. On 27 January 1971 journalist Félix Fuentes claimed that two million pesos a month of the public's money was being spent on these killers.

The torpedoes-hawks also had a hand in the 1968 student repression. They were detected during the peak of the rebellion on 13 August, when a crowd of some two hundred thousand students in a column five kilometers long converged on the central plaza in Mexico City. In the role of provocateurs they infiltrated the ranks of the marchers, as they would do later, on 10 June, shouting "Vivas" to Che Guevara and "To war, let's get on with it!"[55]

But, by and large, they played a minor role in the 1968 events. In September the government took the offensive. The paratrooper battalion and the infantry, the armored cars filled with presidential guards, the red trucks full of firefighters, the traffic police, antiriot tanks, and the paddy wagons cleared the students from the central plaza. In October the army prepared to shoot and kill.

In June 1971 a different spectacle greeted the public eye. The regular infantry was conspicuous by its absence, the *granaderos* were present in the role of bystanders, and the police looked on passively until the gunfire was over and then began arresting demonstrators. Snipers were stationed on the rooftops overlooking the marchers, while lumpen gangs might be seen on street corners armed with long clubs. In the Cosmos Moviehouse, the Fish awaited the marchers with his gang of torpedoes.

The signal for the offensive was a burst of machine-gun fire from an adjacent building. The pseudo-student *porros* who had infiltrated the marchers then went into action. Their hair was cut short, they wore tennis shoes and light-colored shirts so that they might recognize one another. When they attacked with clubs and pistols, they were supported by gunfire from the roofs. There was so much confusion during the mêlée that some of the torpedoes-hawks beat one another. After their wounded were taken to the hospital, they raided it from top to bottom and rescued their comrades to keep the operation a secret. In the best S.S. style, they ripped bottles of blood serum from the arms of students they had wounded and left as they had arrived—kicking and shouting.

Before the shooting started, Col. Angel Rodríguez, chief of the Police General Staff, tried to discourage the leaders and organizers of the march from proceeding further. "In the Cosmos Moviehouse," he warned, "there is a gang of armed youth with clubs and guns who are going to attack you." [56] Later, when President Echeverría learned of the massacre, he is reported to have wept. [57] Prominent officials were fired for allowing matters to get out of hand. Alfonso Martínez Domínguez and Rogelio Flores Curiel, chief of the Metropolitan Police, were removed on 15 June.

Bloody Thursday, said Revueltas, "stands for nothing else than the '68 Movement under new conditions." After the extraofficial repression of 10 June, the government adopted "an 'intelligent position' with respect to the movement"—the prelude to a democratic opening. [58] The government gave up trying to implement Mussolini's slogan: "Nothing against the state, nothing outside the state, everything inside the state." [59] As in 1968, the student movement turned out to be consequential in achieving at least some of its objectives.

Taking a long view, Revueltas concluded that Bloody Thursday, like Tlatelolco, signified a defeat rather than victory for the ruling party. Its lasting effect was to have raised the students' collective consciousness and commitment to freedom from arbitrary rule. In calling for democratization of the political system and the trade unions, for workers' control and self-management of state and mixed enterprises, students had embarked on a course of recovering independence for other sectors of the Left.[60] The march had begun with chants of "Mexico! . . . Freedom! . . . Mexico! . . . Freedom!" This cry had an anarchist, not just a liberal, ring.

There was a lesson to be learned from these bitter experiences. The torpedoes-hawks became for the students what the rural political bosses were for peasants like Jaramillo and rural schoolteachers like Gámiz, and what the corrupted labor bureaucrats were for industrial workers like Campa and Rodríguez. All of these parasites were in collusion against the popular resistance that might undermine the political mafia in power. Students had arrived at an inescapable conclusion: the PRI government was their enemy, not just Mexican capitalism and U.S. imperialism. So they called for a new praxis "by means of arms as a last resort."[61]

THE SEPTEMBER 23 COMMUNIST LEAGUE

With vivid recollections of the 2 October and 10 June massacres, students in the Communist Youth took to armed struggle in self-defense. As a leader of the September 23 Communist League from Baja California recalled the origin of the students' armed struggle, it emerged in response to and "after the cruel repressions of '68 and '71."[62]

The umbrella organization known as the September 23 Communist League was the students' collective response to the armed gangs in their midst. The league's founders were disaffected members of the Communist Youth at the National University and the Polytechnic Institute in Mexico City, and at the Autonomous University of Nuevo León in Monterrey—the principal centers of *porro* violence.[63] Later they were joined by student leaders from the University of Guadalajara, who likewise were being victimized or targeted by *porros* in the pay of the ruling party.[64]

As a group of student leaders from Guadalajara testified in a prison interview published in *¿Por Qué?* (3 August 1972), they had begun armed actions prematurely in response to beatings and killings by *porros*. They had turned to armed struggle "because arms are necessary for the personal protection of members of the Frente Estudiantil Revolucionario [Revolutionary Student Front]"—the leftist student association at the university. They had armed themselves in order to continue carrying out revolutionary tasks because the *porros* in the Federación de Estudiantes de Guadalajara (Guadalajara Student Federation) "refuse to let us do so except by defending ourselves with the same means used by them."[65]

Mexico's urban guerrillas were an integral part of the continuing student rebellion dating from 1968. If we break down the social composition of the seven principal urban guerrillas since 1969, it is noteworthy that students predominate in all of them with one exception, the Frente Urbano Zapatista (Zapatista Urban Front, FUZ).[66] If one adds to this list the social composition of Cabañas's guerrillas after 10 June 1971, of Carmelo Cortés's breakaway Revolutionary Armed Forces, of the Guajiros (a Chihuahua-based group), and the Lacandones (drawing on former students from the National University and the Polytechnical Institute), the evidence overwhelmingly supports this conclusion.[67]

Further evidence for this student connection appears in an article in *Tiempo* on the third anniversary of the 10 June massacre. Although the language smacks of a police report, the information supports what was later learned about the origins of the urban guerrillas. In October 1970, almost exactly two years after the 2 October massacre, an unusual meeting took place on a side street of the La Pinzona barrio in Guadalajara: "There were close to thirty persons gathered in the house, nine of them women, and there were representatives of the Cabañas and Vázquez groups, as of members of the Committees of Struggle of the different schools and departments of the universities in Mexico City, Guadalajara, and Monterrey."[68] That tells a lot, as does the six-point program they allegedly agreed on. It called for bank and commercial "expropriations," attacks on police stations and small military posts for the purpose of seizing weapons, abductions with the double aim of obtaining funds and exchanging prisoners, a campaign of terror with homemade bombs against government agencies and foreign businesses, the sabotage of government installations, and an urban guerrilla war spreading "chaos and anarchy."

Considering that disaffected members of the Communist Youth played a leading role in most of the urban guerrillas, it is a safe guess that they intended to implement the PCM's program for a new revolution by means of armed actions.[69] In effect, they opted for the anarchist strategy of directly confronting and smashing the bourgeois state. Nor was that the only trace of anarchism in their makeup.

The FUZ was Guevarist in orientation. In December 1969 it launched its first assault on a supermarket in Mexico City. This action was followed by a hit on a branch of the National Bank of Mexico in October 1970 and by the spectacular kidnapping in September 1971 of Julio Hirschfeld Almada, a government bureaucrat and millionaire. The purpose of the kidnapping was not to raise funds for the guerrillas, since the ransom of three hundred thousand pesos was distributed entirely among the needy as a symbolic return of money taken from the poor through government and private exploitation. In a prison interview published in *Punto Crítico* (June 1972), the FUZ's spokesperson, Paquita Calvo Zapata, explained that the organization consisted of both an underground armed commando and an aboveground apparatus for legal aid and recruiting. Following Guevara, the FUZ's fundamental objective was consciousness-raising aimed at "setting off a political explosion . . . in order to take power."[70] The FUZ hoped to accelerate the march of history through the creation of Guevara's "new man."[71] A precursor of the September 23 Communist League, it labored to unify the revolutionary Left, to coordinate its actions with those of other urban and rural guerrillas, as a "first step toward unification in a massive [umbrella] organization for armed struggle on a national level."[72]

In the state of Jalisco, the Fuerzas Revolucionarias Armadas del Pueblo (People's Armed Revolutionary Forces, FRAP), the armed fist of the Revolutionary Student Front, also followed in Guevara's footsteps. As the FRAP declared in a 5 May 1972 manifesto to the nation:

> As long as a socially privileged class exploits and becomes rich through the work of other classes, there will be a class struggle and corresponding violence: the violence of the exploiters to uphold their economic interests, and the violence of the exploited to free themselves. . . . [Meanwhile], the workers' living conditions are each day more desperate; each day the rich become richer and the poor become poorer. . . . The responsibility of the vanguard is . . . to make the social revolution.[73]

As in the case of Cabañas's Party of the Poor, the FRAP's program aimed at abolishing the distinction between rich and poor, thereby going beyond the establishment of socialism to an egalitarian, communist society.

Most of Mexico's leaders in urban guerrilla warfare eventually joined the umbrella organization, the September 23 Communist League. They also subscribed to its unique mix of anarchist and communist themes. Organized in Guadalajara in March 1973, it brought together the original September 23 Communist Movement centered in Monterrey, the Revolutionary Student Front, the Lacandones, and the Revolutionary Action Movement (Korean-trained guerrillas operating in Michoacán).[74]

The roots of the league go back to the Communist Youth's Third Congress in December 1970. Inspired by Revueltas's thesis of the inexistence of a communist vanguard, the Communist Youth resolved on creating one. That was not their only inspiration. They also drew on the legacy of Bakunin and of Ricardo Flores Magón, on the "new anarchism" of Daniel Cohn-Bendit, on the anarcho-Marxism of Herbert Marcuse, on such heterodox Marxists as Trotsky, Mao, and Guevara, on the examples of urban guerrilla warfare in the Southern Cone (Argentina, Uruguay, Brazil), and indirectly on the mentor of urban guerrilla warfare, Spanish Civil War veteran and neoanarchist Abraham Guillén.[75]

The doctrines of the league were developed in the form of three programmatic statements—the Madera documents I, II, and III. Their fundamental thesis was the proletarian character of the student population. Regardless of each student's class origins, according to the Madera documents, they belonged to a new stratum of the proletariat in their day-to-day activities.[76] The massification of centers of higher learning and their transformation into veritable knowledge factories had as their overriding concern the reproduction of capitalist social relations, so that students were effectively working to perpetuate the system. Their programs of studies had become necessary to the extraction of surplus value under conditions of advanced technology, the scientific-technical revolution, and new methods of doing business. Since they were not paid for working, students appeared to be the most oppressed and exploited segment of the proletariat and at the same time the best suited by virtue of their education to become its revolutionary vanguard.

Bizarre as this thesis must have sounded to the Old Left, there was a Marxist logic undergirding it. If commercial workers belong to the proletariat, as Marx argued in volume two of *Capital*, then why not students? Like commercial workers, they produce neither commodities nor surplus value, but are nonetheless exploited. Unlike independent workers such as peasants and artisans, they labor under the supervision of teachers in a role corresponding to that of industrial workers under a foreman. Although some complete their program of studies to become junior members of the privileged class of bureaucrats, only then do these former students graduate from the ranks of the proletariat.

Given the proletarian content of Mexico's student rebellion, the league's strategy was to clean house by sweeping out the "democrats." These included all who participated in bourgeois politics in opposition to the ruling party. Like the political parties of the Left that had settled for negotiations with the government, trade unions were regarded as obstacles to independent political action. Thus, in a revival of the anarchist legacy of direct action, the league opted for a strategy of industrial sabotage, bank robberies, kidnappings, and outright assassinations not only of the "pig police," but also of PCM militants who stood in its way.[77]

David Jiménez Sarmiento, a young student in the Faculty of Philosophy and Literature at the National University and a member of the Communist Youth, had taken part in the student actions of 2 October 1968. Disillusioned by what he saw at Tlatelolco, he gathered other young Communists who decided to form guerrilla commandos without previous approval from the party. They finally formed three groups: Lacandones, Patria o Muerte, and Arturo Gámiz.[78] The first was the most famous, named after Indians of the Chiapas jungle who resisted Spanish colonization for centuries and were pacified only in the 1940s. The influence of the Cuban Revolution was obvious in the second name, for that was Fidel Castro's slogan during the height of resistance to U.S. aggression at the Bay of Pigs. And the last name also showed Cuban influence, for Gámiz's guerrillas were the Mexican counterpart of the July 26 Movement and Castro's assault on the Moncada barracks. Guevara's well-known essay, *Guerrilla Warfare: A Method*, gave a political orientation to the commandos.[79]

They began their actions in Mexico City, Monterrey, and Chihuahua. The Lacandones specialized in assaults on stores and businesses from 1969 until 1975. On 18 January 1973 they carried out an expropriation of the Bimbo Bakery—the Mexican front for Wonder Bread.[80] As a result of this action they lost their best cadres. But they replaced their losses and reappeared in 1974–1975 as members of the September 23 Communist League.

In an immediate response to the fusillades at Tlatelolco, there arose another urban guerrilla group made up of Mexican students who were studying at the Patrice Lumumba University in Moscow. This group was the creation of former schoolteacher Fabricio Gómez Souza, who was studying in that special university for Third World students. When he heard what had happened in Tlatelolco he held a meeting in his dormitory with a dozen other Mexicans, who decided to join him in a guerrilla war. They formed the Revolutionary Action Movement.[81]

As the movement's leader, Gómez Souza interviewed representatives of the Soviet, Cuban, and Vietnamese governments to get help for an armed vanguard. For diplomatic reasons, these governments refused to become involved. So in November 1968 he journeyed to Pyongyang, capital of North Korea, where he got what he wanted. On his return to Moscow he received twenty-five thousand dollars from the North Korean embassy so that he and other comrades could travel to Mexico to gather at least fifty revolutionaries for training in North Korea.

Gómez Souza arrived in Mexico at the beginning of 1969. A student recruit from the Communist Youth in Morelia, Angel Bravo Cisneros, took over the leadership of the first contingent. It included Marta Maldonado, daughter of a former governor of the state of Baja California, who was to become the Patty Hearst of Mexico. Two more contingents followed them to North Korea for training. After long and hard workouts at a camp fifty kilometers to the northeast of Pyongyang, they all returned to Mexico in September.

In North Korea they received a strong communist indoctrination. According to the concept of "Juche" in the thought of North Korea's leader Kim Il Sung, the guerrillas should become self-reliant. They should get their arms from raids on the army and police, their finances from bank assaults. Each of the 50 guerrillas should recruit 10 others until there were 550 ready to begin the armed struggle. Then each of these 550 should recruit 10 more, and these still others in geometric progression. Right away they set up training centers in Mexico City and in the states of Michoacán, Querétaro, Jalisco, and Guerrero.

The first guerrilla action was an assault on a cashier from the Commercial Bank of Michoacán who was carrying funds from Morelia to Mexico City—more than a million pesos. This took place in the "Tres Estrellas" bus terminal in the capital on 19 December 1970. On 10 September 1971 came the second attack, an assault on the Bank of London branch in León, Guanajuato. That year forty members of the organization, including Bravo Cisneros, Gómez Souza, and seventeen others trained in North Korea, were captured. But the movement survived repression until in March 1973 it united its cadres with the September 23 Communist League.

Another guerrilla movement of importance came out of the Revolutionary Student Front at the University of Guadalajara.[82] The front made its debut on the political scene in September 1970 when it confronted the mafia of bureaucrats, professors, judges, and politicians who ran the university with the help of *porros* in control of the Guadalajara Student Federation. The federation's connection with the state government was obvious to all, for it functioned as a springboard to political posts.

In these circumstances the front carried out its first action on 24 September 1970. It expelled the tramps and freeloading carousers from Student House, seizing and holding the place until forced to surrender to soldiers and police. The day before there had been a shoot-out between members of the front and the Student Federation, resulting in three dead and dozens wounded. The federation's gangsters had started the fight. None of them went to jail, but members of the front were put behind bars. The embryonic front then decided to go underground, and in this clandestine status prepared for an armed struggle.

The violence was not confined to the university. Gunfights and vendettas between the two student factions wound up with the front carrying out bank assaults and kidnapping VIPs. The first bank assault occurred a year later. On 25 November 1971 came an attack on the Zamora Bank with a booty of 130,000 pesos, followed on 23 December 1971 by an assault on the Refaccionario Bank of Jalisco with a take of 100,000 pesos. At the end of 1972 and the beginning of 1973 there were raids on several banks and businesses. The driving force in this group was made up of the Campaña López brothers: Carlos, Alfredo, Juventino, and Ramón. The first two were students at the university and members of the Communist Youth.

For these assaults Carlos and Alfredo were arrested, along with two other comrades. It was then that Juventino, who went by the nickname "Ho Chi Minh," founded the FRAP. On 4 May 1973 he kidnapped the U.S. consul in Guadalajara, George Terrence Leonhardy, and asked for a million pesos in ransom. For the consul's life, "Ho" asked for the liberation of thirty political prisoners, among them Carlos and Alfredo. They were freed, and a special plane took them to Cuba.[83]

On 2 June 1973 the fourth brother, Ramón, kidnapped industrialist Pedro Sarquis Morrows, picking up a ransom of three million pesos.[84] Juventino was caught in August and shortly after, Ramón was arrested. But the FRAP went on with its struggle. On 25 August 1974 it snatched Gen. José Guadalupe Zuno, brother-in-law of the president of Mexico. This man was a progressive identified with *cardenismo*. A ransom of twenty million pesos was demanded for his release, but the government refused to negotiate with "terrorists."[85] Its only concession was to broadcast a tape that defended the guerrilla war. Two days later the FRAP's "Che Guevara" women's commando kidnapped millionaire Margarita Saad. The family handed over four million pesos, but Margarita was found slain with no explanation.[86] This deed caused the national press to turn against the guerrillas.

Although the Lacandones and the Revolutionary Action Movement joined the September 23 Communist League at its founding in 1973, the FRAP refused to do so. About the same time, one of the original members of the league, David López Valenzuela, went over to the FRAP.[87] He left the league because he was opposed to its tactics of spectacular deeds and targeting of police as a means of raising public consciousness. The FRAP was one of the few urban guerrilla movements that was born with links to the masses. But mass support began to fade in the course of the armed struggle.[88]

The most important of the urban guerrillas was the September 23 Communist League. It was the brainchild of Raúl Ramos Zavala, former leader of the Communist Youth.[89] After he broke with the PCM at the end of 1970, he interviewed representatives of other revolutionary movements to try to overcome their divisions and fuse them into a single nationwide movement.

Ramos made his first contacts with the Professional Student Movement, a Christian-communist organization counseled by Jesuit priests in the Monterrey Technological Institute. In this movement Ignacio Salas Obregón, the future leader of the league, distinguished himself. Later Ramos journeyed to Chihuahua, where he contacted Diego Lucero Martínez, a survivor of the assault on the Madera barracks. Lucero belonged to the September 23 Movement, also known as the Armed Commandos of

Chihuahua, named to honor the assault on 23 September 1965. In Mexico City, Ramos established contact with David Jiménez Sarmiento of the Lacandones. Following up on his project of unifying the Left, he then went to Guadalajara. There, with the mediation of Diego Lucero, he interviewed Fernando Salinas Mora, also of the September 23 Movement. By then the September 23 Movement had grown to include dissident members of the Revolutionary Student Front who called themselves the Vikings, directed by Juan Manuel Rodríguez. In this way Ramos brought under one executive command five organizations committed to armed struggle, including the former members of Monterrey's Communist Youth.

All linked, they went into action with two simultaneous bank assaults in Monterrey on 14 January 1972, and three more the next day in Chihuahua City. Their aim? To build up funds for the formation of a guerrilla organization on a national scale.

The first guerrillas fell in Chihuahua, where Diego Lucero and two comrades were killed and eight more went to prison. Ramos, the leader of the organization, died in a shoot-out with a police patrol in Mexico City. It was then that new leaders emerged, Ignacio Salas and a former member of the Communist Youth in Monterrey, José Angel García Martínez. These two met in the Pantitlán neighborhood in Mexico City, where they agreed to continue Ramos's project of organizing a national guerrilla movement.

On 15 March 1973 the first meeting to found the future league took place in Guadalajara. The various representatives met in the house of Fernando Salinas Mora, alias "el Richard." Besides representatives of the initial movements brought together by Ramos, there were delegates from five other groups: the survivors of the Revolutionary Action Movement, the "Sickies of Sinaloa," the Spartacus Communist League, the FUZ, and Lucio Cabañas's Peasant Justice Brigade. Cabañas hoped that the new national movement would take the name of his Party of the Poor. But in memory of the first Cuban-type guerrillas led by Gámiz, the official name adopted was September 23 Communist League. A national coordinator with a directing bureau of five people was chosen. Cabañas was not one of them.

A second national meeting of the league's delegates took place in Guadalajara in July and August 1973. There a majority agreed to the following set of proposals: first, to apply firepower in support of mass demonstrations; second, to develop actions to liberate political prisoners; third, to expropriate arms; fourth, to expropriate banks; fifth, to kill prominent chiefs of police and army officers, and also union bureaucrats who had sold out to the bosses and the government. Because it disagreed with this last clause, the FUZ left the league. Disagreements also caused the exit of the Revolutionary Action Movement, the Spartacists, and Cabañas's Peasant Justice Brigade. So as a result of internal dissension the league was reduced to its initial members plus the "Sickies of Sinaloa," whose political weight increased with passing time.

The league "sickened" under the influence of the Sinaloans and the Jesuits. The directing bureau under the control of Monterrey's revolutionary Christians formed one faction; the group operating in the Autonomous University of Sinaloa formed the other. The struggle inside the league took up much of its attention. Each faction accused its rival of petty bourgeois opportunism, and each became more leftist in response to the other's criticism. The only winner was ultraleftism.

Unlike other urban commandos, the league paid each guerrilla a monthly salary. This amounted to housing, food, and three thousand pesos at predevaluation rates. Later the guerrillas got a raise of 23 percent, so that the police worked for lower wages than the league.[90] The league was made up of mercenaries of the revolution. Of the seventy-six police killed by various guerrilla groups in a two-year period, the league could claim credit for most. League members murdered police in cold blood without even trying to seize their arms. They hoped to demoralize them, to create panic among their relatives, and to pressure them to seek other jobs.

At the beginning of its struggle the league embraced between 200 and 250 militants. Three and a half years later it was as strong as when it began. By December 1976, 21 heads of the organization were still at large.[91] Since each one commanded a dozen cadres, police and military repression had yet to make a difference.

The first action of the league was an abortive attempt to kidnap Monterrey industrialist Eugenio Garza Sada in September 1973. Because he resisted, he was killed. In October came the second action with the double kidnapping of Monterrey businessman Fernando Arguren and the British consul in Guadalajara, Anthony Duncan Williams. Since the government refused to negotiate with "criminals," the league killed the businessman and freed the consul. After the failure of these two efforts, it concentrated on bank assaults, until in 1976 it took to more kidnappings, obtaining five million pesos ransom for the daughter of the Belgian ambassador. But it failed in the effort to seize the sister of the president-elect, José López Portillo. Meanwhile, it continued to target Mexico City's police.

The political principles underlying these armed actions were elaborated by Gustavo Hirales Morán in the *Manifesto to the Student Proletariat*, signed by the coordinating commission of the Student Federation of the University of Sinaloa and circulated among students nationwide in May and June 1973. The Old Left immediately stigmatized it as the declaration of principles of the "Sickies of Sinaloa."[92] What kind of sickness? They were allegedly victims of the political disease of "infantile leftism" criticized by Lenin in his famous *"Left-Wing" Communism: An Infantile Disorder.*

The student rebellion was interpreted by the league as a revolutionary struggle of the proletariat, a struggle that in 1968 "only the opportunism, myopia, and cowardice of the democrats had stopped . . . from turning into an armed insurrection to destroy bourgeois power."[93] This thesis was hardly new, having first been formulated by Students for a Democratic Society, the militant organization of the New Left in the United States.[94] Herbert Marcuse, a philosophy professor at the University of California and a former member of the Frankfurt School, was heralded as the mentor and champion of this new anarchist current. The September 23 League was indebted to its thesis of an antibureaucratic revolution, not just an anticapitalist one. Wrote Marcuse: "The new radicalism militates against the centralized bureaucratic communist as well as against the semi-democratic liberal organization. There is a strong element of spontaneity, even anarchism, in this rebellion."[95]

Hirales eventually returned to the Communist party and denounced the "Sickies." Behind their strategy of permanent harassment of the police and their struggle to the death against reformist tendencies within the league, he detected a non-Marxist and quasi-religious conception of the world. They interpreted the proletariat not only as a product of historical evolution, but also as "the avenging and executing arm called to destroy injustice, secular evil and sin, and to regenerate this corrupt society through an inevitable blood bath."[96] The league's ideas purported to have a Marxist pedigree. But they derived from anarchists old and new, from Bakunin and Daniel Cohn-Bendit, the ideologue of the student movement in France in 1968, not from Marx or Lenin.

COMMITTEES OF SELF-DEFENSE

Mexico's New Left had two wings: one committed to armed struggle, the other to community organizing. Although they sometimes overlapped, they pursued different ends. Armed struggle was ideologically motivated to write off the capitalist system and to replace it with a socialist society or possibly an egalitarian-communist one. Community organizing focused on less transcendent, more mundane objectives involving local and neighborhood issues, such as the lack of proper sewage, potable water, electrification, roads, decent housing, public transportation, and schools. To these divergent strategies corresponded different forms of organization. Armed struggle was undertaken by political-military, clandestine elite formations. Community organizing became the work of popular defense committees focusing on open, mass struggles, and the articulation of a mass political line.

Students played a key role in each. They were the spinal column of the self-defense committees in Nuevo León, Chihuahua, Durango, Morelos, Oaxaca, and the Federal District, as well as of the committees of struggle engaging in armed resistance at the universities in Mexico City, Guadalajara, and Monterrey. Political commentators agree that they had a common source in the student rebellion of 1968, a "watershed year" in Mexico's turbulent political history.[97] Following the explosive student occupations of the central square in Mexico City, a new popular leadership emerged, "the generation of 1968." Despite continuities with popular resistance struggles in the past, their contemporary resurgence "required the students."[98]

Since 1968 students by the hundreds, possibly thousands, had opted for an intense political commitment both in the countryside and the city. Converted to political activism, these "seeds of a new political culture . . . served as catalysts of a new political perspective that was national in scope." Besides involvement in the armed struggle, "student cadres would participate in all the important popular movements."[99] It is unlikely that they created those movements, but it is a fair guess that "they became organic leaders of them . . . , that they sought out communities with a tradition of protest, that they gravitated to situations and localities where movements were brewing."[100] The self-defense committees assimilated elements of the anarchist ideology shared by the guerrillas. This would explain their common commitment to *autonomía* (independence of the Establishment) and *autogestión* (self-rule by each member).

The committees of workers, peasants, and students functioned as veritable "soviets." Besides sharing a common life in poverty, they made up an informal party of the poor. They came together under the banner of a preferential option for the poor and were conceived as making up "'the poor' in opposition to the rich and the state."[101]

The focus on the poor drew on a diversity of sources, on anarchism, on liberation theology, and on the heterodox Marxism dominating student politics at the National University and the Polytechnical Institute. Unlike the political-military vanguards under mainly Guevarist influence, the popular defense committees drew especially on Maoism and Maoist populism, whose slogans they adopted—learn from the people, go to the people.[102]

In Monterrey, the leaders of the *colonia* (neighborhood) Tierra y Libertad, a squatters' encampment, embraced a Maoist ideology and sponsored land invasions and self-government.[103] They explicitly rejected negotiations over squatters' rights and showed no interest in electoral participation. In the state of Morelos, off the old Cuernavaca-Acapulco road near Temixco, the *colonia* Rubén Jaramillo also showed signs of Maoist influence. Founded in March 1973 by a charismatic young peasant, Florencio Medrano Mederos, alias "el Güero," it was conceived as the first socialist commune in Mexico and as the staging ground of a prolonged people's war.[104]

Reinforced by liberation theology and by revolutionary Christian practice focusing on the creation of *comunidades básicas* (grassroots communities), the Maoist current spawned in 1981–1982 the Movimiento Revolucionario del Pueblo (People's Revolutionary Movement) and the Organización de Izquierda Revolucionaria/Línea de Masas (Organization of the Revolutionary Left/Mass Line). Both concentrated on organizing the urban poor through collectivist and cooperative experiments of various kinds.[105] Besides making their presence felt in the *colonia* Tierra y Libertad in Monterrey and the *colonia* Rubén Jaramillo in Morelos, they were demonstrably active in the *colonia* 2 de Octubre in the Federal District, a relative newcomer established in 1975.

Maoism stands out among the heterodox Marxisms as having the greatest affinity for anarchism. In the mid-sixties Mao launched the Cultural Revolution, whose leveling tendencies and egalitarian aspirations became anathema in the Soviet bloc. No other currents within Marxism, not even the ultraleft Trotskyist groupuscules, exhibit the Maoists' intense aversion to bureaucracy and its pyramids of power. Led by Mao Tse-tung, the Cultural Revolution was Trotsky's promised antibureaucratic revolution engineered through a rebellion of China's youth. It is hardly a coincidence that the student rebellions unleashed in France in May and in Mexico in July 1968 had as their immediate precursor the Chinese Cultural Revolution.

Mexico's student rebellion responded to a chain of events that began in China. "In June 1966, an unprecedented event took place in the history of student movements: it was the beginning of the so-called 'Great Proletarian Cultural Revolution' in China. Mao Zedong . . . once again assumed his role of fifty years before—that of student leader."[106] In what amounted to a student strike, the middle schools and universities were shut down for a year as students marched and demonstrated against expressions of bureaucracy in its sundry forms. Organized as Red Guards, they began their rebellion by reducing school principals and some teachers to the status of maintenance workers sweeping floors and growing vegetables.[107] It was a great leveling experience, a tribute to consciousness-raising to witness this reversal of roles. As Mao added fuel to the students' anti-intellectualism: "Intellectuals usually express their general outlook through their way of looking at knowledge. Is it privately owned or publicly owned? Some regard it as their own property, for sale when the price is right. . . . Such are mere 'experts' and not 'reds.' "[108]

The Cultural Revolution did not emerge in an ideological vacuum. From the beginning, Maoism had a strong anarchist component. As a student, Mao read pamphlets on anarchism and translations of books by Bakunin and Kropotkin; these account for his leveling tendencies. Before joining the Chinese Communist party, he established close associations with anarchist groups in Peking and corresponded with anarchists in other parts of China. "One of his early articles, 'A Broad People's Alliance' (1919), supported the political views of the anarchists for having a wider appeal and also for being more profound that those of the Marxists."[109] Paradoxically, anarchism always had a populist appeal, so that Mao's blend of anarcho-Marxism was especially suited for community organizing among Mexico's urban and rural poor.

The Coalición Obrero Campesino Estudiantil del Istmo (Worker-Peasant-Student Coalition of the Isthmus, COCEI) in Juchitán, Oaxaca, stands out as the most-discussed and influential of these broad people's alliances. Established in 1973, it attracted the support of small merchants, independent craftspeople, and the local intelligentsia. It was especially noteworthy for its victory in Juchitán's municipal elections in alliance with the Communist party.[110] The COCEI was not Maoist-inspired, but it shared Mao's anarcho-populist orientation and the New Left's political agenda.

The clearest instance of a Maoist popular coalition was the Asociación Nacional Obrero, Campesino, Estudiantil (Worker, Peasant, Student National Association, ANOCE) organized in 1973 in Acatlipa, Morelos. This was the mass front behind the successful takeover of Villa de las Flores, some sixty hectares of choice real estate awaiting the development of vacation homes for the rich from Mexico City. Beginning with an invasion of thirty families on 31 March 1973, the renamed Colonia Proletaria Rubén Jaramillo grew to ten thousand in June and had a population of nearly fifteen thousand in September.

The ANOCE was the mass front of the Maoist party organized in Cuernavaca in response to the Sino-Soviet split in 1964. By then the Partido Revolucionario del Proletariado (Proletarian Revolutionary party) had been taken over by "el Güero" Medrano. Medrano was born in 1946 of peasant stock in Limón Grande, Guerrero. He had been an activist in Vázquez's Civic Association, then in the PCM, until in 1966 he and his peasant followers joined the Proletarian Revolutionary party. Impressed by his leadership qualities, the Chinese embassy invited him and eight other Mexican delegates to spend six months in the People's Republic of China in 1969. On his return, after the party's president and other intellectuals were hunted down and imprisoned for their role in an insurrectionary bombing in Mexico City, he named himself president of the Maoist party.

The ANOCE's community of squatters represented more than a revival of Rubén Jaramillo's earlier project in the plains of Michapa and El Guarín. El Güero planned to convert the community into a liberated territory, a state within the state of Morelos, and then to look for other bases for his proposed new revolution. Meanwhile, it became an armed camp that barred the police and army from entering. In September, when the government finally intervened on the pretext that Cabañas's guerrillas had found shelter there, it took three thousand soldiers, five hundred local police, and three hundred agents of the judicial police to restore "law and order." The community had become such a hotbed of anarchy that the army continued to occupy it until 1980.

Besides being the first Chinese-type self-administered commune in Mexico, the community served as a recruiting ground and haven for el Güero's guerrillas. "Although the ANOCE was openly an association of workers, peasants, and students, the 30 members of its Committee of Struggle received guerrilla training . . . [and] studied Maoism."[111] El Güero had trained them with another contingent of peasants from Guerrero, who remained in the sierras waiting for his call to launch a people's war.

Under the supreme command of el Güero's brother Primo, the "Armed Forces of the Rubén Jaramillo Colonia" not only kept the police and army at bay, but also planned and carried out clandestine assaults in neighboring towns and rural areas without the community's knowledge. In one of those operations Primo was killed and seventeen other guerrillas forced to disband. Anticipating government repression, el Güero and his Committee of Struggle eluded capture by abandoning the community on the eve of the army's invasion in September.

In January 1974 he organized a new Maoist party, the Partido Proletario Unido de América (United Proletarian Party of America) with the germs of a popular army, the Ejército Popular de Liberación Unido de América (United Popular Liberation Army of America). Among the Liberation Army's successful actions were the February 1974 kidnapping of a rich landowner in Puente de Ixtla, Morelos, followed by the kidnapping of Sara Martínez de Davis, wife of a wealthy U.S. citizen in Cuernavaca. Their haul amounted to several million pesos from these two operations.

The new Maoist party and popular liberation army were active not only in Morelos, but also in the neighboring states of Guerrero and Oaxaca, where they participated in the COCEI's land invasions. Interviewed in the Sierra Madre del Sur in October 1978, el Güero declared: "If I'm eliminated, I'll die in peace because nobody can stop the movement of the indigenous villages and ejidos of Guerrero, Oaxaca, Veracruz, Chiapas, Campeche, Michoacán, and Durango."[112] Fifteen days later, after his guerrillas had taken over a small town in the Sierra of Oaxaca, the army surrounded them. The guerrillas escaped, but he was wounded in the skirmish. He died shortly thereafter.

The prototype of the new mass fronts was the *colonia* Francisco Villa, which emerged in response to a peasant land invasion in Chihuahua in June 1968.[113] From it sprang the first Popular Assembly and its directing organ, the Comité de Defensa Popular (Popular Defense Committee, CDP) established in the capital of Chihuahua in January 1972. Although the Communist party had a hand in organizing them, the links were severed in 1974 when the CDP embraced a more radical political rhetoric.

A month before the days of rage in Mexico City, Chihuahua City residents mobilized on the city's outskirts to protest their lack of decent housing. They occupied vacant lands and, later, fertile fields belonging to the old landlord Luis Terrazas, who before the 1910 Revolution had owned the state lock, stock, and barrel. They seized a piece of his Quinta de las Carolinas. The first land invasion was followed by others, all in response to a decade of struggles and to the military repression following Gámiz's guerrillas. Thus the settlement Francisco Villa came into being three years after the death of Arturo Gámiz and one year after the guerrilla war of Oscar González. In 1980 the settlement had some twenty-five thousand inhabitants.

The Chihuahua Popular Defense Committee serves as a model for understanding the general role of CDPs in the resistance sparked by the student rebellion of 1968.[114] It tried to create a parallel society based on a network of local trade union, peasant, student, and neighborhood associations. For the first time, women took an active political role through the neighborhood committees. Like other popular defense committees, the Chihuahua CDP made a special effort to capture new political space through the democratization of municipal agencies and mobilizations of the local poor.[115]

The Chihuahua Popular Defense Committee came as the sequel to several other popular fronts. The Popular Solidarity Front was organized in 1969 to combat the treachery of the union bureaucracy in the Pepsi Cola Company of Chihuahua. The front included students as well as workers mobilized through local committees. The Struggle Committee against Electoral Farce also won the support of students. It brought off a gigantic meeting against President Díaz Ordaz and Luis Echeverría. The Committee for Struggle against the High Cost of Living denounced the rising price of sugar and sales taxes with colorful protest actions. Thus a broad front emerged that helped to raise people's consciousness.

The resistance to the union bureaucracy at the Pepsi Cola Company was followed in 1971 by a similar effort by militants in the Movimiento Sindical Ferrocarrilero (Railway Union Movement) to regain control of their union. They seized the local of this sold-out union and held it. Expecting repression, they tried to form a new solidarity front like the one in 1969. They began by seeking support from the Francisco Villa settlement, from the Chihuahua Steelworkers' Union, from the local branch of the Sindicato de Trabajadores Electricistas de la República Mexicana (Mexican Electrical Workers Union), from Section Eight of the Revolutionary Teachers' Movement, and from the local Student Council. They planned to sign a pact of alliance in April 1972.

While discussions were in progress, the September 23 Movement (Armed Commandos of Chihuahua) went into action. On 15 January 1972 a group of three commandos simultaneously assaulted three banks in the state capital—the Mexican Commercial Bank, the National Bank of Mexico, and the Bank of Commerce. In the first two attacks the guerrillas made clean getaways, but three of them fell in the third action, including a woman, Avelina Gallegos, a fifth-year law student at the University of Chihuahua. In this third action, the police killed by mistake a passing student and a woman trying to leave the bank. By then, the local press was supporting any action against the authorities, including this triple action known as Operation Madera.

A reward of two hundred thousand pesos was offered for information leading to the arrest of the fugitives. Soldiers from the Fifth Military Zone and federal police agents launched a manhunt. When a recent recruit of the guerrillas sought protection through a lawyer, he was quickly betrayed. Arrested on 16 January, he was forced to talk. That brought the arrest of other guerrillas, but most of them remained at large.

The same day the police killed in cold blood Diego Lucero Martínez, a graduate of the University of Chihuahua, former president of its Student Society, a survivor of the attack on the Madera barracks, and founder of the Armed Commandos of Chihuahua. The next day the district attorney, Antonio Quesada Fornelli, announced that Lucero had died resisting arrest. The truth was otherwise. Adolfo Anchondo Salazar, who had lent his house as a hideout, had seen Lucero riding around in a patrol car after the arrest. He concluded that the police had murdered him. As the word got out, law students at the university met in permanent assembly. They came out of the assembly en masse to march to the governor's house to demand an investigation. The governor, Oscar Flores, appointed an investigating committee that soon exposed the lies of the district attorney and the police.

For over a decade Chihuahuans had been resisting the political monopoly of the PRI and fighting off its control whenever there was a show of popular solidarity. Meanwhile, the local branch of the Electrical Workers Union, the Chihuahua Steelworkers Union, and the students were trying to create an organization to channel this popular energy surging up against the government. All these elements joined with the nascent anti-police movement in calling for a popular assembly.

The Francisco Villa settlement and the Student Coordinating Committee arranged for a popular assembly to meet in the central plaza on 19 January. There the demonstrators voted a unanimous "no" to the question of whether they considered it a crime of social dissolution for revolutionaries to "expropriate" banks. The Popular Assembly set forth its demands: the removal and prosecution of the district attorney and the chief of police.

The events that followed accelerated and reinforced the popular resistance. On 20 January the police hanged guerrilla Ramiro Díaz; his body showed hemorrhage through the mouth. The next day "Gaspar" suffered the same fate. He was taken from the police station to the town of General Trías, given a running start of five hundred meters, and then brought down "attempting to escape." He had been arrested along with Héctor Lucero Hernández, half-brother of the dead engineer Diego Lucero. Héctor had revealed the place where the loot was hidden.

On 24 January the protestors returned to their struggle in the streets, and on 26 January the Popular Assembly, fifteen thousand strong, again met in front of the state capitol. Then the protestors marched to the governor's house. This time they insisted that he listen to their demand that the authorities responsible for Lucero's murder be prosecuted. Two days later the archbishop of Chihuahua declared his solidarity with the Popular Assembly.

The Popular Defense Committee, an organization for the defense of civil rights, emerged from the assembly. It included delegates from the Chihuahua University Union, from the Student Society of the University of Chihuahua, from the Technological Institute and the Normal School, from Section Eight of the Revolutionary Teachers' Movement, from the Electrical Workers Union, from the Chihuahua Steelworkers, from the Railway Union Movement, and from the Francisco Villa settlement. It defended the poor, but had no permanent leaders. Commissions were formed to discuss matters of common concern, and the Popular Assembly voted on their proposals. In an effort to coordinate their work, the commissions periodically returned to the Popular Assembly for consultation.

On 14 February 1972 the governor, pressured by the popular mobilizations led by the CDP, accepted the "resignation" of the district attorney but not that of the police inspector, Ambrosio Gutiérrez. The first investigating commission with popular participation was dissolved. In order to wash his hands of the affair, the governor then submitted the case to an "Academy of Penal Sciences" composed mainly of members of the state government and his judicial "yes men." With this maneuver the authorities made fools of the protestors by exonerating the state's officials. But the CDP mobilized, closing ranks with the university students on strike, who took advantage of the situation to make new demands of their own. Together they helped to form neighborhood committees, which spread propaganda and soon brought twenty thousand people into the streets.

In this trial by fire the CDP lost the participation of several organizations: the Steelworkers Union, the Electrical Workers, and Section Eight of the Revolutionary Teachers' Movement. But it kept up the struggle with the tactics of mass mobilization and new ways of contacting organizations not belonging to it. Finally, it won from the governor the legalization of the occupied lands with title deeds to them.

The effectiveness of the CDP lay in its ability to mobilize large numbers of people and in its capacity for negotiation with the Mexican state. On 30 September 1976 it had an interview with President Echeverría within its own liberated territory in the colonia Francisco Villa. The president was obliged to enter the encampment without bodyguards. He also had to listen to reproaches from the CDP because of the government's repression and co-optation of union leaders.

By the end of the 1970s, twenty organizations made up the CDP in Chihuahua. Popular defense committees also popped up in other cities throughout the state, in Ciudad Anáhuac, Jiménez, Delicias, Parral, Flores Magón, and Camargo. In Ciudad Juárez a popular defense committee targeted what it took to be generalized corruption. It made alliances with teachers, squatters, and local bus drivers and it organized struggles against landlords and real estate speculators.

The *colonia* Francisco Villa and the Railway Union Movement prepared a discussion program for the CDPs in other states. By organizing the poor in the struggle for local power and by building class consciousness, the CDPs hoped to satisfy their constituents through a popular program addressed to the most urgent needs of workers, peasants, students, and the marginalized poor. Foremost among their demands were wage hikes, shorter hours, and public housing for urban workers; expropriation of large estates, redistribution of government-owned lands, and direct control of the rural credit system with low interest rates and long-term payment schedules for peasants; participation in school administration, more scholarships, easy credit from the state, and complete freedom to demonstrate for students; and the formation of neighborhood committees in tenements and shantytowns, defense of squatters's rights, grassroots control over the prices of basic foodstuffs, and real social assistance for the unemployed and the marginal poor. These concerns were capped by the common demand for the immediate release of all political prisoners and an end to torture during interrogations.

For some, the popular defense committees were local germs of a future national assembly, like the one sharing political power in Bolivia during Gen. Juan José Torres's administration in 1971.[116] For others, they were the germs of a soviet-type government based on a worker-peasant-student alliance. In Russia between February and October 1917, soviets of workers', peasants', and soldiers' deputies achieved dual power and then seized national power through an armed uprising under the leadership of a vanguard party. The question was whether the CDPs were capable of matching the Russian experience.

The anarchist character of the popular defense committees should be evident. A majority of Russian anarchists defended the soviets in 1917 as the "best form of political organization that had ever existed."[117] That was because they enabled their constituents at any time to recall and replace deputies by others who better expressed their will and because they were the spontaneous creations of a popular movement of self-defense.[118] In Mexico as in Russia, a clash soon developed between the self-proclaimed political vanguard and the soviets. But unlike in Russia, where the soviets were deprived of power and came under the heel of the Communist party, in Mexico the CDPs retained their independence of the PCM's front organizations.

Direct action is the anarchism of our times, writes Abraham Guillén, "anarchist in its concept of direct democracy, self-managed enterprises and federations of freely associated workers."[119] Because it challenges the bureaucratic state, direct action "has to have an anarchist content."[120] These words target the monopoly of political power in the Soviet Union in the late 1960s and apply with equal force to the 1968 student rebellion against the PRI government and to Mexico's urban guerrillas and popular defense committees of the 1970s.

SIX

THE REVIVAL OF
ANARCHIST THEORY

After the lapse of half a century during which anarchist theorizing virtually disappeared from the Mexican scene and Marxism replaced it as the core ideology among radicalized workers, a renewed interest in anarchism occurred in the wake of the guerrilla resurgence and student rebellion of the late 1960s. Between the last issue of Ricardo Flores Magón's *Regeneración* in March 1918 and the beginnings of the student rebellion in April 1968, the only work of significance to anarchist theory was Revueltas's 1962 essay on Mexico's headless proletariat. Not until 1968 did a handful of Marxist and Marxist-influenced intellectuals begin to respond to Revueltas's initiatives. After that, he was no longer the lone voice crying in the wilderness.

Following Revueltas, a new crop of intellectuals emerged who increasingly distanced themselves from the mummified Marxism of the Communist party. In the course of a reexamination of Mexican history and the country's most pressing problems, they discovered that the bourgeoisie had become decapitated along with the proletariat and that the great mass upheaval of 1910–1917 had played into the hands of a bureaucratic class. The resulting hypothesis of a "ripped-off revolution" had an anarchist pedigree that once again placed anarchist theory on the intellectual agenda.[1]

The practical import of this new theory was that, rather than continuing to defend the Mexican Revolution against a bourgeoisie intent on regaining political power, the Left should prepare for a new revolution. Besides fueling anarchist impatience with the electoral process and with drawn-out legal reforms addressed to symptoms instead of causes, the new theory helped to revive Mexico's indigenous legacy of direct action transmitted by Ricardo Flores Magón, Emiliano Zapata, and Rubén Jaramillo.[2]

The new theory was indebted to Trotskyist as well as anarchist sources.

But it was not long before its Marxist component gave way to a theory of bureaucratic society with a built-in critique of Marxist socialism in principle as well as practice. While an effort was made to salvage Marxism by reading into it an anarchist content, the effort to understand its historical role eventually discredited it as the ideology of a new exploiting class.[3]

Beginning in the 1970s, Mexico's New Left took a fresh look at the world revolution. In a series of major works flowing from his research at Cuernavaca's Centro Intercultural de Documentación (Intercultural Documentation Center, CIDOC), Ivan Illich counterposed the new industrial order under the control of a new class of professional and managerial workers to both the old industrial order in decomposition and the alternative of a decentralized, self-managed, egalitarian society free of ecological crises.[4] About the same time, the Mexican Left began assimilating the intellectual contributions of anarcho-Marxists whose works in Spanish translation began appearing in bookstores in the nation's capital.[5]

The upshot of this struggle on the theoretical front was an enrichment of anarchist theory in the works of a new generation of anarchist intellectuals.

A HEADLESS PROLETARIAT

Among Mexico's radicalized intellectuals, José Revueltas (1914–1976) was the first to come forward with a new theory. Besides the political and economic struggles for proletarian emancipation, his *Ensayo* acknowledged a third struggle on the theoretical front.[6] With Lenin he agreed that "without revolutionary theory there can be no revolutionary movement," which meant "placing the theoretical struggle on a par with the first two."[7] By the summer of 1968 in the heat of the student rebellion, he began formulating a rationale for armed actions in what he called the "theorization of the movement."[8] While concurring with his Marxist forebears that every step of the actual movement is worth more than a dozen programs, he refused to bargain over principles or to make theoretical compromises.

What kind of man was Revueltas? To his daughter Andrea he wrote on 30 March 1971: "We must rely on nobody but ourselves: to think, write, and struggle with courage, free of all fetishes and dogmatism, no matter where it take us."[9] Because of his rebellious disposition, he felt a natural kinship with Trotsky, who also took an independent stance and made his presence felt in Mexico. Like Trotsky, he gave himself body and soul to what he called the "New Revolution." "It offers us countless opportunities to die," he reflected on the eve of his arrest and imprisonment in November 1968, "and for that reason one must learn how to die well, so that our death serves the purpose of our life." [10] This was no passing sentiment. Revueltas was one of Mexico's great contemporary writers and his novels abound with characters on the razor's edge.

In the course of reviving the Magonist legacy, Revueltas set forth a novel interpretation of the Mexican Revolution. As the text on the back cover of the second 1980 edition depicts the purpose of his *Ensayo*:

> Belatedly, in 1962, the *Ensayo* accomplished its urgent mission, to present the history of Mexico from a Marxist point of view and, at the same time, to present the history of the Left and of the Communist party . . . to analyze the formation of the Mexican nation on the basis of class interests, to strip bare the bourgeois nationalist ideology that still prevails in Mexico, and to rescue and exalt the importance of Ricardo Flores Magón as a precursor, yes, but not of the revolution of 1910, rather of the Mexican socialist revolution.

Revueltas's *Ensayo* was a virtual declaration of war on the theoretical front. Basic to his reinterpretation of Mexico's history was the rejection of the Old Left's thesis of a fundamental rupture between the 1910 Revolution and the *porfiriato*. Revueltas shared Flores Magón's belief in the continuity of Mexican liberalism from Benito Juárez's Revolution of Ayutla in 1855 to the governments of Madero and Carranza more than half a century later. His new history confirmed the suspicion that the 1917 Constitution was a demagogical concession to the social revolution and that, unable to carry on in the old way and fearful that the popular explosion might get out of hand, the bourgeoisie had deferred to the revolutionary generals and their populist rhetoric. [11]

Mexico's peculiarity, according to Revueltas, was to have gone through a bourgeois revolution in 1910–1917 without the bourgeoisie's having previously developed a systematic ideology. Compelled to improvise one in the heat of the armed struggle but without a political party of its own, it took over the prevailing ideology of the Revolution, which was agrarian, nationalist, and proletarian. Thus the new 1917 Constitution postulates a Mexican state that allegedly transcends class interests.

The irony is that the adoption of an agrarian, nationalist, and proletarian ideology was "eminently positive and advantageous for the industrial bourgeoisie from a class point of view." [12] It helped to overcome the remnants of feudalism and peonage in the countryside and to provide a pool of free laborers for industrial development. Although the ideology of the revolution was resisted by leading members of the bourgeoisie until it proved its worth, President Cárdenas's expropriation of the foreign-owned petroleum industry in 1938 marked the turning point, after which the bourgeoisie caught up with the thinking of its class ideologues.

Revueltas identifies the ideologues of the bourgeoisie with the revolutionary generals in the Constitutionalist army, victors in the struggle against Villa and Zapata as well as against the arch-bourgeois Carranza. This struggle issued in a period of unstable, confused, and occasionally contradictory relations between the Mexican state and the business community. The official party of the revolution founded by General Calles in 1928, the Revolutionary National party, was not a creation of the bourgeoisie. Nonetheless, it turned out to represent the interests of native business.

Even Carranza showed an appreciation for the new ideology. With the worker and peasant masses on the move, he pictured the interests of his class within a framework of popular demands. As a classic example of the bourgeois promotion of popular expectations, Carranza presented his Constitutionalist revolution as the prelude to a social revolution. Thus Revueltas cites his speech in Hermosillo (26 May 1913):

> It is high time to stop making false promises to the people. . . . The Plan of Guadalupe contains no utopia, nothing unrealizable, no bastard promises made with the intention of ignoring them. . . . But the Mexican people should know that, once the armed struggle convoked by the Plan of Guadalupe is over, the formidable and majestic social struggle, the class struggle, will have to begin—whether we like it or not, and no matter what forces are opposed to it. New social doctrines are bound to take hold of our masses, not just about redistribution of the land and natural resources, effective suffrage, more schools, and an equal share of the nation's wealth, but about something greater and more sacred: the establishment of justice, the search for equality, and the disappearance of the powerful. . . . We will have to change everything, to create a new Constitution whose beneficent effect on the masses nothing and nobody will be able to prevent. We need laws that favor the peasant and the worker. But these will be promulgated by the peasants and workers themselves, since they are sure to triumph in the social and revindicating struggle.[13]

With Carranza's Plan of Guadalupe, Revueltas argues, the national bourgeoisie took over the reins of government. But with his assassination in 1920, the revolutionary generals came to the fore without breaking with his doctrine. "This unique political form of bourgeois-democratic consciousness has continued to represent the basic orientation and dominant element in the ideology of all the governments emanating from the Revolution."[14] Thanks to the defeat of Zapata's popular-agrarian revolution, it was able to do so. Thus there were two revolutions, and the one that prevailed made it imperative for the one that failed to launch a new revolution.

Is it possible to trace the intellectual inspiration behind this novel interpretation of Mexico's history? A 1967 interview with Revueltas by Norma Castro Quiteño provides a clue. In ideological matters, he confessed, José Carlos Mariátegui had always been his master. "It was he who opened the eyes of my generation to the need to adapt Marxism to the national and continental conditions [of the Americas] and, rather than accept the ignorant repetition of formulas of an imported Marxism, the need to capture the national reality."[15]

To his novel interpretation of Mexico's political history and his picture of a prevailing bourgeois-democratic ideology in proletarian and peasant garb, Revueltas added his reassessment of the role of the Communist party. The PCM had been the tail of the working class instead of its head; the proletariat had in turn wagged the tail of Mexico's capitalists.[16] On the widely shared but false assumption that the 1917 Constitution contains the ingredients for the promised socialist development of the Revolution, the party had become the extreme expression of bourgeois-democratic ideology. So the PCM was not a proletarian vanguard but a vanguard party of the bourgeoisie.

The pervasiveness of the ideology of the Mexican Revolution, says Revueltas, has diverted workers from recognizing their class interests. Mexican workers lack an awareness not of the immediate and visible injustices of Mexican society, but of its "essential injustice," its basically exploitative character. Labor struggles by themselves are not a sign of independence. For that, there must be proletarian ideologues capable of becoming the "*collective brain* that thinks *of* the class, *for* the class, and *with* the class."[17] The PCM had failed dismally in this task.

Without a collective brain that thinks both for and with the workers, he reasoned, there are only two possible outcomes. First, there is the "*opportunism* of being with the masses without any finality"; second, there is the "*sectarianism* of not being with the masses" because of the insistence on final aims.[18] In the first case, the fundamental interests of the proletariat are dismissed or ignored; in the second, its immediate interests. Opportunism and sectarianism were flip sides of the same Communist party coin.

Ironically, the PCM faulted reformists in the labor movement for selling out the working class and collaborating with the bourgeoisie, when the party had been doing precisely that throughout most of its fitful history. The sole exception was its sectarian line from 1929 to 1935. However, in this 180-degree turn, it merely shelved its opportunist policies for future use.[19] Meanwhile, its rupture with the bourgeoisie, its confrontation with the government, and its preparations for armed struggle did not elicit the popular response anticipated. So, when its sectarian strategy led to abject defeat, the PCM reverted to a policy of pushing forward Mexico's bourgeois-democratic revolution.

To Revueltas's credit, he singled out Ricardo Flores Magón as Mexico's foremost representative of an authentic proletarian ideology. A bona fide communist, unlike his counterparts in the Communist party, Flores Magón directed the struggles of workers and peasants in "absolute independence of the bourgeois-democratic conspirators, who only in 1910 proposed to lead the people in armed struggle." In an effort to discredit him, the ideologues of the bourgeoisie have placed the principal stress on his anarchism. But because the principal purpose of his struggle was not the anarchist's obsession with abolishing the state, his detractors "fail to perceive in the doctrinal anarchist that was Flores Magón the proletarian ideologue *that he also was*."[20]

After the Revolution, advanced workers continued to flow with the anarcho-syndicalist current and to represent what Revueltas calls the proletariat's instinct of independence. But while reformists had the support of successive governments of the Revolution, anarcho-syndicalists did not. As an organized movement, anarcho-syndicalism was deliberately stamped out, precisely because it alone "led the workers in great independent actions and, therefore, was the only current capable of assimilating proletarian ideology."[21]

Revueltas credits the anarcho-syndicalists with leading the single most important strike in Mexico after the Revolution, the CGT-sponsored strike of transit workers in January 1923, the last one in which workers armed themselves in self-defense.[22] Although he acknowledges there were others, such as the railway workers' strike in January–February 1927 and again in 1958–1959, workers stopped short of the defiance shown in 1923 when they directly challenged the repressive powers of the Mexican state. While conceding that anarcho-syndicalism held aloft the banner of working-class independence, however, he depicted it as a sectarian deviation.

Revueltas was a transitional figure in the anarchist intellectual revival. Although he charted the path the new theorizing would take, he followed it only part of the way. By 1968 he began to have second thoughts about the residues of orthodoxy in his famous essay. But he became increasingly ill and died before he could formulate them satisfactorily and bring them to fruition.

THE DECAPITATED BOURGEOISIE

Mexican Trotskyists were among the first to assimilate and to make political capital of Revueltas's theory. Although Trotskyism is usually described and classified as a variant of the Old Left, in 1968 Trotskyist youth in Mexico as well as France and the United States acquired the trappings of a New Left. Like Revueltas, they had a foot in both camps.

Trotsky's writings had a special appeal for the New Left because of his barbs against Stalin's dogmatism and the Soviet bureaucracy's betrayal of the communist revolution. With the outbreak of World War II, Trotsky was among the first to broach the hypothesis of the Soviet bureaucracy's degeneration from a parasitic caste into an exploiting class. Transformed into a theory by his former friends and followers, this hypothesis was eventually applied to Mexico's ruling party. Like Revueltas's theory, it too had an anarchist pedigree.

As the titular head and leading exponent of Mexican Trotskyism in the 1970s, Manuel Aguilar Mora paid homage to Revueltas while advancing a parallel thesis that incorporated the libertarian features in Trotsky's critique of the Soviet bureaucracy.[23] In a work first published in 1970, which went through several printings before being republished in an expanded edition in 1977, he argues that the Mexican proletariat was not alone in being headless—the bourgeoisie also lacked a head.

The Mexican bourgeoisie had become an economic titan but was still a political pygmy. During the Revolution of 1910–1917, the defeat of the "only proletarian alternative at the time, *floresmagonismo*, . . . [signified that] there was no triumphant 'bourgeois-democratic revolution,' but rather an incomplete permanent revolution."[24] Although an attempt was made at a bourgeois-democratic revolution beginning with Madero, "Carranza's assassination is, above all, the symbol of the incapacity of the Mexican bourgeoisie to maintain its hegemonic position." The resulting political vacuum was filled by those Aguilar Mora identifies as "the modern urban petty-bourgeois sectors headed by the military chiefs Obregón and Calles."[25]

The form of government that emerged under the revolutionary generals was not bourgeois, says Aguilar Mora, but "Bonapartist." In referring to the regime of Napoleon III in France as a model of "Bonapartism," he notes that it represented a third position between capital and labor while finding its principal base of support in the peasantry, the most numerous class in society. As in France from 1851 to 1870, Aguilar Mora contends that in Mexico it became the only form of government possible under conditions in which the bourgeoisie had lost the capacity to govern and the proletariat had yet to acquire that capacity. These two great classes responsible for the Mexican revolution found themselves in a condition of equilibrium, which enabled the revolutionary generals to rise above both in the role of moderator. Thus the "revolutionary regime installed by Obregón, whether it evolved toward the Right (Calles) or toward the Left (Cárdenas), may be considered a unique case of Bonapartism."[26]

Trotsky had been among the first to characterize the governments of the Revolution as "Bonapartist." During his political exile in Mexico from January 1937 until his assassination by a Kremlin agent in August 1940, the Mexican Revolution had Trotsky for its defender because of its massive expropriations of the oil and railroad industries. "Governments in backward countries, which is to say colonial and semi-colonial ones, everywhere assume a Bonapartist or semi-Bonapartist character, differing from one another in that some take a democratic direction in seeking the backing of workers and peasants, while others install a form of government bordering on a military-police dictatorship."[27] Mexico, he contended, had taken the first of these two paths.

The predicament of a Bonapartist government, Trotsky argued, is that it periodically "veers between foreign and domestic capital, between the weak national bourgeoisie and the relatively powerful proletariat." Although seemingly suspended above the warring classes, it can govern only by becoming an instrument of foreign capital or by making concessions to labor and, with labor support, standing up to foreign economic pressures. Through its policy of expropriations, the Cárdenas regime had bolstered the country's political and economic independence, strengthened the role of state capitalism, and raised the prospect of workers' self-management in nationalized industries.[28] But the Mexican proletariat had yet to take advantage of this springboard by creating a genuine vanguard party. Contrary to expectations, Aguilar Mora concludes, a political bureaucracy recruited from the so-called urban petty bourgeoisie had filled the power vacuum left by the decapitated bourgeoisie.[29] What Mexico needed, therefore, was a revived proletarian revolution to remove the bureaucracy from power.

In a book Aguilar Mora cites as a model, Adolfo Gilly (1928–) argues that the Mexican Revolution was a *permanent* but interrupted social revolution by workers and peasants, *combined* with a political revolution in the form of a Bonapartist transitional regime.[30] Although Ricardo Flores Magón and the PLM lacked the means for an effective alliance with the peasantry, they played a key role in the mobilizations of the proletariat, which "found an echo and a bond of union in the revolutionary restlessness that silently agitated the peasants, until the immense peasant mass found a guide and opening to the future for its demands in an alliance with the revolutionary urban forces."[31] Power was conquered by the "petty bourgeoisie," which established an intermediate and shaky regime that maintained itself by playing off the interests of capital and labor. By the "petty bourgeoisie," Gilly understands not only Marx's petty proprietors, producers, and vendors, but also intermediate salaried employees, such as accountants, schoolteachers, nurses, journalists, military officers, and government officials—the core of the Bonapartist bureaucracy.[32] Since repeated efforts to replace the bureaucratic regime with a form of bourgeois rule had failed, he believed it could end only with the triumph of a proletarian revolution.

The Mexican Revolution, Gilly contends, was neither an unfinished bourgeois-democratic revolution nor a finished one, but a potentially socialist revolution from the beginning interrupted by a transitional Bonapartist regime. It developed through three stages. The first, that of Villa and Zapata, launched the land reform but was stopped. The second, that of Cárdenas, nationalized the principal means of production but was also interrupted. The third, catalyzed by the 1968 student revolt, aims at completing the interrupted revolution.[33] Thus Gilly believes that the Cárdenas regime and the 1968 student rebellion revived the socialist impetus implicit in Zapata's land reform and the revolutionary legacy going back to Flores Magón.

The Mexican form of Bonapartism, argues Aguilar Mora, is in a category by itself. Defined by the institutionalized succession of "sexennial Bonapartes" based on rule by a political bureaucracy, the Mexican political system exhibits a flexibility uncommon among Bonapartist regimes in guaranteeing a change at the helm every six years.[34] This unique feature supposedly accounts for its unusual stability and continuity.

But can this Trotskyist paradigm explain the role of the Mexican bureaucracy as the principal beneficiary of the political system? Since the organization of the first government party in 1929, Mexico has chafed under one-party rule, a party controlled by bureaucrats with an elected dictator for a head. If the political bureaucracy were merely a stratum linked to a class of petty proprietors, one might expect the bourgeoisie to recapture the government that eluded its control. The more credible interpretation is that the political bureaucracy is the political sector of a new exploiting class, as Gilly was on the verge of recognizing in his 1980 work on priests and bureaucrats—a re-creation of Marxist theory that was indirectly indebted to anarchist sources.[35]

MARXISM RE-CREATED

Historically, anarchists have responded to the Marxist challenge to their theory and practice in two ways: by re-creating Marxism in their own image and by unmasking it as the ideology of a new exploiting class. Considering the scope and complexity of Marxist theory, it is not surprising that these options are not exclusive.

The classic example of the first option is Lenin's re-creation of Marxism in the partial image of French communism and Russian anarchism. Lenin was the first to transform Marx into an egalitarian on the property question and to successfully pass off his re-creation as the genuine article.[36] However, the only anarchists who have followed in Lenin's footsteps have been anarchists by another name. Rather than professing anarchism, they have professed Marxism.

The principal Mexican exponent of anarchism in the name of Marxism is the enfant terrible of liberation theology and the bête noir of the Catholic Church in Latin America, José Porfirio Miranda (1924–   ). A former Jesuit and for many years an adviser and lecturer for workers' groups, his critique of Marxism is directed not at its professed communism but at its mistaken predictions.[37] Miranda's tour de force is to re-create Marxism in the image of the communism practiced by the early Christian communities, which makes it a conscious continuation of early Christianity. Redefining his terms so that "communism is the one and only logical realization of the humanism that the West claims and professes," Miranda calls this startling re-creation the "Christian humanism of Karl Marx."[38]

Before examining Miranda's re-creation, one should consider its purpose. In his prologue to *Marx en México* (1972), he complains of the ineffectiveness of Mexican Marxists in mobilizing the proletariat toward a revolutionary goal because of their defective analysis of the sociopolitical structure of Mexico. His book is a reply to those who believe that every consequential Marxist must become an ally of economic development and political democracy. On the contrary, Miranda argues that developmentalism places Marxism at the service of Mexican capitalism and that democratism harnesses workers to the reformist ideology of the Revolution, which makes a new revolution unnecessary.[39]

The normal form of government under capitalism, says Miranda, requires the separation of political from economic power; that means a Bonapartist political dictatorship coupled with capitalist free enterprise, such as exists in Mexico.[40] His reservations concerning the struggle for political democracy within a capitalist framework stem from this historical observation concerning the relation between the economic structure and the political superstructure. He believes that the events on 2 October 1968 and 10 June 1971 confirm these reservations.

An authentically revolutionary strategy is "100 percent incompatible with collaboration by Marxists with bourgeois 'peaceful' democratization and development," Miranda concludes, so that a "Marxist strategy must prepare the masses for a series of 'disputes' that we know beforehand must be violent."[41]

Expanding on this theme, he notes that increasing government repression eventually does away with the system of liberal democracy. This normal outcome takes the form either of Latin American military regimes or the Mexican political system in which the lawmaking body lacks real power because of the "political absolutism of the president and undisturbed capitalist rule in the economic sphere." The advantage of Mexico's concealed dictatorship is that it creates the illusion that elected representatives can help the workers in their struggle against the capitalist Leviathan. Thus "the government can enjoy the luxury of multiform populist measures, while the bourgeoisie continues exploiting to the hilt."[42]

The unpopularity of Mexico's bourgeoisie, says Miranda, grows with its economic stranglehold. "The dictatorship of the official party has been a genial solution: the ire of the oppressed may boil over against the capitalists, but in the eyes of the people the official party is not identified with the bourgeoisie."[43] Paradoxically, the rule of the bourgeoisie is strengthened every time there is an election. Because its Partido de Acción Nacional (National Action party, PAN) is invariably defeated, there is the illusion of a popular victory.

"Under capitalism, every 'democratic' maneuver by the state is essentially a trick, a trick of such efficacy that it even fools the government."[44] "Democracy," according to Miranda, dissociates political from economic domination in order to assure the preservation of capitalism. It deceives the people the more the political system appears to be law-abiding. The capitalists accept the government's concealed dictatorship, knowing that it serves them well. That is why there have been no successful military coups in Mexico since bourgeois political rule was overthrown. "Why should there be, if the government enjoys stable dictatorial power that in other countries requires a coup?"[45]

In view of the socialist ideology enthroned in Articles 27 and 123 of the Constitution, the ruling party has an immense advantage. Its demagogy is directly proportional, Miranda believes, to the degree of domination and exploitation by the bourgeoisie, for the more the capitalists exploit their workers, the more must the ruling party appear to be revolutionary. The practical lesson to be drawn is that Mexican workers must break completely with the fetishism of the Revolution and make their own revolution.[46]

Just as workers should abstain from voting in the government-endorsed political charade, says Miranda, they should also give up trying to democratize the trade unions. They cannot afford to adopt the limits and goals inherent in business unionism, because the trade unions detach organized workers from the struggles of the unorganized.[47] The alternative is to create revolutionary unions on the margins of the legal system, to revive the anarcho-syndicalism of the CGT, and to bring about a change in the masses until they opt for a political general strike.

The only hope for Mexico's oppressed and exploited workers, Miranda believes, is a *"new revolution*, rather than a revival and continuation of the old one."[48] Because of "reformist palliatives," he adds, "our revolution was rapidly betrayed and defeated." By "our revolution" he does not mean the liberal democratic one under Madero, much less the Bonapartist dictatorship beginning with Obregón, but the workers' revolution with peasant backing launched by Ricardo Flores Magón and the PLM. This is confirmed by his Magonist faith that "a revolutionary outbreak is certainly justified, notwithstanding the eventual defeat," to which he adds that the "events of 1968 and 1971 and the later activities of rural and urban guerrillas demonstrate this."[49]

Mexico's Marxists make the mistake of continually postponing their new revolution, he argues, "as if the revolution had to wait until capitalism completed its developmentalist trajectory by entering on a definitive crisis and showing itself incapable of resolving economic problems." Revolutions are not economically determined, but may be unleashed by enough popular awareness and indignation to produce an explosion: "What makes a crisis definitive is conscious revolutionary action . . . contrary to the dogma of economic determinism."[50]

Miranda's re-creation of Marxism hinges on his interpretation of Marx's theory of exchange values and table of equivalences, a table of the exchange ratios of commodities and relative worth of individuals who work for wages. Exchange values are a civilized invention fixed by custom whose purpose is, first, to induce workers, peasants, and artisans to exchange their commodities for less labor than it costs them, and second, to get them to work so that they can be exploited.[51] Short of direct force, they can be induced to work for a pittance only by fraud. The resulting "politics of deceit" is fundamental to understanding the process by which human geese are induced not only to lay golden eggs, but also to surrender them voluntarily to their masters in conformity with a table of equivalences.

People must be encouraged to consume more in order to work more: "for surplus value to continue to be extracted without interruption, the mythologization of 'economic development' and the elevation of the level of consumption must be the mystique of all sectors, . . . of all forces 'for progress.' "[52] That, according to Miranda, is Marx's secret of capitalist accumulation through surplus value.

By Marx's "materialism" Miranda understands its philosophical rather than its economic import. To Marx's characterization of exchange value as a mode of existence of a commodity that has nothing to do with corporeal reality, he adds that exchange value is only a "concept . . . that the human mind projects upon things as a means of ordering them." That the values of commodities can be compared in a conventional table of equivalences is a "product of the mind . . . , a societal tenet, an invention of culture." Even Marx did not fully understand "that he had found the key to history when he discovered that exchange-value is a mental construct."[53]

In this reconstruction of Marxism, the value of labor power is a figment of the imagination. Although Marx acknowledged that a historical and moral element enters into the value of the basic necessities that sustain the workers, Miranda goes a step further in characterizing economic custom as an "immaterial force operating in history." That this re-creation violates the sense of Marx's materialism is apparent from Miranda's further observation that "to confront these [immaterial] causes is the mission of existentialism," not Marxism.[54]

While Engels justified the historical role of slavery with his adage, "Without the slavery of antiquity, no modern socialism," Miranda wants to "rid Marxism of its residue of Hegelian necessitarianism, which justifies all crimes past and present as necessary." As Engels noted in a review of volume one of *Capital* (28 March 1868), although "Marx stresses the evils of capitalist production, so also does he clearly prove that this social system has been necessary so as to develop the productive forces of society to a level which will make it possible for *all* members of society to develop equally in a manner *worthy of human beings*."[55] Since Marx insists on leveling upward instead of downward, however, the humanist pie will be shared only in the by-and-by, provided there is enough to go around for everybody.

Against the majority of Marxists in Mexico, Miranda dissociates the motive for a new revolution from the desire for affluence. The system of wage labor is at issue, the equation of the wage system with a modified and piecemeal form of slavery, not an improvement in the workers' standard of living.

In Mexico, the materialist interpreters of Marx have focused on the increasing pauperization of workers and on the lack of genuine democracy as the mainsprings of social discontent. But these are motives for reform, says Miranda, not for revolution: "Marx's economic message was designed to enable them [workers] to fight for motives that elevate the moral level of all humanity" by abolishing wage slavery. "Capitalism consists in the fact that proletarians are not permitted to labor to maintain themselves—to live, in other words—unless they agree to labor for nothing a certain number of hours during the day."[56] Because of the deprivation of human freedom, this condition of degradation is far more repugnant to Miranda than the lack of decent food and housing. That is the gist of his argument for revolution, a moral struggle against exploitation rather than an economic struggle for the good things of life.

Miranda believes that a moral imperative underlies Marx's vision of a communist society. Against the unequal distribution of income and the national product, Marx appealed to a concept of justice that would have "'each individual contribute according to his capacities and receive according to his needs.'" This principle "clearly dissociates the individual's standard of living from the differential table of equivalences." Miranda imputes to Marx the same principle of justice that governed the early Christian communities.[57] However, he ignores the limits on sharing in the *Communist Manifesto* and Marx's objection to "social leveling in its crudest form."[58]

For Miranda, "the communist movement wants to break the link between the diversity of remuneration and the diversity of contributions through labor." That explains his objection to actually-existing socialism in the Soviet Union and Eastern Europe, where the table of equivalences remained in force. "If exchange-value (that 'imaginary entity') and the desire for personal gain continue to exist, they will inevitably create other oppressive and exploitative economic systems. They have in fact already done so . . . [therefore] the revolutionary must reject as superficial the abolition of capitalism, if the 'mental' causes that engendered it remain operative."[59]

Like his anarchist precursors, Miranda targets Mexico's political regime and religious institutions as well as its economic system. What makes his anarchism unique is that he stresses their common denominator in everyday life—the assignment of human worth according to rank in a table of equivalences. For authority he cites a footnote from *Capital*: "one man is king only because other men behave toward him as subjects."[60] As Miranda puts it, "Capitalist oppression could not have endured if all of us, or nearly all of us, had not been its accomplices."[61] Thus, exploited workers must share responsibility with their oppressors for the hierarchical ordering of human society.

Miranda's critique of religion is as unsparing as his attack on the other members of his sinister trinity. "The God of the Bible is incompatible with religion . . . Jesus Christ not only stressed this unmistakable trait of Yahweh but also expressly attacked the cultic worship and the temples that were allegedly dedicated to the true God." [62] Like Ricardo Flores Magón, Miranda upbraids organized Christianity for being an oppressive institution and ally of capitalist exploitation. "Perhaps the greatest disaster of history was the reabsorption of Christianity by the framework of religion." "Religion does not alter the prevailing order," but is a "stratagem for preventing the revolution." Therefore, "Rebellion against religion is mandatory for anyone convinced that justice must be achieved." [63]

In the final analysis, Miranda believes that neither Marx nor the Marxists were sufficiently radical in their critique of oppressive institutions. Marxists have yet to challenge socially acquired power through education. Even more telling, they have yet to dispute the role of noneconomic hierarchies based on rankings of sex, age, and physical fitness. "In Marxist communism, there can be no justification for care of the old, the mentally retarded, the born cripple." Those are biblical, not Marxist, concerns. "A Marxism that overlooks the absolute in the outcry of the neighbor in misery must 'ground' the imperative [of humanity] in its effect on productivity. It is on this point that present-day Marxism is not radical enough." [64]

RECONCEPTUALIZING THE WORLD REVOLUTION

For anarchists, the alternative to re-creating Marxism in an anarchist mold is to demonstrate that its vaunted communism is not what it pretends to be. We have seen that Marxism is a sword that cuts two ways. Having examined Miranda's re-creation of it, let us consider the critique of Marxism and what it led to, beginning with Revueltas and his immediate circle. As we shall see, one alternative to Miranda's anarchized Marxism is González Rojo's de-Marxified anarchism.

Within two years of the publication of his major work on Mexico's headless proletariat, Revueltas concluded that Stalin had decapitated the Soviet working class. The celebrated workers' state "had evolved at a steady and onerous pace toward its conversion into a nonproletarian state" that represented the interests of the Soviet bureaucracy. The outcome was a narrowly "national state on the margin of the universal interests of the working class," so that "'socialist' Stalinism became transformed through a policy of opportunism into its opposite—bourgeois Stalinism."[65] That is not to say that the Stalinist bureaucracy had become bourgeois, but rather that it had become tempted by a bourgeois style of life into reaching a national settlement with the international bourgeoisie.

Revueltas had made a major breakthrough by extending his original 1962 thesis, applicable only to capitalist Mexico, to the quite different context of the first socialist state. For this, his former comrades in the Communist party accused him of "Trotskyism." But unlike Trotsky, he still believed that socialism was the fruit of Stalin's 1929 revolution.

In an August 1966 essay, he took the further step of interpreting the socialist revolution in the Soviet Union and Eastern Europe as oppressive independently of its Stalinist deformation. In a major concession to anarchist theory, he claimed that "socialism cannot be reduced solely to the socialization of the means of production, nor can communism be limited to the principle that society receives from each according to one's capacities and distributes to each according to one's needs." From its inception, socialism had "real liberty," or "human disalienation," as its ultimate objective. Without such liberty, Revueltas argued, antagonisms develop between workers and the state, between socialist society and the national interest, between the national interest and international socialism with the prospect of armed conflict among socialist countries. As a purely economic transformation, "without freedom of criticism, without workers' self-management, and without democracy, socialism is a new form of human alienation."[66]

In 1968, Revueltas's dosage of anarchism received another boost from three related events, which he took as a portent of a new revolution international in scope. Following the simultaneous appearance of the May student rebellion in France and the "Prague Spring" in defiance of a Communist party in name only, there occurred the massive student rebellion in Mexico. This combination of events had as its common denominator a cry for freedom in the form of demands for student and worker self-management. Wrote Revueltas in July 1968: "The essential question of the contemporary world is the struggle for liberty, that is, for the free exercise of critical discourse . . . [which] can no longer be conditional upon the old stereotypes of 'bourgeois liberty' or 'proletarian liberty.'"[67] The next month he interpreted this struggle as aiming at "real human disalienation . . . as a daily practice, not as a distant and abstract 'ideal.'"[68]

Not just socialist practice but Marxist theory faced a crisis, because of the "insufficiency of Marx's thought for understanding the contemporary world." The fundamental problem was not that Marx was mistaken in this or that claim concerning the nineteenth century, Revueltas argued, but that events had passed him by. "The common language of 1968 in Tokyo, Berlin, Paris, and Mexico City condenses more than fifty years of a betrayed and alienated contemporary history, which it seeks to liberate [from a false historical consciousness]. . . . It restores Trotsky alongside Lenin, it recovers Rosa Luxembourg, it disseminates the work of Che Guevara, it pays homage to Mao."[69] In each of these dissident, anarchist-prone Marxisms new ground was broken toward understanding our times.

The absence of a vanguard party in Mexico and the rest of Latin America, according to Revueltas, had resulted in a failure to probe the underlying causes that sidetracked the communist movement after the Bolshevik Revolution. The political awareness and historical knowledge possessed by the proletariat had been filtered through the lens of nominally Communist parties that had been reduced to instruments of Soviet foreign policy and that neither knew nor responded to the unique conditions of their countries. Thus Mexican revolutionaries needed to restudy the "vicissitudes, calamities, and failures of the international communist movement . . . that began with the death of Lenin and have yet to reach their end."[70]

In this perspective, the fundamental struggle for liberation was not that between the socialist and capitalist camps periodically threatening a nuclear holocaust, but the independent struggle by workers of all countries against both capitalist hegemony and socialist bureaucracy. Without a struggle on both fronts, Revueltas believed, there was no realistic prospect of liberating the peoples of Latin America.[71]

Revueltas maintained that, since World War II, the struggle between capitalism and socialism had been partially resolved in favor of the latter. But it could not be fully resolved except through a transformation of the Communist parties into real Marxist-Leninist vanguards or, failing that, the creation of new proletarian vanguards. In either event, this would depend on overcoming the traces of nationalism that divided them and set them against one another. Such a task, Revueltas contended, devolved on the creation of a new Communist International.[72]

A pretty large dose of anarchism was needed for him to reach the conclusion that a nuclear confrontation between socialism and capitalism is incompatible with an independent strategy of the proletariat. An independent strategy called for a ruthless criticism of the Stalinist scenario of world revolution. Marx had traced the impending collapse of capitalism to two main factors: first, the antagonism between the developing productive forces and the fetters imposed on them by private property; second, the class struggle between proletariat and bourgeoisie. Lenin noted two other factors: interimperialist rivalries over the division of the world's markets, and the antagonism between a handful of capitalist powers with huge colonial possessions and the immense majority of peoples compelled to fight for their independence. To these destabilizing factors Stalin added the rivalry between the capitalist and the socialist camps.[73] Revueltas's lasting contribution was to have challenged the consequences of accepting and following this Stalinist scenario.

It remained for Enrique González Rojo (1928–), Revueltas's protégé in the Spartacus Communist League, to carry his mentor's critique to its logical conclusion. In a book appropriately dedicated to Revueltas's memory, he argues that the class struggle in Mexico is mainly one between capitalists and bureaucrats, old masters and new, a struggle in which socialist ideology plays into the hands of professional bureaucrats.[74] It was a tour de force, the first concerted effort by a Mexican Marxist to go beyond Lenin as well as Marx.

González Rojo's major work, *La revolución proletario-intelectual* (1981), revives Bakunin's scenario of a worldwide bureaucratic revolution as reformulated by the Polish revolutionary Waclaw Machajski (1866–1926). Wrote Bakunin in 1873, referring to the nightmare that Marx's socialist followers planned to launch in broad daylight, "They will establish . . . the direct command of government engineers who will constitute a new privileged scientific political class."[75] To this Machajski added that socialism "leaves inviolate all the incomes of the 'white hands,'" while intellectual workers get their maintenance from the unpaid product of the proletarian's labor dressed up as a reward for their skilled labor power.[76] Such is the cold reality of which a Bonapartist and postbourgeois regime is only the tip of the bureaucratic iceberg.

Admittedly, González Rojo's knowledge of Machajski was secondhand. Having no direct access to Machajski's writings in Russian, he relied on the prologue by Henry Mayer to a book on Bakunin, on a history of Russian political thought by Soviet academician S. S. Utechin, and on an article by Nico Berti on anarchist prognoses of an emerging class of "new masters." He also consulted Trotsky's 1931 autobiography, in which Trotsky refers to Machajski's "amazing conclusion that socialism is a social order based on the exploitation of the workers by a professional intelligentsia."[77]

Taking his cue from Bakunin's French precursors as well as from Bakunin's Polish successor, González Rojo points to the failure of socialist revolutions to establish a "Republic of Equals." Instead, they end by substituting one form of exploitation for another.[78] Trotsky's thesis that the Soviet Union became a degenerate workers' state with bureaucratic deformations is rejected on the grounds that from its very beginning the "Bolshevik Revolution was a revolution made *by* the workers, *for* the intellectual class." Rather than a deformed workers' state, "what we have is a mode of production distinct from capitalism and socialism . . . [because] the state nationalizes the *material* means of production, but leaves intact private property in the *intellectual* means of production." This new mode of production is described as "techno-bureaucratic," and the revolution that brings it about as a "proletarian-intellectual revolution." [79]

What is it, he asks, that made possible the substitution of a proletarian-intellectual for a proletarian revolution in the Soviet Union? His answer is that "intellectuals do not constitute a stratum, a layer, a sector, but a class." Unlike the so-called labor aristocracy constituting the crowning layer of the proletariat, intellectual workers have independent interests plus the capacity to acquire power and to establish a new economic order. The Marxist version of world revolution is scientifically obsolete, because it fails to acknowledge the role of this new class, "its tendency to acquire power by means of the struggle between labor and capital." Is Marxism, then, useless as an ideology? On the contrary, it is eminently suited to become the "ideology of the intellectual class" because it denies that intellectuals have any class interests distinct from those of the proletariat as a whole. [80]

By returning to the origins of modern communism in the French Revolution, González Rojo assesses Marxism for what it is, a deformation of communist ideology. The first to have coined the word "communism" was Babeuf's mentor, the prolific French journalist Nicolas Restif de la Bretonne. Having written in 1781 a fantasy of an egalitarian society and having introduced the goal of a community of goods in 1782, he decided in 1793 to use the word "communism" for his anticipated new order. Babeuf's term "communist" had exactly the same meaning, likewise with reference to a community of goods. [81] But in stark contrast to Lenin's revival of Babeuf's usage, the *Communist Manifesto* has for its goal only a community of property in the means of production. So why call it communist?

González Rojo sides with the French egalitarians against Marx's concessions to differential payments during the initial stage of communism. [82] As Marx notes in his "Critique of the Gotha Program," during this lower stage "a given amount of labor in one form is exchanged for an equal amount of labor in another," which implies an unequal share because "one man is superior to another physically or mentally, and so supplies more labor in the same time." [83] Marx shrugged off this inequality as a defect peculiar to a communist society that has only just emerged from capitalism. But why call it a defect of communist society rather than an asset in a techno-bureaucratic one?

Contrary to Marx and Engels's assumption that the abolition of bourgeois property means the abolition of exploitation, González Rojo argues that it signifies only the abolition of capitalist exploitation. He had learned this from reading Trotsky, who knew what was at stake but hesitated to affirm that the Soviet bureaucracy was not just an exploiting stratum but an exploiting class.[84] Not until World War II did Trotsky have second thoughts when he opened a Pandora's box by declaring that, should the bloodletting not lead to a worldwide revolution, then the "inability of the proletariat to take into its hands the leadership of society could actually lead . . . to the growth of a new ruling class." In that event, Marxists would have to revise their interpretation of the Soviet Union, for it would have become evident to them that "in its fundamental traits the present USSR was the precursor of a new exploiting regime on an international scale . . . [and that] the bureaucracy will become a new exploiting class."[85]

González Rojo owes an additional debt to Trotsky, whose detailed explanation of bureaucratic exploitation in the USSR shares common ground with Machajski's conclusion that socialism is a social order based on the exploitation of manual workers by intellectual workers. Guillén was not the first to have noticed Trotsky's indebtedness to anarchist sources. Max Nomad believed that Trotsky derived his strategy of permanent revolution from Machajski, not just his theory of bureaucratic exploitation underlying his critique of the Soviet system.[86] That Trotsky shared common ground with anarchism is further evident from his demand for equality through a leveling down of Soviet incomes and from his commitment to the dying away of the state as a condition of even the most elementary socialism.[87]

Because of his criticism of socialism, González Rojo opened himself to the charge of "Trotskyism." In a series of essays in 1967, his mentor Revueltas had already vindicated Trotsky's critique of the Soviet Union, while in 1968 he had joined with Mexican Trotskyists to found the short-lived Grupo Comunista Internacionalista (Internationalist Communist Group).[88] Like his mentor, González Rojo continued to maintain close relations with Mexican Trotskyists. Indeed, two decades later we find him joining the Trotskyist-inspired Movement toward Socialism, in the conviction that mass mobilizations in support of Cuauhtémoc Cárdenas's presidential bid might become the springboard to a new revolution.[89]

Revueltas and González Rojo were not the only ones on the Mexican Left to have come under the influence of Trotsky's incipient anarchism. In 1977, Carlos Sirvent published his monograph *La burocracia*. Following Trotsky's usage, he uses the term "bureaucracy" to cover administrators, managers, and supervisors in industry as well as government. Although Sirvent concedes that under capitalism the top bureaucrats belong to the bourgeoisie, he argues that under socialism the bureaucracy constitutes a new exploiting class.[90] Among his sources he mentions a 1960 article by Claude Lefort, who broke with Trotskyism in 1949, and a 1965 work by two leaders of the "Left Opposition" in Poland, Jacek Kuron and Karol Modzelewski.[91] Some twenty thousand copies of Sirvent's influential monograph were published in the first edition and it was adopted by the National Association of Universities and Institutes of Higher Learning in Mexico for training secondary school teachers in the social sciences.

POSTINDUSTRIAL ANARCHISM

We have seen that Mexican anarchists added a new monster to Flores Magón's sinister trinity of Capital, State, and Church—the octopus of Bureaucracy in business and the professions, in organized labor and politics. Their critique of contemporary society did not stop there, but took a novel turn with their focus on a different set of problems that adversely affected not just Mexican workers but all social classes. "Industrialism" was its name, the common denominator of the new bureaucratic Behemoth and of the old capitalist Leviathan.

By the 1970s, Mexico City, the industrial heart of Mexico, had become the most populous urban center in the world and had almost the number of Mexicans in the rest of the republic. There were some six million denizens in the capital's industrial slum of Nezahualcóyotl alone. Plagued by rats and refuse in the streets, without drinking water, sewers, and indoor plumbing, they breathed in dust from the contaminated excrement the winds picked up and blew across the valley. Downtown, amid traffic jams that defy description, the burning eyes of pedestrians cried out as each passing bus spewed forth new doses of carbon monoxide. The stifling, pushing crowds in bus terminals and subways accentuated the discomfort, all under a cloud of smog that hung over the city. With its unsurpassedly low quality of life, Mexico City was a morbid texture of Third World poverty and advanced technology gone haywire. It was an ecological disaster.

Could a credible case for anarchism be made by addressing these social ills that made life unfit in the capital city? During the late 1960s and the early 1970s they came under the scrutiny of Ivan Illich's controversial Intercultural Documentation Center (CIDOC), founded in Cuernavaca in 1964. A Viennese priest, Ivan Illich (1926–) studied theology and philosophy at the Gregorian University in Rome and obtained a Ph.D. in history from the University of Salzburg. But CIDOC was a Mexican institution where from 1964 through the mid-1970s, he directed research seminars on institutional alternatives in a technological society with a special focus on Latin America.

Illich's summaries of the discussions and theses he presented at these seminars received worldwide attention when they were published.[92] The first of the Spanish translations appeared in Mexico in 1978, *Nemesis médica*. In 1985, J. Mortiz published *La sociedad desescolarizada* and *Energía y equidad*, and in 1990 *El género vernáculo*. The only one of his CIDOC works not contracted with a Mexican publisher was *La convivencialidad*, which appeared in Barcelona in 1978. But like his works published in Mexico, it was read and discussed in intellectual circles in the nation's capital.

Among the unique features of Illich's anarchism is the connection he perceives between industrial growth and the mushrooming of bureaucracy. Bureaucratic escalation can be checked, he argues, only by slowing down and reversing industrial growth. This calls for austerity and abstinence with respect to progeny as well as material production. It requires a frugal society in place of rising demands and expectations.[93] Beyond a given threshold, "further energy inputs increase inequality." Thus, a Republic of Equals depends on a "post-industrial, labor-intensive, low energy . . . economy."[94]

The alternative to managerial fascism dominated by experts, according to Illich, is a nonbureaucratic, workers' self-managed economy.[95] The choice is between enjoying less by having more or achieving freedom and happiness for everyone with less technology, less production, less consumption, and less pollution. The pervasiveness of scarcity obliges us to practice voluntary poverty for the sake of peace, "to limit procreation, consumption, and waste . . . [and] our expectations that machines will do the work for us."[96]

For Illich the fundamental enemy is not capitalism but industrialism and its perverse prophets of progress. The economic systems fathered by Adam Smith and Karl Marx shared the perverse premise that the fundamental problem of humankind is not too much but too little production. They did not foresee the large-scale industrial pollution from overproduction, overconsumption, and overpopulation that combined to accentuate inequality under both systems and to break the ecological balance between human beings and their physical environment. Toward a solution of these problems, Illich urges an inversion of current values plus the courage to face up to the liberals' and socialists' challenge of being antipeople, antieducation, and antiprogress. For him the only acceptable solution is the "Neanderthal" socialism highlighted in the epigraph to *Energy and Equity*: "Socialism can arrive only on bicycle!"

Illich believes that the history of humankind is one long catalogue of enslavement and exploitation, but that it was not until modern times that the peaceful professions, the arts and sciences, began to compete with war in pillaging their victims.[97] This indictment of civilization suggests a reversion to Rousseau and to the anarchism of Sylvain Maréchal's 1796 "Manifesto of the Equals." "Let all the arts perish, if necessary, as long as real equality remains," wrote Maréchal. "Disappear at last, revolting distinctions between rich and poor, great and small, masters and servants, governors and governed!"[98]

The common theme through Illich's writings is his commitment to a "convivial" society in which people treat one another as brothers and sisters. Conviviality opposes privileged access to education, tools, transportation, and medicine and the privileged participation in their benefits. Its goal is to increase equality through "equal control over inputs . . . [and] an equal distribution of outputs." Equal opportunity may be secured by matching maximum and minimum incomes. But it is far from enough, since it has "no effect on equalizing the privileges that really count in a society where the job has become more important than the home . . . [where] workers are graded by the amount of manpower capital they represent . . . [and] those who hold high denominations of knowledge stock will be certified for the use of all kinds of time-saving privileges."[99]

Fundamental to Illich's anarchism is the imperative to level downward instead of upward. Although the purpose of obligatory schooling is to equalize educational opportunities, it has the opposite effect of polarizing society into "knows" and "know nots."[100] Given the escalating costs of education and the failure to impose an upper limit on the personal stockpiling of expertise, he contends, it is an illusion to attempt to achieve equality by spending more money on the poor. "Today's managers [and professional workers] form a new class of men. . . . This class of power-holders must be eliminated, but this cannot be done by mass slaughter or replacement. . . . Management can be done away with only by eliminating the machinery that makes it necessary and, therefore, the demands for output that give it sway."[101]

Illich's fellow Austrian at CIDOC, Leo Gabriel (1945–), helped spread the new gospel of conviviality. After living through the student uprising in Paris in 1968 and completing his doctorate in social anthropology at the Collège de France under Claude Lévi-Strauss, in 1970 he journeyed to Mexico in search of an alternative to the culture of Central Europe in which he had grown up. Like others of his generation, he aspired to what he calls a "social utopia," a self-managed community of individual freedom and solidarity aimed at improving the quality of everyday life. In Mexico he found what he was looking for in the mutual aid among peasants struggling for land, the solidarity among strikers in defense of a living wage, the shared experience of neighborhood organizations in the shantytowns of the big cities, and the semireligious fellowship of guerrillas fighting against oppression.[102] But there was a notable difference between his aspirations and those of the popular movements and organizations in which he discovered a kindred spirit. While he longed for a community of equals bound together by ties of friendship, they struggled mainly to survive.

Through his Grupo Informe de Cuernavaca, Gabriel became an active participant in their struggles. An anarchist commune of actors, musicians, and amateur filmmakers, the Grupo Informe engaged in "consciousness raising" by transmitting the experiences of struggle of the various resistance movements to other communities facing similar problems. It performed "guerrilla theater," inspired its audiences with songs of protest, and showed films of popular mobilizations. Before and after these performances for peasants and townspeople in remote villages of Morelos and in the neighboring states of Guerrero, Puebla, and Michoacán, Gabriel did a lot of talking behind closed doors—a form of direct action with the risk of deportation. As he recalls, "In this work we had to expose ourselves to the same danger that the popular organizations experienced, that of being hunted down by the army and police." [103]

To Illich's brand of peaceful anarchism, Gabriel added a touch of violence. Committed to direct action, in 1973 the Grupo Informe made a pilgrimage overland through Central and South America to the Mecca of urban guerrilla struggles in Argentina. Besides performing for the Argentine guerrillas, Gabriel interviewed their leaders and agreed to collaborate with their cadres in exile. On returning to Cuernavaca in 1974, he and another member of his group pieced together a two-hour film from the guerrillas' archives in Buenos Aires, which they used for propaganda in their clandestine work with the September 23 Communist League.

Unlike Illich, Gabriel believes that guerrilla violence is neither doomed nor bound to become self-defeating. He was induced to collaborate with the September 23 League because of his unique synthesis of Illich's gospel and Guillén's strategy of the urban guerrilla. Once the guerrillas were suppressed in Mexico and the Grupo Informe dissolved in 1976, he went to Nicaragua to work for the Sandinistas. Following the Sandinista victory in July 1979, he established the Alternative Information News Agency of independent journalists in Managua and began collaborating with Radio Liberación and the guerrillas in El Salvador. After a decade of journalistic activity, Gabriel summed up his experience of the Central American revolutions in a book published in Mexico that is as remarkable for its combination of personal testimony and historical objectivity as it is for its novel thesis that, without conviviality, without the collective memories and shared sufferings of a "popular culture," there can be no revolutionary movement. [104]

It was not the first time that visitors from abroad would contribute to the struggle on the theoretical front. Plotino Rhodakanaty, the first advocate of anarchist doctrine in Mexico, where he arrived in 1861, was born in Athens, Greece, of a Greek father and an Austrian mother. The Spanish émigré José Muñuzuri became the first editor of *El Hijo del Trabajo*, the official organ of the anarchist circle La Social organized by Rhodakanaty, and a fellow Spaniard, Juan B. Villarreal, became president of one of the first labor congresses in Mexico dominated by anarchists.[105] Shortly before the revolution a Catalonian political exile, Amadeo Ferrés, carried the doctrine of anarcho-syndicalism to the Mexican working class. Assisting him was Juan Francisco Moncaleano, a political fugitive hunted by the Colombian army, who arrived in Mexico with his feminist wife and three Cuban anarchists on the heels of Madero's uprising. Moncaleano laid plans for the first Rationalist School in Mexico while publicizing the cause of Ricardo Flores Magón and the PLM. After his arrest and deportation in September 1912, the House of the World Worker paid tribute to him as its founding martyr.[106]

So it was that anarchist theory received a boost on Mexican soil with help from foreign thinkers and agitators. Although they were mainly active before or during the Mexican Revolution of 1910–1917, they have become influential again in conjunction with the revival of anarchist theory after the 1968 student rebellion.

ANARCHISM WITHOUT ILLUSIONS

Preoccupation with the ultimate goals of anarchism may be rewarding for intellectuals and visionaries like Illich, but, as Gabriel notes, it is eminently unrealistic for those who must carry on a daily struggle merely to survive. It is also dangerous to survival in a country where the ruling party silences critics by jailing, murdering, or "disappearing" them. It became imperative therefore to bring anarchist theory down to earth without sacrificial lambs. One way of doing so was to show how anarchism might be relevant to the solution of mundane problems cutting across class lines. Illich made a stab at it, but his research was not grounded in the realities of Mexican politics.

Mexican anarchists already had more than one program, a maximum and a minimum. Their maximum program amounted to a declaration of war against capital, the state, and the clergy, a struggle on three fronts on behalf of an egalitarian communist society, a program revived by Miranda in the 1970s. By then the struggle to abolish capitalism had resulted not in the emancipation of workers by the workers themselves, but in the political ascendancy of a bureaucratic class and the transformation of the socialist dream into a bureaucratic nightmare. So this maximum program needed to be revised by identifying the fundamental enemy with the advancing bureaucratic system threatening to replace capitalism. That was González Rojo's special contribution.

Meanwhile, the anarchists' minimum program, a preeminently democratic program of basic reforms under capitalism, had become obsolete. Its commitment to fair elections and an end to the political monopoly of the ruling party threatened to open the floodgates to an electoral landslide by the bourgeois National Action party (PAN).[107] To be effective, an anarchist program would have to countervail the threat of this fastest-growing party in Mexico by targeting capitalism as the fundamental enemy and by mobilizing against it virtually all sectors of the Mexican Left, including nationalists in the ruling party.

A centerpiece in the revival of anarchist theory during the 1970s, the publishing house of El Caballito helped to reorient anarchists to the need for a new minimum program. Its director and managing editor, Manuel López Gallo (1929–), believed that a new program might give some substance to the mirage of social revolution forever receding on the political horizon. Although incapable of being realized, anarchist ideals might still be useful in changing the way people think. They might even help in spreading Marxism, whose maximum program of communism contained an anarchist component.[108]

What was needed was an anarchism with political clout, an anarchism without illusions. President Echeverría had made use of the rising tide of social discontent since 1968 by backing the organization of a new Marxist party, the Partido Socialista de los Trabajadores (Socialist Workers party), as a means of offsetting the PAN's growing electoral strength. In the same spirit, López Gallo and his circle began asking whether neo-Trotskyist and neoanarchist theories might help to dam the currents of bourgeois influence in Mexico. Thus the 1970s witnessed the encouragement and publication of works with a Trotskyist and anarchist slant by representatives of the Mexican Left who had no illusions about either one of these "isms."

López Gallo's interest in the Left stretched across the political spectrum to include an influential sector of the ruling party. El Caballito became an outlet for his own books and churned out others he could agree with. Its publishing program aimed at presenting alternatives to both liberal capitalism and bureaucratic socialism while unifying the Mexican Left around nationalist as well as socialist objectives.[109]

For López Gallo, these two enemies of the working class did not have the same weight. He identified the workers' fundamental enemy not with the new class of bureaucrats directly over them, but with Mexico's absentee owners responsive to the multinationals. So it behooved the Left to join with its immediate enemy to fight the enemy of its enemy, the private sector in league with foreign interests. In effect, he supported a third position, which postponed the confrontation with the bureaucracy and leaned toward a bureaucratic solution to Mexico's social ills.[110]

An anarchist Realpolitik was dictated, he argued, by the ideological backwardness of Mexico's workers. The Mexican people were not ready for democracy, because in political matters a majority of them still thought and behaved like children incapable of recognizing their real interests. *Pan* means "bread" in Spanish, and for countless numbers of ignorant peasants the PAN was the party that provided for their daily bread and cared for their elementary needs. The potentially revolutionary classes were politically illiterate and got their politics from the pulpit, radio, and television. Among their leaders, talented and ambitious individuals had been repeatedly co-opted by the ruling party. In this perspective, López Gallo believed that a program for greater democracy would play into the hands of reactionaries.[111]

Although genuinely sympathetic with the neoanarchist and neo-Trotskyist projects he sponsored, he had no illusions about them.[112] The anarchist's dilemma is that workers must emancipate themselves or be emancipated by others, when most workers lack an understanding of their political interests and their leaders are unreliable. Thus López Gallo concluded that the only viable strategy for anarchists is to serve as a counterweight to the ideology of Mexico's private sector.

It is worth recalling that not all anarchists have been practicing democrats. In the aftermath of the 1848 February Revolution in France, Proudhon noted that without far-reaching social and economic reforms, universal suffrage becomes a device for legitimizing the status quo. Against the exaggerated claims for representative democracy, he denied that an elected assembly could faithfully represent the workers' interests in a class-ridden society. In practice, democracy was counterrevolutionary. "One way or another, preponderant strength in government belongs to the men who have preponderance of talent and fortune. . . . Instead of saying, as did M. Thiers [a constitutional democrat], The King reigns and does not govern, democracy says, The People reign and does not govern, which is to deny the Revolution!"[113] López Gallo agreed with this prognosis, that democracy in Mexico is an electoral noose for strangling the people's interests.

In 1980 El Caballito announced its plan for a "libertarian library." The first volume in the series was an anthology of recent essays by Spanish, North American, and British writers celebrating the rebirth of international anarchism after the seeming deathblow inflicted by the Spanish Civil War.[114]

The rebirth of anarchism, according to the introductory essay, had come in response·to the overriding bureaucratization and centralization of authority in contemporary societies.[115] The vast literature on behalf of workers' self-management had found supporters among influential persons in almost every country and had stimulated interest in the writings of nineteenth-century anarchists.[116] Although El Caballito folded in the mid-1980s and its libertarian library was nipped in the bud, the publishing house of J. Mortiz responded to the growing appetite for anarchist theory by publishing the works of Ivan Illich.

Besides translating and publishing the works of neoanarchists, López Gallo imported their books, which were otherwise inaccessible to Mexican readers. In addition to the publishing house, his family owned the centrally located basement bookstore El Sótano, across from the Alameda Park in Mexico City. Through his bookstore, López Gallo imported the works of French neoanarchists in Spanish translation. He also made available to Mexican readers a two-volume collection of Cornelius Castoriadis's writings, originally published in French, along with Heleno Saña's examination of the anarchist undercurrent in the political thought of Lenin, Trotsky, Mao, Castro, Guevara, and Marcuse—books published in Barcelona and Madrid while General Franco was still in power.[117]

As one of the original importers of Guevara's complete works and Fidel Castro's speeches, López Gallo arranged for the export of El Caballito's books to Havana. On friendly terms with the Cuban leadership, he became closely identified with Fidel Castro's policy of promoting the unity of the Left, a strategy that paid political dividends in Cuba, Nicaragua, El Salvador, and Guatemala. He also shared Castro's unique blend of socialism and revolutionary nationalism. Among the books he marketed in Havana was Gilly's *La revolución interrumpida*, a synthesis of Marxist theory and Mexico's national revolutionary tradition. Castro read it and, notwithstanding Gilly's Trotskyism, made it required reading for the Central Committee of the Cuban Communist party.[118]

An intellectual in his own right, López Gallo befriended Gilly during the Argentine's imprisonment in Lecumberri, Mexico City's notorious penitentiary and custodian of political prisoners. He was instrumental not only in getting Gilly to write a book on the Mexican Revolution, but also in securing Gilly's release following its publication. With Gilly's help, he launched a Latin America neo-Trotskyist quarterly with himself as editor. The first issue of *Coyoacán*, named after Trotsky's place of residence in the capital during his final years of exile, appeared in October 1977.

These works helped sustain López Gallo's theory of the worldwide emergence of a bureaucratic elite on the road to class power. This former economics professor at the National University wrote a major treatise on economics and politics in the history of Mexico in which he argued that the central political bureaucracy had effectively consolidated its power during World War II, after which the authority of the president had become uncontainable.[119] But he stopped short of developing a general theory of the bureaucratic class and of the bureaucratic mode of production, along the lines of Sirvent's 1977 monograph and González Rojo's book in 1981.[120]

Sharing López Gallo's theory was an important segment of the Mexican Left that still looked to the ruling party for leverage in moving the country away from capitalism. Lombardo Toledano's split from the PRI, the Popular Socialist party, was among the most articulate representatives of a Mexican road to socialism based on the expansion of the public sector.[121] As a party that embodied Enrique Flores Magón's belief in a continuing Mexican Revolution and the socialist postulates inscribed in the 1917 Constitution, it shared the legacy of the PLM's reformists, minus their anarchism.[122]

Although a firm believer in the consolidation of the central bureaucracy since World War II, López Gallo has promoted books on the erosion of bureaucratic power since 1940. He finds this rival theory supportive of his own, because they share a fundamental premise: the destruction of the liberal-oligarchic state during the Mexican Revolution and its replacement by a bureaucratic regime in which the bourgeoisie has been relegated to the political sidelines. Because the era of military coups ended in 1940, López Gallo believes that the central political bureaucracy is today more entrenched than ever. But two of the books El Caballito published in 1976, Mario Huacuja and José Woldenberg's *Estado y lucha política en el México actual* and Juan Felipe Leal's *México: Estado, burocracia y sindicatos*, argue that it is more vulnerable than before because the influence of Mexico's bourgeoisie has grown, budded, and bloomed.[123]

In 1977, López Gallo published Donald Hodges and Ross Gandy's *El destino de la revolución mexicana*, which upholds the fundamental premise shared by López Gallo and the authors of the books just mentioned. He also made plans to publish a second edition based on the English version, *Mexico 1910–1982: Reform or Revolution?*—a project that was never consummated because shortly afterward El Caballito folded. I mention the two editions because each rejects "López Gallo's thesis of bureaucratic consolidation . . . [and] supports the hypothesis of an *erosion of bureaucratic power*."[124] In 1977 El Caballito also published Hodges and Guillén's *Revaloración de la guerrilla urbana* and, in the following year, Hodges's *Marxismo y revolución en el siglo veinte*. Like the book with Gandy, these two works paved the way toward a more realistic theory of revolution than the prevailing ones with their Marxist and Leninist pedigrees, a theory López Gallo shared.

Notwithstanding some theoretical differences, El Caballito's books placed on the political agenda the question of how the Mexican Left should respond to the bureaucratic new order threatening to replace capitalism. Should it opt for a struggle on two fronts or throw its support behind the class of professionals and administrators seeking to replace the proletariat as the vanguard of a new revolution? López Gallo and company chose to revive Enrique Flores Magón's strategy of conspiring against both houses while swimming with the current. In pushing forward the bureaucratic revolution in the economic sphere, they hoped to bury capitalism and have a chance, however slim, of directing the revolution into new channels.[125]

The logic of their anarchist Realpolitik accounts for the support they gave in 1987 to the Democratic Current inside the ruling party. It was led by three of the PRI's top leaders: Porfirio Muñoz Ledo, the tough, flamboyant populist who was secretary of public education under López Portillo and later ambassador to the United Nations and president of the PRI; Cuauhtémoc Cárdenas, Lázaro's son and past governor of Michoacán; and Ifigenia Martínez, one of Mexico's most brilliant economists and a PRI celebrity. They made a lot of speeches and public appearances and were soon joined by some outstanding personalities of the independent Left, among them Enrique González Rojo and Adolfo Gilly.

As the momentum increased for Cuauhtémoc Cárdenas's presidential candidacy, almost all the parties on the Left struggled for a place on his political bandwagon. The most glaring exception was the Revolutionary Workers' party, which split over Cárdenas's candidacy after Gilly went to a shindig thrown by the Democratic Current to do some politicking and find out what was going on. The next day the Trotskyist party called a meeting of its Central Committee and Gilly, who was a member, showed up. He was ordered to explain what he was doing at the PRI's social affair, the implication being that only sellouts would go to it. White in the face, Gilly rose to his feet and said, "Explain? There is nothing to explain!" and walked out.[126]

Within weeks, Gilly had taken some three hundred cadres out of the party with him and organized a new political movement, the Movimiento al Socialismo (Movement toward Socialism). Meanwhile, the student movement had flared up and began fielding some three hundred thousand in the Zócalo week after week in a huge strike protesting the closing of automatic admissions at the National University. The exploding student movement went for Gilly when the Trotskyist Antonio Santos and his friends among the student leaders joined Gilly's movement. So the Movement toward Socialism acquired a mass base and parleyed with the Democratic Current while the Revolutionary Workers' party sat in its corner and sulked.

Was this the fate of Fidel Castro's united Left strategy in Mexico, to curry favor with former leaders of the ruling party? What a comedown from the 1982 elections, when anarchist students went around painting on walls "No Votes" (Don't vote) and "Alto a la Farsa Electoral" (Stop the Electoral Farce). They were rounded up and thrown into prison.[127]

Mexico is neither a democracy nor on the threshold of democracy, and the ruling party has yet to give up office when it can resort to repression to quash opposition and use fraud to win an election. As the computers counted the first wave of results flooding in from the cities, it was a landslide for Cárdenas. So the computers promptly "broke down," to the amusement of every cynic and the horror of the National Democratic Front, giving the PRI time to rig the election. It may not have won the votes, but it certainly won the count, giving it a majority in the Congress and winning the presidency.

Did López Gallo's cobelievers expect more from the political system than it could possibly deliver? No, there was more to their support for Cárdenas than meets the eye. The ruling party had made a marked turn to the right by giving up on nationalism and joining the PAN in a drive for privatizing the public sector and downgrading the populist legacy of the Revolution. The PRI was becoming a bourgeois party, so that the pragmatic Left had to search for allies elsewhere. The Democratic Current and its progeny, the Frente Democrático Nacional (National Democratic Front), fitted the bill.

In 1983 Gandy and I questioned López Gallo's theory of bureaucratic consolidation,[128] with good reason, since the transformation of the ruling party under President Miguel de la Madrid (1982–1988) and his successor, Carlos Salinas de Gortari (1988–1994), has confirmed our initial skepticism. Mexicans can no longer say with López Gallo, "Thanks to the Revolution and its political instrument, the PRI, our nation is not completely in the hands of reaction,"[129] for what was credible in 1983 ceased to be so by the time of the 1988 elections.

When the economic crisis hit in 1982, de la Madrid used it to create a bank parallel to the nationalized one. During the second half of his administration he ripped down part of the tariff wall. Salinas took over and ripped down the rest. He destatified the bank, drove wages through the floor, used the corporate state to hold the unions in line, and went for a free-trade zone. Salinas did what the business community wanted in an effort to get its cooperation. Because the bourgeoisie can speculate against the peso, because it can make more money abroad than it can at home, the economy is in ruins, capital flight continues, and the growth rate in the 1980s was nearly zero.

Ross Gandy, who has lived in Mexico since 1970 and, like Gilly, is a political friend of López Gallo, summarizes the PRI's predicament in a letter to me dated 7 March 1991:

> Salinas is doing what the bourgeoisie wants in order to stop the flights of capital. He gave them back the bank. He smashed workers' wages. He dropped the subsidies. He gave up the populist rhetoric. He sold half the state sector. He tore down the tariff wall, WITHOUT MUCH RECI-PROCITY! Every time Salinas gives the bourgeoisie something, it asks for more. The bourgeoisie wants the ejidos. It wants to shrink down the National University by ending free admissions and imposing stiff entrance examinations. The hundreds of billions of megabucks it took out since 1960 are not coming back until it also gets control of foreign policy and finally the government.[130]

So the PRI government has become a de facto hostage to economic black-mail with no rescue in sight, because the bourgeoisie has put down roots abroad that have become profitable and hesitates to bring its money home for fear the country may blow up.

By 1991 Cárdenas's new Partido de la Revolución Democrática (Party of the Democratic Revolution) had taken up the positions of the old PRI, the commitment to revolutionary nationalism, an independent foreign policy, preservation of the ejido sector and state-owned industries. Meanwhile, the PRI had adopted most of the positions of the bourgeois PAN. And the PAN? It cannot compete with the PRI's new line, and the bourgeoisie no longer has any need for it, except as a foil in case the PRI relapses into a populist rhetoric. So Cárdenas's new party has become the political heir to the dormant legacy of the Mexican Revolution, which the Left interprets as a step toward socialism.

Under these circumstances, the logic of López Gallo's anarchist Real-politik means support for Cárdenas's new party. That is precisely Gilly's position and that of his Movement toward Socialism. In a country where everyone loves to talk and the Left is a tremendous *noise*, its only realistic posture is to keep the bureaucratic revolution afloat. The thorny question is whether the Revolution can be kept going by the traditional Left's unilateral reliance on an electoral solution.

The strategies currently available to Mexican anarchists are not mutually exclusive. It is possible to support simultaneously the bureaucratic revolution from above against the threat of a bourgeois political restoration, and the simmering revolution from below against the prospect of bureaucratic consolidation. At the same time, it is a mistake to expect PRI politicos like Muñoz Ledo and Cuauhtémoc Cárdenas to do much more than Salinas himself. In Gandy's appraisal of the situation, which he shares with Gilly, history teaches that such people move only when mobilized masses make them move.

It is the popular resistance that we should pay more attention to. The Base Christian Communities, 90,000 of them, sent their representatives to a Congress in Veracruz last month [October 1988]. This is more important than Cárdenas's National Democratic Front. The Urban Popular Movement, the grass roots organizations of the shanty towns all over Mexico that struggle for water, drainage, roads, etc., just held a national congress. The spontaneous peasant land seizures, the building of independent peasant leagues, the tremendous student movement, the National Council of Indian Peoples representing independent organizations of twenty-six of the fifty-two tribes, I could go on and on; this is what is important, not the antics of the Left parties in the rubber stamp Congress, not their bullshit in coming "elections!"[131]

CONCLUSION

Today, the Mexican Left is in total disarray. With the fall of communism in Eastern Europe, the drive toward privatization throughout the Third World, and the emergence of a so-called new world order, the Bolshevik Revolution has become a dead letter. With the transformation of the Communist parties in the former Soviet bloc into social democratic parties and the democratization of the Communist parties in Western Europe, there is no longer a middle ground between social democracy and anarchism. We are back where we started at the beginning of the century, before bolshevism emerged and filled the vacuum.

The history of the PCM is symptomatic of what has happened to the rest of the Mexican Left. After making a left turn in 1960 that lasted until the late 1970s, the Communist party cadres moved steadily to the right until they became completely submerged in the tidal wave of democracy engulfing Latin America and the rest of the world.

On the eve of the party's self-dissolution in 1981, the delegates at its 19th Congress voted by a narrow margin to give up the Leninist slogan of "dictatorship of the proletariat" and to replace it with "democratic workers' power." Shortly afterward, Mexico's Communists changed their name while simultaneously rejecting the structure of a vanguard party for that of a socialist mass organization. In 1987 they took the further step of abandoning the "hammer and sickle," the traditional Communist emblem, and of rejecting the trademark "scientific socialism" as tying them too closely to Marxism. Simultaneously, they broke off their ties to the various parties constituting the international Communist movement. The final step was taken in 1989, when they completed their backsliding by forming a democratic party.

With the disappearance of the Soviet Union in January 1992, the Mexican Left despaired about the future. Marx and Lenin were both in the doghouse. Wrote Ross Gandy to me in a letter from Cuernavaca dated 15 September 1992: "Down here the Left has retreated to a social democratic position. It hangs tough on old standbys like nationalism and government intervention in the economy, but has modified its position on collectivism and planning. Collectivism is no longer seen as a panacea, and planning has become auxiliary to privatization within a market economy. There is a lot of yapping about electoral democracy. In other words, the social democratic option."

Evidently, the wind is blowing in a social democratic direction. However, Gandy overheard one Marxist professor at the National University saying to his colleagues: "The Marxists are wrong, the anarchists were right!" Gandy too has resisted the temptation to abandon ship. As he remarks in the same letter: "Yes, I have been spreading the new anarchism among students at the ENEP-Aragón-UNAM [a division of the Universidad Nacional Autónoma de México on the capital's eastern rim at Aragón]. Not that I need to spread anarchism among them: they tend that way spontaneously. Yes, I've lectured on Bakunin and anarcho-Marxism!"

From what we have seen, anarchism too is enjoying a revival. Meanwhile, it too has undergone a sea change.

The most enduring expression of the old anarchism was its assimilation of Marx's theoretical contributions and Blanqui's strategy of a revolutionary vanguard. In Mexico, Ricardo Flores Magón was its apostle. Later, Spanish anarchists would weld together features of these two legacies. Guillén is a prime example. A vanguard of professional revolutionaries is better prepared to seize power than the workers' traditional political and trade union organizations but, once the enemy is defeated, Guillén believed, power should be relinquished to workers' councils and committees of self-management operating within a system of direct democracy.[1] "All power to the soviets!"—that is the only way David can defeat Goliath.

Alongside this refurbished anarchism a new anarchism has come to life. It takes its cues not from stalwarts like Flores Magón, but from the New Left. Under the inspiration of such diverse currents as the Cuban Revolution, liberation theology, and the new science of ecology, Miranda and Illich argue that David's victory will be self-defeating unless he learns to master himself. Rather than overhauling the pecking order, workers try to use it to their own advantage. Mexican anarchists have yet to make the connection between human and animal exploitation, between eating meat and being treated like meat.[2] The most striking illustration of the adage "Power corrupts, absolute power corrupts absolutely" is humanity's relationship to other animals. Unknowingly, workers become accomplices of their own exploitation.[3] Besides keeping the wheels of industry rolling, they share in the benefits of greed from technological progress and modernization, in the victimization of nature and the destruction of the planet. Far from workers not consuming enough, in advanced countries they consume too much.[4] So to an updated indictment of ruling elites, the new anarchism adds a critique of the working class.

Diego Abad de Santillán, the renowned Spanish disseminator of Flores Magón's political philosophy, disputes the widely accepted belief that anarchism is in crisis, an obsolete ideology, and thus condemned to die. He concedes that it has lost the support of organized labor and no longer serves as a catalyst of revolutionary trade unionism. But he argues that it has acquired other believers, which enables it to flourish without a self-conscious and organized political movement.

"What is anarchism?" he asks. It is a doctrine that "proclaims the dignity and freedom of human beings whatever the circumstances." It is tied neither to a specific economic and political program nor to a given strategy, conspiratorial or otherwise. Only by forcing anarchist beliefs into a fixed mold and artificially coupling them to the life cycle of a particular doctrine can one make a convincing case for the obsolescence of anarchist ideology.[5]

Few schools of anarchism have endured without significant revision. Proudhon's mutualist anarchism of independent producers in a free market gave way to Bakunin's collectivist anarchism, which gave way to Kropotkin's communist anarchism. The doctrinaire element in each was an asset in winning proselytes, but a liability in holding them. Put to the test in the utopian communities erected on the margins of the capitalist system, anarchist recipes of perfection did not fare well when faced with economic realities.

So a new generation of Spanish anarchists in the 1920s and the 1930s tried to excise the element of ideology.[6] "Anarchism without a program" was their battle cry. What made anarchism a constant factor in human society was its inchoate spirit of rebellion, declared such luminaries as Ricardo Mella in Spain, Gustav Landauer and Max Nettlau in Germany, and, belatedly, Errico Malatesta in Italy.[7] A certificate of citizenship was given to all the historical forms of anarchism through the recognition of their common denominator.

"Does the river create the bed on which it flows or does the river bed create the river?" Abad asked in an article written in 1922–1923. He answered that the river creates the channel, that anarchists should not reverse the natural order, and that the mission of antiauthoritarians in a revolution is to be provokers, not liberty killers. "They must not impose socialism or any other value on the masses but should stimulate them to reach their conclusions naturally . . . [which] is why we reject constructive programs . . . [and] do not want syndicalism or anarchist communism when it is presented as . . . a completed system." The social currents released by revolutions should be free to flow: "We do not want to dig the river bed, but rather to enlarge and stimulate the river to determine its own course."[8]

Shortly after writing these lines, Abad shifted positions. He took a new and favorable look at anarcho-syndicalism and its communist program, as can be seen in his book on Flores Magón.[9] It is not enough to provoke a revolution, he says in a February 1926 article rethinking his earlier view. Rather than "passive spectators of social struggles . . . we can be a proletarian force capable of speaking our piece."[10] In opting for the channeling and directing role he had previously repudiated, he no longer believed that anarchism should be an undefined ideological current.

He returned to his original position several decades later. By then it had become evident that anarchism had no future as a program for a labor movement that was no longer revolutionary. The three-thousand-year-old history of anarchism without a program had persuaded him that the recovery of that legacy was a guarantee of its survival. As an antidote to the bureaucratization of the contemporary world, anarchism had become "more viable than ever, more so than in the epoch in which it embraced the labor movement, more than during its explosions of heroic rebellion, more than in its exemplary opposition to war."[11] This claim strikes me as exaggerated and I am at a loss to explain how it might be tested. But what can be corroborated is that anarchism has not withered away, as anticipated.

Abad's mistake was to have reduced the anarchist options to anarchism with and without a clear-cut program. He failed to consider a third possibility—an anarchist program without the trademark. Invisible to potentially hostile critics, this alternative anarchism is far from obsolete, as the Mexican experience shows.

In contemporary movements of social protest there is a place for programmatic as well as unprogramed anarchism. During the 1968 student rebellion, the inchoate anarchism of the students at the Polytechnical Institute played a vital role in mobilizing popular resistance and sparking the student strike. Almost all popular movements of this kind have been libertarian in their early phases.

Where should one look for traces of this anarchist revival? Abad's answer is in philosophy and the social sciences, and in the efforts of rebellious youth to knock down the pillars of old society.[12] "The rebirth of anarchism in the twentieth century," writes another commentator, "has been due to a general disaffiliation of 'intellectuals' . . . from the general celebration of the affluent society . . . [where they are] 'on tap' but rarely 'on top.'"[13]

If anarchism is a going concern, it is because of new recruits among the most rapidly growing segment of society, among students and intellectuals disaffected by the chasm between knowledge and wealth, clarification and manipulation. The Magonist legacy survived during the 1930s and the 1940s through the efforts of the *jaramillista* movement at the sugar mills in Atencingo and Zacatepec. But a new chapter began with the student rebellion and anarchist intellectual revival of the 1960s and the 1970s.

Has the anarchist project changed? Not really. As heretofore, it aims to melt down the pyramids of power and privilege in all dimensions of social life—racial, sexual, familial, political, cultural, economic. Admittedly, the anarchist project is more ambitious than the socialist and communist projects. But anarchism is less sectarian in addressing all features of the social question.

For bearers of the Magonist legacy, the economic dimension is still of premier importance. As long as human geese go on laying golden eggs for their masters and social betters, they can count on wild and woolly anarchists as their champions. Objectively speaking, anarchists still represent the economic interests of exploited workers far more than those of intellectuals.

There are anarchists in principle and anarchists in deed. We have seen that Guillén includes Lenin and Trotsky among anarchists in principle. Both Lenin and Trotsky framed a revolutionary dictatorship that put doctrinaire anarchists out of circulation, but they made an exception of anarchists who supported the October Revolution.

Is there a touchstone for identifying anarchists? Words are not enough; "by their fruits ye shall know them" (Matt. 7 : 20). Wrote Bakunin: "Let us learn a little from the wisdom of our adversaries. All governments have the word 'liberty' in their mouth, while their actions are reactionary. So revolutionary leaders . . . should adopt a more moderate language, as peaceful as possible, but *make* the revolution. . . . Let us be silent about our principles when exigency requires, but always implacable and consequential in *deeds*." [14] Between an armchair anarchist and a revolutionary who talks a different language, Guillén advises anarchists to throw in their lot with the latter. Despite their authoritarianism, says the leading exponent of Spanish anarchism today, Babeuf, Blanqui, Lenin, Trotsky, Mao, Castro, and Guevara should be emulated because of their revolutionary propaganda of the deed. [15]

Direct action is the key to anarchist strategy. In the form of direct democracy and workers' self-management, it contributes to dismantling the machinery of oppression. In nullifying rule from the top down, in takeovers of fields, factories, and workshops, it dispenses with intermediaries. "The proletariat can become free and master of its destiny only on condition of acquiring possession of the means of producing and distributing the economic surplus, without the intermediary of the bourgeoisie or bureaucracy, through workers' councils in self-managed enterprises."[16] As a strategy of direct action, anarchism leads not just to socialism, but to self-managed socialism and then to communism.[17]

"Is anarchism a philosophy condemned never to be realized?" asks Juan Gómez Casas, secretary of the Spanish National Confederation of Work. His answer confirms the conclusion of the present study, that an anarchism without the label is neither obsolete nor inconsequential. The modern idea of self-management is the most conspicuous example.[18] Despite indiscriminate use and abuse of the term "self-management," it designates a society conformable to anarchist principles as well as strategy, ends as well as means. The great popularity enjoyed today by the philosophy of self-government demonstrates that anarchism is not a worn-out ideology.[19]

While acknowledging that the anarchist tradition is an extremely complex one, John Hart charts the decline of Mexican anarchism after the Revolution by focusing on its organized expressions in the Communist party, the Casa, the CGT, the Mexican Anarchist Federation, the Grupo Cultural "Ricardo Flores Magón," and Tierra y Libertad.[20] The fate of the CGT determined, in his judgment, the fate of Mexican anarchism as a whole. As late as 1928 its national membership had grown from some fifty thousand to more than eighty thousand members concentrated mainly in the Federal District.[21] But the ruling party put an end to the General Confederation of Workers with the July 1931 passage of the Código Federal de Trabajo (Federal Labor Code), giving the government the power to recognize unions, to legitimate strikes, and to intervene in labor conflicts. That spelled the demise of any direct role for anarcho-communist ideology in the ranks of organized labor.

The new labor code destroyed not only the confederation, but also the political mind-set of its former members. The resulting ideological confusion demoralized the confederation's leadership, led to desertions, and transformed the rank and file from intransigent believers in direct action into docile supporters of government arbitration and of a bureaucratically managed collaboration between labor and capital. As a former CGT leader interviewed in 1933 cynically described the transformation that had taken place over barely a two-year period: "When the leaders are anarchist they [the workers] are anarchist; when the leaders are 'governmental' they are governmental, too."[22]

By consolidating the grip of the political bureaucracy on the nation in 1929, the new ruling party effectively wiped out thirty years of organizing activity by anarchists, which had helped to make the 1910–1917 Revolution. But did this spell the decline of Mexican anarchism or only of its association with organized labor?

The Magonist legacy received a boost during the 1930s and the 1940s through the efforts of the *jaramillista* movement in Morelos and Puebla, but it also survived in the speeches and articles of Enrique Flores Magón. After he returned to Mexico in 1923, his rhetoric underwent a change. He began calling for the rights of workers and peasants under the 1917 Constitution. The defense of their constitutional rights, he believed, was the best guarantee that "the Revolution is not over" and "'will not be over until you, the people, destroy the [remaining] injustices.'"[23] Instead of armed struggle, he called for the implementation of the articles on labor and agrarian reform written into the Constitution. In place of the PLM's 1911 program, he resurrected its 1906 program professing liberal rather than anarchist principles.[24]

Librado Rivera interpreted this change of face to mean that Enrique was a deserter from Magonism.[25] Although the mortal enemy of Presidents Carranza, Obregón, and Calles, Enrique became an "unconditional supporter" of President Cárdenas.[26] He actively campaigned for the election of Avila Camacho, Cárdenas's appointed successor, and accepted a position as legal counsel in the Secretariat of Agriculture during Avila Camacho's presidency.[27] He also supported the official party after its transformation into the PRI, as did the Communist party during the 1950s. However, he remained faithful to his revolutionary principles in turning down two generous offers, a life pension in 1934 and a cabinet position in Cárdenas's government in 1939.

Notwithstanding Rivera's criticism, to Enrique Flores Magón's credit he became the bearer of a new anarchist current after the Revolution, an anarchism without adjectives and under a different name. Like Abad de Santillán, he reconciled his anarchist principles with a program for structural reforms. In Mexico this led to a popular front with the ruling party and to support for Cárdenas's revolution by quotas. Enrique was not alone in adopting this new strategy. It also induced the Jaramillo brothers and Rodríguez to make common cause with the Communist party. It helped to make them politically effective. So Enrique's revival of the PLM's 1906 program may be chalked up to common sense rather than to a betrayal of his brother's political legacy.

Anarchist ideology not only predates but also postdates its association with the word "anarchism." Beginning with Enrique Flores Magón, Mexican anarchists increasingly depicted themselves in other terms. The Jaramillo brothers did not describe themselves as "anarchists." None of the recognized leaders of Mexico's rural and urban guerrillas in the 1960s and the 1970s subscribed to the anarchist label. Revueltas revived the anarchist legacy but did not apply the term to himself; neither did González Rojo. Rodríguez and Raya still prefer the adjective "communist." Miranda calls himself a communist, and Illich adopts the respectable cover of the word "socialism."

While anarchism after the 1930s goes by another name, is it exclusively or mainly an anarchism without adjectives? Guillén, the most widely published contemporary anarchist, upholds communism as a solution to the social question for the largest political party in the world, "the party of discontent."[28] This was also the focus of Enrique Flores Magón's anarchism after the Revolution.

The traces of anarchism in the thinking of former Communist cadres have another name, but not without adjectives. As late as 1989, the cadres in the Mexican Socialist party who had given up the hammer and sickle still clung to the "Internationale" as the party's anthem. Written in June 1871 by the French Communard and revolutionary poet Eugène Pottier, when the Communards of Paris were being hunted down and slaughtered by the hundreds, its original verses reflect the political thinking of Proudhon and Blanqui far more than that of Marx and Engels. Its Spanish adaptation is even more controversial, as in the following line sung by former Mexican Communists: "No queremos ni autoridad, ni Estado, ni burgués, ni Dios" (We want neither authority, nor the State, nor bourgeois, nor God). What is this, if not a composite of Proudhon's open and Blanqui's veiled anarchism? It is the anarchism implicit in Proudhon's maxims, "Property Is Theft" and "Nobody Is King," and in Blanqui's precept, "Neither God nor Master."[29] It is Blanqui's noxious "triumvirate of Loyola, Caesar, and Shylock."[30] It is Flores Magón's dark trinity of "Capital, State, and Church."

To summarize in philosophical or broad outlines the results of this study, Mexican anarchism has become progressively less sectarian without ceasing to be communist. The most dramatic instance of this development may be seen in the different faces of Magonism in response to changing political circumstances over the six decades since the Mexican Revolution. The preoccupations of anarchists in the 1940s and the 1950s were not those of anarchists in the immediate wake of the armed struggles of 1910–1917, nor were these the concerns of the anarchizing current during the 1968 student rebellion and its aftermath. These changes are reflected in the personalities I have chosen from three successive generations to illustrate the continuing relevance of Ricardo Flores Magón's legacy.

If we take a generation as consisting of from twenty to thirty years, the time typically required, depending on native customs and circumstances, to generate offspring, then the original generation of Magonists, dating from Ricardo Flores Magón's birth in 1874 and of his brother Enrique in

1877, came of age around 1900 and made its principal impact on history prior to Ricardo's death in 1922. Mónico Rodríguez's father belonged to Ricardo's generation, having been born in 1864, the same year as Librado Rivera. Despite successive splits between PLM moderates and extremists, the overriding concern of this first wave of Magonists was to make a revolution with the popular fervor generated by the proletarian and peasant explosions from 1910 to 1917. But after Zapata's assassination in April 1919 the steam evaporated from the revolutionary kettle.

Flores Magón's generation was followed by the first generation of his political heirs. Influential after the Revolution, this new generation dates from the birth of Rubén Jaramillo in 1900 and of his brother Porfirio in 1902. Like the preceding generation, it divided into two wings: Librado Rivera's followers, committed to a new revolution outside the 1917 Constitution; and the followers of Enrique Flores Magón, dedicated to the more modest task of implementing the PLM's 1906 program written into the Constitution. Like Enrique, Rubén became an unconditional supporter of General Cárdenas throughout most of the 1930s,[31] but unlike him, both Rubén and Porfirio joined the Communist party. Porfirio stayed with the party, while Rubén took a more intransigent stand by launching his plan for a new revolution in 1943. Thus the Jaramillo brothers and their followers split over the same question of strategy that some two decades earlier had divided Librado Rivera and Enrique Flores Magón.[32]

The next generation of Magonists may be dated from Mónico Rodríguez's birth in 1919. Like Rubén, he read Flores Magón's writings as others read the New Testament but, unlike Rubén, took a more sanguine view of the PCM. Whereas Rubén quit the party after a year because of differences of principle, Mónico became a party professional and stuck with it until 1958. After the Jaramillo brothers parted company, he tried to soften their political differences and continued to collaborate with both. He swore by the PLM's 1911 program but, like Enrique Flores Magón, also threw his support behind a re-edition of the PLM's 1906 program.

For the last generation of Magonists, Juan Vargas may be taken as representative. Vargas was born in 1942 and came of age in the early 1960s, when Rubén Jaramillo was making headlines because of the land invasions in Michapa and El Guarín. A native of Morelos, he admired the exploits of this latter-day Zapata. Like others of his generation, he subsequently came under the influence of Gámiz, Cabañas, Vázquez, the anarchizing current in the student rebellion, and its aftermath in the urban guerrillas of the 1970s. His anarchism was already half-formed when Rodríguez introduced him to Flores Magón's *Semilla libertaria* and to Revueltas's essay on Mexico's headless proletariat. It was further enriched by José Miranda's liberation theology, by Ivan Illich's work at CIDOC, and by Leo Gabriel's

Grupo Informe de Cuernavaca. Che Guevara's exploits made a deep impression on him, as did Guillén's brand of anarcho-Marxism. Not the least of his differences with Rodríguez was his affiliation to the Communist party in 1977.

What were the motives or reasons that led Flores Magón's political heirs to join the PCM, given the impossibility of resurrecting the alliance with Mexican anarchists during the early 1920s? In 1919 anarchists looked on the October Revolution as a beacon light for oppressed workers everywhere. Many of them sincerely joined the party as the Mexican section of the Communist International. But did their successors join it for the same or similar reasons?

There is a pattern in the circumstances of Rubén's affiliation to the Communist party in 1938, his reaffiliation in 1961, and Vargas's affiliation in 1977. By April 1938, after General Franco's forces had pushed back the Loyalist armies with the help of one hundred thousand Italian troops and Italian and German warplanes, the Second Spanish Republic was all but doomed. The menace of fascism had repercussions not just in Spain but in Mexico in bringing together rival and bickering sectors of a hitherto divided Left. In 1961 the nascent Cuban Revolution was threatened by hostile foreign forces and by the prospect of renewed intervention after the Bay of Pigs invasion in April. So a sense of solidarity with the Spanish Republic in 1938 and with the Cuban Revolution in 1961 may account for Rubén's decision to join the party in times of trouble.

In Vargas's case, I do not have to guess. The arguments Cuban comrades used in 1968 to convince me to rejoin the American Communist party I later used to persuade Vargas to join the PCM. It was not easy to contest their argument, first, for solidarity with the Cuban Revolution and with the revolutionary movements in Guatemala, Nicaragua, and El Salvador, and second, for militancy in a Communist party as a condition of being politically effective on the Left. Besides these arguments, the failure of the armed struggle in Mexico and a "Letter to Campa" on May Day 1976 by former members of the Communist League in which they acknowledged their errors and readiness to return to the PCM, were the deciding factors in Vargas's decision.[33]

Whatever may have been the motives for compromising their anarchist principles, Flores Magón's political heirs testify to the declining fortunes of Magonism as an independent political tendency. Jaramillo made national headlines, founded a political party, twice ran for governor in the state of Morelos, wrote a widely read autobiography, and received national recognition in the histories of Mexican insurgency alongside Villa, Zapata, and Ricardo Flores Magón. In sharp contrast, Rodríguez was a professional organizer for the Communist party, the leader of a former faction occasionally mentioned in party documents and party histories, but became a living legend only in Morelos as its last great battler for social justice.[34] Lacking the stature of his two predecessors, Vargas presents a shadowy figure remembered, if at all, in connection with the Grupo Informe and the 1980 state elections as the PCM's candidate from Cuernavaca. If these samples from successive generations are a faithful index of the latter-day history of Magonism, one must conclude that the future of Mexican anarchism belongs to others.[35]

POSTSCRIPT

Nothing and nobody can detain the triumphal march of the revolutionary movement. Does the bourgeoisie want peace? Then let it become the working class! Is peace what the authorities want? Then let them take off their coats and take up the pickaxe and cudgel, the plough and the hoe! Because as long as there is inequality, as long as some work so that others consume . . . there will be no peace.

RICARDO FLORES MAGÓN

These words have turned out to be prophetic.[1] On New Year's Day 1994 Mexicans were startled by the news of an Indian peasant uprising in the state of Chiapas. San Cristóbal de las Casas (the state's second largest city with a population of 85,000), and three other sizable towns at the entrance to the Lacandon rain forest were occupied by masked peasants of the Zapatista Army of National Liberation (EZLN). In the most spectacular guerrilla offensive since the 1970s and the largest since Rubén Jaramillo's peasant uprising in 1953, Emiliano Zapata's and Ricardo Flores Magón's latest political heirs declared war on the government in the name of the country's impoverished Indian population. Although the future of Mexican anarchism may belong to others, there were still strong residues of the revolutionary idealism and guerrilla mystique of the 1960s.

A few days before the army ambushed his guerrillas in October 1978, El Güero declared that the Mexican government and its armed forces could never contain the "movement of the indigenous villages and ejidos of Guerrero, Oaxaca, Veracruz, Chiapas, Campeche, Michoacán, and Durango."[2] He was the first to support with firepower the demand for autonomy by Mexico's Indian population, the largest in the Americas, consisting of some ten million according to recent estimates. He would not be the last.

In an action reminiscent of Bakunin's September 1870 takeover of the Hôtel de Ville in Lyons in southern France and his repeated exhortations to burn all titles to property and other official documents, the rebels broke through the barred doors of San Cristóbal's town hall, destroyed the financial records and land titles, hurled computers out of the windows, and set the first story ablaze.[3] In Altamirano, one of the other towns they occupied, they swarmed over the concrete town hall, smashing it apart with sledgehammers. They had come to destroy the hated symbols of a government whose legitimacy they disputed for having stolen the Indians' traditional lands, for having fraudulently remained in power in 1988 when Cuauhtémoc Cárdenas won the elections but lost the count, for legally terminating in 1992 the system of agrarian reform established by the 1917 Constitution, and for signing the North American Free Trade Agreement that promised more riches for Mexico's wealthy but also more misery for the country's marginalized and indigenous poor.

Unlike the sectarian programs couched in Marxist rhetoric of the 1960s and the 1970s, the EZLN called not for a new revolution but for structural changes akin to Zapata's 1911 Plan of Ayala. Its program included a sweeping land redistribution, an overhaul of the political system to guarantee full democracy, a reorientation of the government's market-oriented economic policies, and political autonomy for the Indian regions of the country. In a propaganda battle that has reshaped the public's image of the guerrillas, they explained that they had gone to war to ensure fair elections in August 1994, to secure democracy for all Mexicans, and to make themselves heard.[4]

But there was more than meets the eye to their eleven-point program "for work, land, housing, food, health care, education, independence, freedom, democracy, justice, and peace."[5] Although launched in Zapata's name, the armed assault by two thousand combatants on New Year's Day was not just another peasant and Indian uprising. The red and black badges on their uniforms reminded them of the fighting tradition of Mexico's workers on strike, but the EZLN's black flag of anarchism with a communist red star suggested something far more radical.

The EZLN does not espouse an anarchist or communist ideology, or any other doctrinaire "ism." But its most eloquent voice, that of Subcomandante Marcos, says of the Indians' eleven-point program, "those points are summarized in a single word: socialism." What kind of socialism? Not the mimetic, West European or Marxist-Leninist variety championed by other sectors of the Mexican Left. It is a socialism of the poor, one in which "everybody will be equal," an indigenous socialism of sharing based on the pre-Hispanic communal traditions of the Mayan Indians, a socialism depicted as "utopian" and "millenarian" rather than rational and materialistic.[6]

In sharp contrast to earlier guerrilla movements in Mexico, the Zapatista Army's commanders are subordinate to an Indigenous Revolutionary Clandestine Committee consisting of representatives of the Indian communities in Chiapas. The white and mestizo political-military vanguard has a strictly limited role, that of political counselors and military strategists for the Mayans who determine policy. The result is an anarchist dream come true: a grassroots structure with the bottom in control rather than an armed vanguard imposing its policies from on top. It was the legacy of El Güero, fed in Mexico by the same anarchist philosophy that led Mao Zedong to make common cause with the Bolshevik Revolution, to lead an armed struggle for national liberation during the thirties and forties, and to launch an antibureaucratic cultural revolution in the sixties.

Like the guerrillas in neighboring Guatemala, the EZLN embraced a Maoist strategy with a strong dose of anarchism. Guatemala's Revolutionary Movement of 13 November (MR-13) charted the way, followed a decade later by the Organization of the People in Arms (ORPA) and the Guerrilla Army of the Poor (EGP) launched from Mexico.[7] The Guatemalan guerrillas were the first to apply a Maoist strategy, the first to live among the indigenous peoples and to share their way of life. Almost a decade of consciousness-raising and military training preceded the ORPA's and the EGP's armed struggle with combatants consisting overwhelmingly of Mayan Indians.[8] However, it is important to stress that there is no evidence of any links between them and the EZLN.

The EZLN's ties to earlier guerrilla formations are to be discovered elsewhere. The day after the occupation of San Cristóbal, federal and local officials linked the organization to two tiny radical holdovers from the 1970s, remnants of Cabañas's Party of the Poor and the less well-known Revolutionary Workers' and Peasants' Party of Popular Unity, the second being a splinter of an extinct guerrilla group operating in Oaxaca.[9] These suspicions were partly confirmed during an interview with Subcomandante Marcos at a clandestine camp in the Lacandon rain forest. In the first account of how the rebel movement came together, he told reporters from the Mexico City newspaper *La Jornada* that more than ten years ago he had come to the Lacandon with a small group from outside Chiapas who were looking for ways to foment a new revolution with the support of workers, peasants, students, and intellectuals. Together with a local peasant league, they helped Indian villagers defend themselves against the ranchers' hired guns in fights over disputed land. Although he did not identify the peasant group, its political front appears to have been the now-dissolved Emiliano Zapata Independent National Peasant Association (ANCIEZ).[10]

In 1980 Cabañas's group shed its last vestiges of Guevarism by adopting a Maoist strategy of prolonged people's war. It also began to collaborate with another Maoist organization, People's Union, which changed its name in 1972 to the People's Union Clandestine Revolutionary Labor Party (PROCUP), after which it engaged in bank expropriations and bombings of commercial establishments and government bureaus for the next five years. The two parties continued to operate independently, but they supported each other's actions and together published the bimonthly Maoist bulletin *Proletario*. Although the origins of the EZLN are still shrouded in mystery, government sources declared on 3 January 1994 that "the PROCUP'S propaganda has been discovered in the guerrillas' encampment" and that "there are clear signs that the EZLN and the PROCUP are closely related."[11]

The Sandinista Army shares several features with Cabañas's party and with the PROCUP that are not found in other Maoist organizations. Their center of operations is in southern Mexico in Guerrero, Oaxaca, and Chiapas; they are the nucleus of a people's revolutionary army committed to disarming the enemy culturally and politically as well as militarily; their mass organizations operate clandestinely; and, like those of the PROCUP, their leaders wear hoods, roughly similar badges on their uniforms, and a red star.[12]

Besides militants from the PROCUP and the Party of the Poor, the EZLN includes survivors from the shipwreck of other movements of the sixties and seventies. In 1974, rebels of the Armed Forces of National Liberation (FALN) were overcome by the federal army in the township of Ocosingo. Militants of Popular Politics, the Organization of the Revolutionary Left/Mass Line, a faction of the September 23 League under the name of the Emiliano Zapata Revolutionary Brigade (BREZ), and the People's Union also did organizing work in Chiapas. The government was not alone in making these claims.[13] However, the first book-length study of the EZLN gives more credence to its ties to the Movement of Revolutionary Action (MAR). An EZLN commander confessed that he received his ideological and military training in North Korea during the late sixties, that he recently adopted a "Maoist line," and that after the hue and cry over the fraudulent elections in 1988 he "decided to go to Chiapas in search of his former comrades." Thus the MAR militants who remained at large completed "a long journey of more than twenty years to begin another history on New Year's Day."[14]

Maoism in Mexico has two principal sources: the People's Union, operating mainly in central and southern Mexico, and Popular Politics, having its original base in the northern cities of Torreón, Durango, Chihuahua, and Monterrey. Popular Politics appeared on the eve of the 1968 student rebellion in the form of student brigades, which afterward inserted themselves in the grassroots and neighborhood movements across the country as far south as Chiapas. Community organizing was their forte and Maoist populism ("go to the people, learn from the people"), the ideology most suited to their organizing activities. From Popular Politics sprang Proletarian Line (LP) and Mass Line (LM). In addition to their Maoist ideology, they also drew on Christian millenarianism and on Mexico's anarchist legacy.[15]

In 1976 militants of the People's Union began working with Christian catechists among the Chiapas Indians. Two years later they were followed by militants of Popular Politics represented by Proletarian Line. The initial consciousness-raising among the Indians was the work of catechists under the influence of Vatican II and liberation theology. But it was the Northerners from Torreón who sought to link the Indians' struggle for emancipation with that of workers, peasants, students, and small business people. Participatory democracy was the common theme on which they founded their utopia: "a society without exploiters and exploited."[16]

The Northerners representing Proletarian Line and Mass Line were successful in winning over not only several Indian communities, but also the catechists. "Some two hundred catechists went to two hundred communities to spread the new ideas . . . but they had changed their mode of thinking. . . . In this context appeared the EZLN's declaration of war."[17] As part of their organizing work, the Northerners were instrumental in founding the Emiliano Zapata Peasant Organization (OCEZ), the Chiapas counterpart of Michoacán's Emiliano Zapata Communal Union (UCEZ). Their intellectual roots go back to the Emiliano Zapata Coalition of Brigades (CBEZ), the student brigades with Maoist proclivities that emerged from the Spartacus Communist League in 1968.[18] However, both Proletarian Line and Mass Line stopped short of advocating armed struggle, which suggests that the militants who founded the EZLN took their cues from other sources.

In a second interview on 17 February 1994, Marcos recalled that in 1983, when his group of twelve chose Chiapas as a springboard to revolution, they felt invincible because of their political commitment. But they were not a political party in process of formation. "From the beginning, we said we did not want power. We were not going to impose our will on civil society by force of arms." The comrades would apply force only against the government as a means of ending the ruling circle's seventy-year dictatorship. Since the Spanish conquest the Indian communities have been waiting five hundred years to liberate themselves, and if necessary "we will continue the war for another five hundred." [19]

Before we could politicize the Indians, Marcos said, we had to become accepted into their communities; we had to conform to the Indians' way of life in the mountains. "And they will only accept you when you carry loads equal to theirs and walk the same distances." This egalitarian ethos not only shaped the Indians' political demands, but also transformed the political outlook of the vanguard. Just as the speed of a guerrilla column can be only as fast as its slowest member, Marcos reflected, so Mexico's economic growth must be no faster than that of the poorest state. The scenario of two or even three Mexicos developing at unequal rates is intolerable to the Chiapas Indians. "Therefore, it cannot be that one part of the country enters the First World while another, our own, [lags behind or] is annihilated." [20] In effect, the Indians' and the EZLN's egalitarianism has more in common with Mexican anarchism than with the vanguard's original brew of Marxism-Leninism.

The most important of the Indians' demands was for administrative and political autonomy not only for themselves, but also for the rest of Mexico's ten million Indians. The comrades want a collective government at all levels, said Marcos. They want every issue to be discussed, decided, and enacted by everybody. "The community reaches an agreement which everybody must abide by. . . . This same form of democracy is what later transformed the EZLN." The Zapatista Army was not born democratically; "it began as a political-military organization," but as the army grew in numbers "the organizational structure of the Indian communities so permeated our movement that we had to become democratic." As a result, "the real leadership of the Zapatista Army is Indian." The Indigenous Revolutionary Clandestine Committee from which it takes orders is an umbrella organization for the many clandestine committees that get together and decide what will be done. It was the self-managed Indian communities, not the EZLN, that decided to declare war on the government. [21]

When Marcos and his friends arrived in 1983, they had to compete with the Christian catechists and Popular Politics for the Indians' allegiance. They were told that the Indians' miserable conditions could be changed only by medical and economic projects of assistance and by participation in the political life of Chiapas. "We arrived and said: 'we have to prepare for something else.' . . . If there wasn't an open clash [with the catechists] it is because we avoided one." The nucleus of the EZLN believed that reality was the best teacher and that the repressive nature of the Mexican state would in time demonstrate that the Indians should choose the armed rather than the peaceful road. And so it happened that ten years later the tables were turned. Said the Indians preliminary to their declaration of war: "What is the problem if we all face death [from malnutrition and lack of health care]? Except that now we're going to decide how to die. Are you with us or are you leaving?" To this Marcos could not reply, "No, wait another five years to see if the new government will change," because each year that passed the government was killing them simply through neglect.[22]

Anthropologists familiar with the Indian and peasant organizations in Chiapas lend credence to Marcos's account of a process in which the urban cadres, which came to Chiapas to foment a revolution, gradually ceded control to representatives of the Indian communities from which they drew their support. In any event, the vanguard benefited. "'If we had continued with that form of organization we would still be deep in the rain forest with 15 or 20 guerrillas,' Marcos said of the Zapatistas' early incarnation as a traditional guerrilla group run by a small cadre of unchallenged leaders."[23]

The decision of veteran leftists of the generation of 1968 to subordinate their revolutionary leadership to that of representatives of the Chiapas Indians highlights a fundamental difference between the EZLN and other armed organizations in Mexico and Central America. That the Zapatista Army is unique in the annals of guerrilla warfare, that it is not a recycled Marxist-Leninist vanguard, was underscored by a Mexican think tank consisting of former guerrillas of the September 23 League, the Movement of Revolutionary Action, and holdovers from Genaro Vázquez's Revolutionary National Civic Association. Others agree that it combines the actions of guerrillas with those of a "real army."[24] The EZLN has columns that advance against the enemy and occupy enemy positions, as in Ocosingo, which was held for three days. "Neither Lucio Cabañas nor Genaro Vázquez were able to mobilize so many people." Never before was an insurgent army able to appear without the government being alerted to its formation. Hiding two thousand combatants among the local population was an astonishing feat.[25]

The novelty of the EZLN's strategy was evident in its first communiqué. In its declaration of war on 1 January it announced that it would protect the lives of civilians in its march to the nation's capital, treat prisoners with compassion, and turn over all wounded to the International Red Cross. In a communiqué that followed on 6 January, it voiced its "authentic respect" for liberty and the people's democratic will, for human rights, and for the Constitution. It declared that its arms and equipment were collected little by little, that it had not "resorted to robbery, kidnapping, or extortion" to obtain them, and that it adhered to the laws of war approved by the Geneva convention.[26] When the insurgent army launched its attack, it seized the former governor at his ranch and tried him for various crimes, including kidnapping, assassination, torture, and imprisonment of innocent people. But after he was sentenced to life imprisonment and to manual labor in an Indian community to provide for his subsistence, the sentence was commuted in favor of an exchange of prisoners and the release of civilians unjustly imprisoned by the federal army.[27] Thus nobody could credibly charge the EZLN with "terrorism."

There was a precedent for this unusual behavior, but it had not been carried out before. "Revolutionary action is of positive value when it is applied in countries with hated dictatorships under which the masses feel oppressed and exploited, a silent aversion that erupts in insurrectional form when guerrillas know how to challenge tyranny in ways that make themselves loved and admired by the people." So writes Abraham Guillén, the dean of Spanish anarchists. "Revolution is the work of minorities . . . but the minorities that triumph are those that share the life of the oppressed majorities . . . that bring democracy directly to the working masses so that the bottom dictates to the top, not vice versa."[28] The key to a successful insurgency lies not only in fighting together and then dispersing, but also in winning over workers, peasants, and the middle classes to a program that is authentically popular—two strategies successfully applied by the EZLN.[29] Could Guillén's lessons for guerrillas have rubbed off on Marcos and his friends?

Whatever may have been its origins, the EZLN's approach to revolution testifies to the wisdom of Guillén's anarchist theory and practice. Because its policies are humane and conformable to the elementary rules of morality, because they strike a chord that almost everyone can agree with, and because Subcomandante Marcos's heart-rending appeals have been widely disseminated in the Mexican press, the EZLN has "won the sympathy of a large part of the population."[30] This explains how it was able to bring the government to the negotiating table and to achieve in eleven days concessions that the Salvadoran guerrillas got only after eleven years.[31]

That the Chiapas rebellion became a shot in the arm for the entire Mexican Left is indisputable. It did so by placing the government and the ruling party in the worst possible light and by drawing attention to their vulnerability. After deploying some twelve thousand troops to eject the Zapatista Army from the cities it had occupied, the government stopped the practice of executing guerrillas after they were captured. Rather than risk public and international censure by a campaign of annihilation against the EZLN's strongholds, it limited itself to rounding up suspected supporters of the Party of the Poor in the state of Guerrero. An enormous demonstration of 150,000 in Mexico City openly supported the guerrillas' demands. The government was induced to change from a hard to a soft line that included dismissing the secretary of the interior (*gobernación*), the attorney general, and the governor of Chiapas.[32] So from a military struggle the confrontation with the EZLN turned into an eminently political contest.

There were other repercussions of the rebellion. On the Monday after the occupation of San Cristóbal, Mexico City's stock market registered a phenomenal one-day drop, falling one hundred points.[33] The violence in Chiapas spread to dozens of small towns where poor peasants seized municipal buildings and occupied lands illegally. Among the spinoffs of the rebellion were the sabotage of high-voltage electrical towers in Michoacán and Puebla, and renewed bombings by leftist groups in Mexico City. In his second bid for the presidency, Cuauhtémoc Cárdenas announced his support for the EZLN's program, if not its methods. The government admitted that the North American Free Trade Agreement had not lived up to expectations and turned its attention to relieving the plight of the Indian communities in Chiapas. In a concession to the democratic opposition, it also relinquished its control of the electoral process. So let no one say that anarchism in Mexico is a spent force or that it has ceased to be an influential factor in the country's politics.

Today, Mexican anarchism is actively represented by the EZLN, whose hope of survival is for the rebel movement to become national. During the 1980s, when new guerrilla movements emerged in Guatemala, whole villages were massacred. To avoid such a scenario in Chiapas, the EZLN has adopted a populist rhetoric. In an April 1994 interview, Subcomandante Marcos said: "If our war gains support all around the country, then the army can't take one place and make a total effort against us. . . . If there are a lot of guerrillas, or social movements, we can divide their forces." He added that the EZLN had learned to avoid the mistakes of the guerrillas in Nicaragua and El Salvador, as well as in Guatemala. "When the guerrillas provided the direction for all the [social] movements, . . . unity became impossible. So we must find the right flag to incorporate all the ways of struggle."[34]

In the aftermath of the Mexican Revolution many anarchists found a haven and cover for their activities within the Mexican Communist party. Later, during the 1960s and the 1970s, Marxist-Leninist vanguards reciprocated by promoting anarchist tactics of direct action and by invoking the names of Ricardo Flores Magón and Emiliano Zapata. Now, for the first time, we witness a Marxist-Leninist vanguard adopting, not just nominally, a Magonist ideology. Said Marcos in the same interview, when asked if the EZLN had been influenced by the Mexican anarchist tradition, especially by Magonism: "Basically, all of our thoughts about the workers and campesinos and the revolution are taken from Flores Magón, Francisco Villa, Emiliano Zapata. Their ideas about the farm workers, the workers in the cities, the hopes of liberty, are our inspiration for this movement."

NOTES

1. THE POLITICAL SUCCESSORS
OF RICARDO FLORES MAGÓN

1. Antonio Díaz Soto y Gama, "A manera de prólogo," in Ricardo Flores Magón, *Antología*, ed. Gonzalo Aguirre Beltrán (Mexico City: Universidad Nacional Autónoma de México, 1972), 78–79. All translations from Spanish are mine unless otherwise indicated.

2. Armando Bartra, ed., *"Regeneración" 1900–1918: La corriente más radical de la revolución mexicana de 1910 a través de su periódico de combate* (Mexico City: Era, 1981), 53–54.

3. Ibid., 54.

4. Ibid., 30–31, 52. See also John M. Hart, *Anarchism and the Mexican Working Class, 1860–1931* (Austin: University of Texas Press, 1978), 176–177.

5. Armando Bartra, *Los herederos de Zapata (movimientos campesinos posrevolucionarios en México)* (Mexico City: Era, 1985).

6. Arnaldo Córdova, *La ideología de la revolución mexicana* (Mexico City: Era, 1973), 135, 136, 144, 173, 179–180, 184–187.

7. José C. Valadés, *Historia general de la revolución mexicana*, 10 vols. (Mexico City: Gernica, 1985), 2:44.

8. José Revueltas, *Ensayo sobre un proletariado sin cabeza*, 2nd ed. (orig. pub. 1962; Mexico City: Era, 1980), 198, 209–210.

9. Gonzalo Aguirre Beltrán, "Introducción," in Ricardo Flores Magón, *Antología*: xxxvi–xxxvii, liv.

10. Donald C. Hodges, *Intellectual Foundations of the Nicaraguan Revolution* (Austin: University of Texas Press, 1986), 82, 83–85.

11. James D. Cockcroft, *Intellectual Precursors of the Mexican Revolution, 1900–1913* (Austin: University of Texas Press, 1976), 233–234.

12. James D. Cockcroft, *Mexico: Class Formation, Capital Accumulation, and the State* (New York: Monthly Review Press, 1983), 146, 242.

13. Hart, *Anarchism*, 183.

14. Revueltas, *Ensayo*, 206; original emphasis.

15. Bartra, *"Regeneración,"* 52.

16. Cockcroft, *Mexico*, 113.

17. Enrique Flores Magón, *Peleamos contra la injusticia: Enrique Flores Magón, precursor de la revolución mexicana, cuenta su historia a Samuel Kaplan*, 2 vols. (Mexico City: Libro Mex, 1960), 2:325.

18. Bartra, *"Regeneración,"* 257.

19. Ibid., 262.

20. Ibid., 263.

21. Ibid., 268.

22. Ibid., 269.

23. Ibid., 308.

24. Ibid., 308–309.

25. Ibid., 304.

26. Ibid., 296.

27. Cited by Aguirre Beltrán, "Introducción," in Flores Magón, *Antología*, li.

28. Bartra, *"Regeneración,"* 326–327.

29. Enrique Flores Magón, "Aclaraciones a la vida y obra de Ricardo Flores Magón," *La Protesta* (30 March 1925). Republished as the introduction to an anonymous selection of articles by Ricardo Flores Magón, *México devorado por el capitalismo americano* (Mexico City: Antorcha, 1977), 12–13.

30. Karl Marx and Friedrich Engels, "Manifesto of the Communist Party," in Robert C. Tucker, ed., *The Marx-Engels Reader*, 2nd ed. (New York: Norton, 1978), 449–450, 490.

31. Bartra, *"Regeneración,"* 290–292.

32. Revueltas, *Ensayo*, 201–202.

33. Marx and Engels, "Manifesto," 484–485.

34. Karl Marx, "Critique of the Gotha Program," in *The Marx-Engels Reader*, 529–531. See Stanley Moore, *Marx on the Choice between Socialism and Communism* (Cambridge: Harvard University Press, 1980), 35.

35. Ricardo Flores Magón, "Vamos hacia la vida," *Antología*, 6.

36. Cockcroft, *Intellectual Precursors*, 118–122.

37. Ibid., 121–122, 161, 192–193. Thanks to this second split, by February 1915 the Casa had been taken over by PLM dissidents: ibid., 229.

38. Luis Araiza, *Historia del movimiento obrero mexicano*, 4 vols. (Mexico City: Editorial Cuauhtémoc, 1965), 3:20.

39. Ibid., 3:63–66.

40. Ramón Martínez Escamilla, ed., *Escritos de Emiliano Zapata (1911–1918)*, 2nd ed. (Mexico City: Ed. Mexicanos Unidos, 1980), 82, 377.

41. David Poole, ed., *Land and Liberty: Anarchist Influences in the Mexican Revolution—Ricardo Flores Magón* (Sanday, Orkney, U.K.: Cienfuegos, 1977), 34, 134; and Cockcroft, *Intellectual Precursors*, 174.

42. Araiza, *Historia*, 4:45.

43. Ibid., 3:19–22, 4:48.

44. Cockcroft, *Intellectual Precursors*, 130, 181, 234–235; Córdova, *La ideología de la revolución mexicana*, 215.

45. Bartra, *"Regeneración,"* 425.

46. Enrique Flores Magón, *Peleamos*, 2:516–517.

47. Bartra, *"Regeneración,"* 435.

48. Ricardo Flores Magón, *Epistolario revolucionario e íntimo*, 3 vols. (Mexico City: Grupo Cultural "Ricardo Flores Magón," 1925), 1:47.

49. Ibid., 1:51.

50. Ibid., 2:45.

51. Cited by Rafael Carrillo, *Ricardo Flores Magón, presidente de la Junta Organizadora del Partido Liberal Mexicano* (Mexico City: N.p., 1945), 51.

52. Ibid.

53. Ibid., 58–59.

54. Córdova, *La ideología de la revolución mexicana*, 95, 209, 215; Cockcroft, *Intellectual Precursors*, 180–181.

55. Barry Carr, "Marxism and Anarchism in the Formation of the Mexican Communist Party, 1910–19," *Hispanic American Historical Review*, vol. 63, no. 2 (1983): 305. See Paco Ignacio Taibo II, *Los Bolshevikis* (Mexico City: Joaquín Mortiz, 1986) 31–32, 66–67, 86–88, 128–129, 148–149, 298, 324–325 n. 93.

56. Enrique Flores Magón, *Peleamos*, 1:209, 2:516–517. This Enrique Flores Magón, Ricardo Flores Magón's brother, is not to be confused with the Enrique Flores Magón who was expelled from the PCM in 1929 after having served as the Comintern's Mexican representative at the founding of the Cuban Communist party in 1925. See Arnoldo Martínez Verdugo, *Historia del comunismo en México* (Mexico City: Grijalbo, 1985), 70 n. 68.

57. Valentín Campa, *Mi testimonio: Experiencias de un comunista mexicano* (Mexico City: Cultura Popular, 1978), 101–102. See also Manuel Márquez Fuentes and Octavio Rodríguez Araujo, *El Partido Comunista Mexicano (en el período de la Internacional Comunista: 1919–1943)* (Mexico City: El Caballito, 1973), 155–157; and Martínez Verdugo, *Historia*, 99–102.

58. N. Bukharin and E. Preobrazhensky, *The ABC of Communism* (orig. pub. 1919; Ann Arbor: University of Michigan Press, 1966), 290, 293. See also V. I. Lenin, "The State and Revolution," in Robert C. Tucker, ed., *The Lenin Anthology* (New York: Norton, 1975), 383.

59. Paul Friedrich, *Agrarian Revolt in a Mexican Village* (Englewood Cliffs, N.J.: Prentice-Hall, 1970), 105.

60. Ibid., 69, 94, 128n; Taibo, *Bolshevikis*, 66–67, 190–192, 263–264, 332 n. 89.

61. Friedrich, *Agrarian Revolt*, 64–69, 139.

62. Ann L. Craig, *The First Agraristas* (Berkeley & Los Angeles: University of California Press, 1983), 87, 161.

63. Ibid., 147–148, 176.

64. Campa, *Mi testimonio*, 34, 60.

65. Ibid., 61.

66. Martínez Verdugo, *Historia*, 27, 35–39, 52; Taibo, *Bolshevikis*, 66–67, 86.

67. Martínez Verdugo, *Historia*, 35; Taibo, *Bolshevikis*: 103, 109.

68. Martínez Verdugo, *Historia*, 33, 35, 37, 56, 61; Taibo, *Bolshevikis*, 87, 94, 110, 180, 185–187.

69. Taibo, *Bolshevikis*, 187.

70. José C. Valadés, *Memorias de un joven rebelde*, 2 vols. (Mexico City: Universidad Autónoma de Sinaloa, 1985), 2:72.

71. Ibid., 2:72–73, 84–85.

72. Ibid., 2:128.

73. Ibid., 2:94.

74. Ibid., 2:103, 126–127.

75. Ibid., 2:128.

76. Paco Ignacio Taibo II, *Arcángeles: Cuatro historias no muy ortodoxo de revolucionarios* (Mexico City: Alianza Editorial Mexicana, 1988), 70–72.

77. Norman E. Caulfield, "The Industrial Workers of the World and Mexican Labor, 1905–1925" (Ph.D. diss., University of Houston, 1987), 88.

78. Ibid., 89.

79. Ibid., 85.

80. Philip S. Foner, *History of the Labor Movement in the United States*, 4 vols. (New York: International Publishers, 1965), 4:18–23.

81. Ibid., 20, 150.

82. Caulfield, "Industrial Workers of the World," 90.

83. Ibid., 150.

84. Valadés, *Memorias*, 2:142, 146.

85. Ibid., 2:153n. See also Taibo, *Arcángeles*, 70, 72, 74.

86. Taibo, *Arcángeles*, 73–74.

87. Ibid., 70–73; and Hart, *Anarchism*, 157.

88. Ethel Duffy Turner, *Ricardo Flores Magón y el Partido Liberal Mexicano* (Mexico City: Erandi, 1960), 310.

89. Taibo, *Arcángeles*, 69.

90. Taibo, *Bolshevikis*, 213.

91. Ibid. See also 67, 159–162, 177, 210–211, 360 n. 28.

92. Arnaldo Córdova, *En una época de crisis (1928–1934)*, vol. 9 in the collection *La clase obrera en la historia de México* (Mexico City: Siglo Veintiuno, 1980), 71; and Rosendo Salazar, *Historia de las luchas proletarias de México* (Mexico City: Avante, 1938), 378–381.

93. Córdova, *En una época de crisis*, 73–74.

94. On Ursulo Galván's support for Lázaro Cárdenas's presidential bid in May 1933, see John W. F. Dulles, *Yesterday in Mexico* (Austin: University of Texas Press, 1961), 571. Enrique Flores Magón also worked actively for Cárdenas's election.

95. See the anonymous article in *El Machete Ilegal* (10 September 1933) and Revueltas, *Ensayo*, 224, 228.

96. Carr, "Marxism and Anarchism," 305.

97. Bartra, "*Regeneración*," 425–6.

98. See the account of this massacre and the events leading to it in Araiza, *Historia*, 4:233–237.

99. Two-day interview with Valentín Campa arranged by Juan de Dios Vargas Sánchez at my home in Cuernavaca, Morelos (10 January 1978), and at the home of Mónico Rodríguez in Chiconcuac, Morelos (11 January 1978). See also Campa, *Mi testimonio*, 169–171.

100. Anonymous, *Rubén Jaramillo: Vida y luchas de un dirigente campesino (1900–1962)* (Mexico City: N.p., n.d.), 18.

101. Ibid., 16. A statement confirmed by my interviews with Mónico Rodríguez, in Chiconcuac, Morelos, 27 July 1975 and 12 December 1977. See Ricardo Flores Magón, *Semilla libertaria*, 2 vols. (Mexico City: Grupo Cultural "Ricardo Flores Magón," 1923).

102. Oral testimony by Rodríguez in Chiconcuac, January 1978.

103. Raúl Macín, *Jaramillo, un profeta olvidado* (Montevideo: Tierra Nueva, 1970), 42–43.

104. See the full translation of the Plan of Cerro Prieto in chap. 3.

105. Interview with Víctor Trujillo González, former *zapatista* director of the Agrarian Labor party, at his home in El Salto de San Antón, Cuernavaca, 13 July 1975. See Ilán Semo, "El ocaso de los mitos (1958–1968)," in Enrique Semo, ed., *México, un pueblo en la historia*, 4 vols. (Mexico City: Nuevo Imagen, 1982), 4:80.

106. Arnoldo Martínez Verdugo, *Partido comunista mexicano: Trayectoría y perspectivas* (Mexico City: Cultura Popular, 1971), 52, 55.

107. Jaime López, *10 años de guerrillas en México 1964–1974* (Mexico City: Posada, 1974), 16, 21.

108. Prudencio Godines, Jr., *¡Qué poca mad . . . era!* (Mexico: N.p., 1968), 39, 52–62, 68–69, 96–98, 106–107; and Elsa Robledo, "Toda la verdad sobre los terroristas mexicanos," *Contenido*, no. 163 (December 1976), 36.

109. José Natividad Rosales, *¿Quién es Lucio Cabañas? ¿Qué pasa con la guerrilla en México?* (Mexico City: Posada, 1974), 82.

110. Godines, *¡Qué poca mad . . . era!*, 99.

111. Ibid., 99–100.

112. Ibid., 123–124.

113. Ibid., 59–60. For the PCM's stake in a new revolution, see Partido Comunista Mexicano, *Nuevo programa para la nueva revolución*, ed. Gerardo Unzueta (Mexico City: Cultura Popular, 1974), 9–10; and Martínez Verdugo, *Partido comunista*, 53–55.

114. Oral testimony by Mónico Rodríguez. By then their roles were reversed. Mónico had been suspended from his position as full-time organizer, but continued to keep in close touch with the party. See the account of his and Edmundo Raya's suspension in "Resolución de la Conferencia del Partido Comunista en el Distrito Federal" (19 September 1957) in Daniel Moreno, *Los partidos políticos del México contemporáneo 1916–1979*, 7th ed. (Mexico City: Costa-Amic, 1979), 215–216.

115. Revueltas, *Ensayo*, 201–208, 240–247.

116. Ibid., 244.

117. Ibid., 244–246.

118. Interview with PCM leaders Cuauhtémoc Sandoval and Gerardo Unzueta at party headquarters in Mexico City, 6 February 1978. See Martínez Verdugo, *Partido comunista*, 20; Gerardo Unzueta, *Comunistas y sindicatos* (Mexico City: Cultura Popular, 1977), 78; and "¡Por la revolución democrática y social! Programa del Partido Comunista Mexicano" (Document approved at the PCM's 16th Congress in October 1973), in José Angel Conchello et al., eds., *Los partidos políticos de México* (Mexico City: Fondo de Cultura Económica, 1975), 157.

119. Oral testimony of a former student activist, Juan de Dios Vargas Sánchez, who wrote the preface to the first edition of my book (coauthored with Ross Gandy), *Mexico 1910–1976: Reform or Revolution?* (London: Zed, 1979).

120. Baloy Mayo, *La guerrilla de Genaro y Lucio: Análisis y resultados* (Mexico City: Diógenes, 1980), 92.

121. Interview with Cuauhtémoc Sandoval on the PCM's links not only with Cabañas, but also with other guerrillas during the 1960s and the 1970s, Mexico City, 6 February 1978.

122. Natividad Rosales, *¿Quién es Lucio Cabañas?*, 82.

123. Baloy Mayo, *La guerrilla de Genaro y Lucio*, 49.

124. Ibid.

125. Luis Suárez, *Lucio Cabañas, el guerrillero sin esperanza* (Mexico City: Roca, 1976), 176, 276.

126. Baloy Mayo, *La guerrilla de Genaro y Lucio*, 45.

127. Interview with Cristóbal Rojas, editor of *¡Presente!*, in Cuernavaca, Morelos, 10 December 1977.

128. Camarada "Ernesto," *El guerrillero*, 2nd ed. (Guadalajara: N.p., 1975), 57.

129. Juan Miguel De Mora, *Las guerrillas en México y Jenaro Vázquez Rojas* (Mexico City: Latino Americana, 1972), 36–37.

130. Cited by López, *10 años de guerrillas*, 62.

131. Ibid., 61. See also Orlando Ortiz, *Genaro Vázquez* (Mexico City: Diógenes, 1973), 187–219.

132. Bartra, *Los herederos de Zapata*, 90.

133. Gustavo Hirales Morán, *La Liga Comunista 23 de Septiembre: Orígenes y naufragio* (Mexico City: Cultura Popular, 1977), 12–13.

134. Interview with Valentín Campa, 10–11 January 1978.

135. Hirales Morán, *La Liga Comunista*, 14–15, 37.

136. Ibid., 14.

137. "Ernesto," *El guerrillero*, 147.

138. Godines, *¡Qué poca mad . . . era!*, 57.

139. Hirales Morán, *La Liga Comunista*, 16.

140. Robledo, "Toda la verdad," 43–44; and "Ernesto," *El Guerrillero*, 147–149.

141. "Ernesto," *El guerrillero*, 64, 72–81.

142. Hirales Morán, *La Liga Comunista*, 18, 20.

143. Ibid., 98.

144. Ibid., 21–24, 84–85.

145. Pablo González Casanova, *El estado y los partidos políticos en México* (Mexico City: Era, 1982), 75. Echeverría's measures of "preventive reformism" sought to avoid or prevent the eruption of social protest and conflicts difficult to control." Américo Saldívar, "Una década de crisis y luchas (1969–1978)," in Enrique Semo, ed., *México: Un pueblo en la historia*, 4:173. See also Moreno, *Los partidos políticos*, 5.

146. Suárez, *Lucio Cabañas*, 26.

147. See Andrea Revueltas et al., "Prólogo" to Revueltas, *Ensayo*, 14–15; original emphasis.

148. Ibid., 15.

149. Ibid., 16 n. 5.

150. Ibid., 27.

151. Ibid., 29. From an interview by Mary Lou Dabdoub, "La maldición de José Revueltas," *Revista de Revistas*, no. 62 (8 August 1973).

152. Revueltas, *Ensayo*, 198.

2. THE CONSPIRACY AGAINST THE SUGAR COMPLEX AT ATENCINGO

1. Letter from Mónico Rodríguez to me, dated Chiconcuac, Morelos, 18 June 1992.

2. Hart, *Anarchism*, vi, viii, 175–177. See also Bartra, *"Regeneración,"* 54; Córdova, *La ideología de la revolución mexicana*, 136, 144, 173; Campa, *Mi testimonio*, 15–16; and Valadés, *Memorias*, 2:44.

3. David F. Ronfeldt, *Atencingo: The Politics of Agrarian Struggle in a Mexican Ejido* (Stanford: Stanford University Press, 1973). The only book-length study of Atencingo cited by Ronfeldt is by Manuel Sánchez Espinosa, *Atencingo de Cárdenas a López Mateos, 1937–1963* (Puebla: N.p. 1963), but there is no record of it in computer listings of library holdings in either Canada or the United States. Ronfeldt's autographed copy is stowed away with other Mexican materials in his garage and is at present inaccessible.

4. Ronfeldt, *Atencingo*, 10.

5. "Meet Mr. Jenkins," *Time* (26 December 1960), 25.

6. Ronfeldt, *Atencingo*, 9. For details, see John Womack, Jr., *Zapata and the Mexican Revolution* (New York: Knopf, 1969), 346–347.

7. "Meet Mr. Jenkins," 25.

8. Ibid., 25–26.

9. Letter from Mónico Rodríguez to me, 4 March 1992.

10. Ibid.

11. Letter from Mónico Rodríguez to me, 30 October 1992.

12. Ronfeldt, *Atencingo*, 12.

13. Ibid., 15.

14. Ibid., 244 n. 9.

15. Ibid., 15–16.

16. Ibid., 27–28.

17. Ibid., 18.

18. Ibid., 36, 49.

19. Unless otherwise indicated, the following account of the chief conspirators is based on Mónico Rodríguez's letters to me dated 21 February, 4 March, 18 June, and 30 October 1992.

20. Data provided by María de Jesús Sánchez Palma, wife of Reyes Jaramillo, on 20 July 1975, and by Reyes Jaramillo, the younger brother of Porfirio and Rubén, on 27 July 1975, at their home in Tlaquiltenango, Morelos.

21. Interviews with Porfirio Jaramillo's widow, Aurora Herrera, Rodríguez's *comadre* (godmother), at her home in Jiutepec, Morelos, 23 July 1975, and with Mónico Rodríguez at his workshop in Chiconcuac, Morelos, 27 July 1975.

22. Interview with Mónico Rodríguez at his workshop in Chiconcuac, 10–11 January 1978.

23. Bartra, *"Regeneración,"* 52, 360; Cockcroft, *Intellectual Precursors*, 210, 223–225.

24. Antonio Díaz Soto y Gama, *La revolución agraria del sur y Emiliano Zapata, su caudillo* (Mexico City: El Caballito, 1976), 203.

25. Renato Ravelo, *Los jaramillistas* (Mexico City: Nuestro Tiempo, 1978), 188–189.

26. Ibid., 188, 189.

27. For these and the foregoing details concerning Rodríguez's antecedents, see Isaías Alanís, Alejo Pichardo, and Agustín Ambriz, "Anecdotario de un viejo luchador social," *Nuevo consenso: Semanario de análisis informativo* (15 September 1991), 8.

28. From Edelmiro Maldonado Leal, *La breve historia del movimiento obrero*, 4th ed. (Culiacán: Universidad Autónoma de Sinaloa, 1981), 83, 85; my emphasis.

29. Alanís, Pichardo, and Ambriz, "Anecdotario," 8.

30. Letter from Rodríguez to me, 18 June 1992.

31. Unless otherwise indicated, the following history is based on Rodríguez's letters to me on 21 February and 4 March 1992.

32. Marcela de Neymet, *Cronología del Partido Comunista Mexicano, primera parte, 1919–1939* (Mexico City: Cultura Popular, 1981), 17, 113–114.

33. Campa, *Mi testimonio*, 67–86, 101–102.

34. Interviews with Rodríguez at his workshop in Chiconcuac, 27 July 1975 and 12 December 1977.

35. Ronfeldt, *Atencingo*, 17n. Ronfeldt cites the 1935 involvement of the Confederation of Mexican Workers (CTM) at Atencingo. But it was not founded until February 1936, when it emerged from the General Confederation of Mexican Workers and Peasants.

36. Letter to me, 18 June 1992.

37. Ronfeldt, *Atencingo*, 21–22.

38. Marcela de Neymet, *Cronología*, 157.

39. Barry Carr, "Mexican Communism 1968–1981: Eurocommunism in the Americas?" *Research Report Series*, no. 42 (La Jolla, Calif.: Center for U.S.-Mexican Studies, University of California, San Diego, 1985), 7.

40. Interviews with Rodríguez at his workshop in Chiconcuac, 12 December 1977 and 10–11 January 1978.

41. Ronfeldt, *Atencingo*, 41.

42. Ibid.

43. Ibid., 41–42.

44. Ibid., 50.

45. Ibid., 68–69.

46. Ibid., 75.

47. Ibid., 82; and Rodríguez's letter to me, 18 June 1992.

48. Ronfeldt, *Atencingo*, 84, 101.

49. Ibid., 89.

50. Ibid., 100.

51. Ibid., 109.

52. Ibid., 122.

53. Ibid., 126–127; and Rodríguez's letter to me, 18 June 1992.

54. Ronfeldt, *Atencingo*, 130.

55. Ibid., 15, 49.

56. Leon Trotsky, *The Russian Revolution*, 3 vols., trans. Max Eastman (Ann Arbor: University of Michigan Press, 1932), 3:168.

57. See the full translation of Point 15 of Jaramillo's Plan of Cerro Prieto in chap. 3.

58. Letter from Rodríguez to me, 21 February 1992.

59. Anonymous, *Rubén Jaramillo*, 13–15.

60. Bartra, "*Regeneración*," 349, 360–362, 377, 398–404, 423–424.

61. Ibid., 398.

62. Díaz Soto y Gama, *La revolución agraria del sur*, 273.

63. Ibid., 274.

64. Bartra, "*Regeneración*," 360.

65. See Womack, *Zapata*, 397–398.

66. Letter dated 31 October 1916, cited by Poole, *Land and Liberty*, 25.

67. Caulfield, "The Industrial Workers of the World," 85, 89.

68. See Hart, *Anarchism*, 176–177.

69. Ricardo Flores Magón, *Semilla libertaria*, 2:90–91.

70. Enrique Flores Magón, "Aclaraciones," 12–13. Republished as the introduction to an anonymous selection of articles by Ricardo Flores Magón, after first being republished in *Tribuna Roja* (Mexico City: Grupo Cultural "Ricardo Flores Magón," 1925); Rodríguez's emphasis.

71. Ibid., 14.

72. Ibid., 14–15.

73. Rubén M. Jaramillo, *Autobiografía*, y Froylán C. Manjarrez, *La matanza de Xochicalco* (Mexico City: Nuestro Tiempo, 1967), 51–52.

74. Ricardo Flores Magón, *México devorado por el capitalismo americano*, 42–43.

75. Ibid., 44.

76. Ibid., 45.

77. Ravelo, *Los jaramillistas*, 188–189.

78. Ibid., 191.

79. Ibid., 191–192. In a 10 December 1977 interview at the office of Cristóbal Rojas, editor of the Cuernavaca daily *¡Presente!*, he volunteered to show me the cave intended to serve as a hideout, the same one used by Jaramillo during the 1943 and 1953 uprisings.

80. Ibid., 193–194.

81. Ibid., 200–201.

82. Ibid., 213.

83. Ibid., 221.

84. Isaías Alanís, "Para Mónico," in Alejo Pichardo's tribute, "Nuestro querido viejo," *Nuevo consenso: Semanario de análisis informativo* (15 September 1991), 8–9.

3. RUBÉN JARAMILLO'S PLAN FOR A NEW REVOLUTION

1. Macín, *Jaramillo*, 22.

2. Cockcroft, *Mexico*, 135.

3. Anonymous, *Rubén Jaramillo*, 22.

4. Luis Javier Garrido, *El partido de la revolución institucionalizada: La formación del nuevo estado en México (1928–1945)* (Mexico City: Siglo XXI, 1982), 261. As functionaries of the National Confederation of Peasants became transformed into government bureaucrats, they ceased to represent the peasants' interests. From its inception, the Confederation of Peasants exhibited an absence of internal democ-

racy. Responsive to those who appointed them, its leaders kept the agrarian reform within bounds and repressed unauthorized land seizures while taking advantage of their positions by selling favors and diverting public monies into their own pockets.

5. Ibid., 259–261.

6. Macín, *Jaramillo*, 42–43.

7. Campa, *Mi testimonio*, 169–171. Campa mistakenly places the massacre at the beginning of 1941. According to his oral testimony at my home in Cuernavaca, Morelos, 10 January 1978, workers' resistance to the new system of presidential despotism dates from this event. For details of the massacre and the events leading up to it, see Araiza, *Historia*, 4:233–237.

8. See below, "The Plan of Cerro Prieto," Point 17.

9. Campa, *Mi testimonio*, 101–102. See also Márquez Fuentes and Rodríguez Araujo, *El partido comunista*, 155–157.

10. Campa, *Mi testimonio*, 101. For details of the plenum of 26–30 June 1937, see ibid., 132–133, and Márquez Fuentes and Rodríguez Araujo, *El partido comunista*, 202–205.

11. Bartra, "*Regeneración*," 261–263.

12. Ibid., 307–308.

13. Ricardo Flores Magón, *Epistolario revolucionario*, 1:47. But see 2:44–45 on his proposal for a united front with "revolutionary Marxists."

14. See Bartra, *Los herederos*.

15. Cockcroft, *Mexico*, 202.

16. Macín, *Jaramillo*, 136.

17. Ibid., 49.

18. Ibid., 101.

19. Ibid., 33.

20. The following biographical details are based on interviews with Mónico Rodríguez at his home and workshop in Chiconcuac, Morelos, on 27 July 1975, 12 December 1977, 10–11 January 1978, and 17 January 1980.

21. See Jaramillo's account of the strike in *Autobiografía*, 44–48.

22. On the events immediately leading to Jaramillo's armed struggle, see ibid., 48–53. For other sources on Jaramillo's first armed uprising, see Macín, *Jaramillo*, 41–120, and Ravelo, *Los jaramillistas*, 51–81.

23. Jaramillo, *Autobiografía*, 95–96.

24. Ibid., 109–112.

25. The following account of the actions at the refinery is based on Mónico Rodríguez's testimony in Chiconcuac, Morelos, 12 December 1977.

26. On Jaramillo's role in Henríquez's campaign, see Enrique Quiles Ponce, *Henríquez y Cárdenas ¡Presentes! Hechos y realidades de la campaña henriquista* (Mexico City: Costa-Amic, 1980), 215–225.

27. Ibid., 272–289.

28. Interviews with Víctor Trujillo González at his home in El Salto de San Antón, Cuernavaca, 13 July 1975, and with Gorgonio Alonso at his store in Emiliano Zapata, Morelos, on the same day; with Reyes Jaramillo and María de Jesús Palma Sánchez in Tlaquiltenango, Morelos, 20 July 1975; and with Aurora Herrera and Arnulfo Cano, her godfather, in Jiutepec, Morelos, 23 July 1975. Among

the few available accounts of Jaramillo's second armed uprising, see Manjarrez, *La matanza*, 137–140, and Ravelo's interviews in *Los jaramillistas*, 121–133.

29. For confirmation of Alonso's story of the assault on Jiutepec, see Quiles Ponce, *Henríquez y Cárdenas*, 292.

30. For Jaramillo's February 1960 and February 1961 land invasions and their political repercussions, I have relied on the testimony of Víctor Trujillo, Gorgonio Alonso, and Arnulfo Cano, who participated in the events. For an additional account, see Ravelo, *Los jaramillistas*, 168–186.

31. Manjarrez, *La matanza*, 146; and Mario Guerra Leal, *La grilla* (Mexico City: Diana, 1979), 178.

32. Manjarrez, *La matanza*, 136.

33. Ibid., 144.

34. See n. 28.

35. Jaramillo, *Autobiografía*, 77–78.

36. Ibid., 84–85.

37. Manjarrez, *La matanza*, 165–167.

38. Macín, *Jaramillo*, 14–16, 39.

39. Anonymous, *Rubén Jaramillo*, 26. In 1915 Obregón persuaded Carranza to give money, buildings, printing presses, and supplies to the House of the World Worker, and to grant its immediate demands in exchange for military help in combating Villa and Zapata—a turning point for Mexico's extreme revolutionary current.

40. Macín, *Jaramillo*, 135–136.

41. Ibid., 146.

42. Data based on interviews with Mónico Rodríguez at his home in Chicon-cuac on 10–11 January 1978, and with Gerardo Unzueta at PCM headquarters in Mexico City on 6 February 1978. See Ilán Semo, "El ocaso de los mitos," 4:79.

43. Ravelo, *Los jaramillistas*, 178.

44. Ibid., 189.

45. See Bartra, *"Regeneración,"* 246, 296, 326–327.

46. Ricardo Flores Magón, *Epistolario y textos*, ed. Manuel González Ramírez (Mexico City: Fondo de Cultura Económica, 1961), 203.

47. Ravelo, *Los jaramillistas*, 188–195.

48. Ibid., 38–39.

49. There are a few notable exceptions. See Hart, *Anarchism*; and Barry Carr, "Marxism and Anarchism."

50. See Campa, *Mi testimonio*, 102.

51. Revueltas, *Ensayo*, 224, 228–229.

52. Ibid., 7.

53. Campa, *Mi testimonio*, 129–136; and Arnoldo Martínez Verdugo, *Crisis política y alternativa comunista* (Mexico City: Cultura Popular, 1979), 278–279.

54. Manuel Aguilar Mora, *La crisis de la izquierda en México* (Mexico City: Juan Pablos, 1978), 96–102.

55. Revueltas, *Ensayo*, 247. Although from 1960 to 1977 the PCM momentarily recovered its independence by calling for a "new revolution" instead of a revival of the old one, it was seduced by the political reforms of 1977 into becoming a parliamentary opposition under new rules aimed at strengthening rather than

weakening the PRI's stranglehold over the nation. The sequel to this right turn saw the party's self-liquidation and replacement by the Partido Socialista Unificado de México (Unified Socialist Party of Mexico) in 1981, followed by the new party's metamorphosis into the Partido Mexicano Socialista (Mexican Socialist party) in 1987, and the latter's dissolution when it joined with the PRI's left wing to become the Partido de la Revolución Democrática (Party of the Democratic Revolution) in 1989.

4. THE RESURGENCE OF GUERRILLA WARFARE

1. Revueltas, *Ensayo*, 46.
2. Barry Carr, *Marxism and Communism in Twentieth-Century Mexico* (Lincoln: University of Nebraska Press, 1992), 233.
3. Letter from Rodríguez to me, 3 October 1992.
4. Fidel Castro, "Discurso pronunciado en el acto conmemorativo del IX aniversario de la acción del 13 de Marzo de 1957," *Discursos pronunciados en distintos actos celebrados desde 1965 a 1968* (Havana: Campamento 5 de Mayo, 1968), 295–296.
5. Moreno, *Los partidos políticos*, 203.
6. Ibid., 215.
7. Ibid., 216.
8. Ilán Semo, "El ocaso de los mitos," 4:59–60; and Martínez Verdugo, *Partido comunista* (Mexico City: Cultura Popular, 1971), 49–50.
9. Martínez Verdugo, *Partido comunista*, 51–52.
10. Campa, *Mi testimonio*, 195–196.
11. Ibid., 196.
12. Martínez Verdugo, *Partido comunista*, 59–60.
13. For a discussion of the takeover and the events leading to it, see Aurora Guadalupe Loyo, "El conflicto magisterial de 1958 en México" (unpublished *licenciado* thesis in sociology, Universidad Nacional Autónoma de México, 1976), 155–180.
14. On the railroad workers' strike, see Antonio Alonso, *El movimiento ferrocarrilero en México 1958–1959* (Mexico City: Era, 1972), 110–152.
15. Interview with Mónico Rodríguez at his workshop in Chiconcuac, 12 December 1977.
16. *Programa del Partido Comunista Mexicano* (Mexico City: Ediciones del Comité Central, 1966), 43. On the struggle against lingering traces of feudalism, see 28, 43; on the bloc of four classes, 46, 48.
17. Martínez Verdugo, *Partido comunista*, 54–55; and Campa, *Mi testimonio*, 277–278.
18. Martínez Verdugo, *Partido comunista*, 78–80.
19. Campa, *Mi testimonio*, 278; and Conchello et al., *Los partidos políticos*, 194.
20. Conchello et al., *Los partidos políticos*, 153–154, 166.
21. Ibid., 166–171.
22. *Programa del Partido Comunista Mexicano*, 9–10.
23. Fidel Castro, "The Duty of a Revolutionary Is to Make the Revolution: The Second Declaration of Havana," in *Fidel Castro Speaks*, ed. Martin Kenner and James Petras (New York: Grove, 1969), 104.

24. *Programa del Partido Comunista Mexicano*, 48–50.

25. Partido Comunista Mexicano, *Nuevo programa*, 25.

26. Ibid., 11, 26.

27. Ibid., 12, 29, 33.

28. Ibid., 35, 40–41, 43–45, 50.

29. Carr, *Marxism and Communism*, 253.

30. Ibid., 252.

31. Partido Comunista Mexicano, *Nuevo programa*, 20.

32. Fidel Castro, "Discurso pronunciado en conmemoración del día internacional del trabajo (l^{ro} de mayo de 1966)," in *Discursos*, 51–53, 55.

33. Partido Comunista Mexicano, *Nuevo programa*, 21.

34. Aguilar Mora, *La crisis*, 151–192.

35. José Revueltas, *México 68: Juventud y revolución* (Mexico City: Era, 1978), 25, 26, 31, 33.

36. Martínez Verdugo, *Partido comunista*, 51.

37. Movimiento de Liberación Nacional, *Programa y llamamiento* (Mexico City: N.p., 1961), 11–18.

38. Ibid., 12, 15.

39. Ibid., 20–21.

40. Fidel Castro, "Turn toward Socialism: Cuba's Socialism Proclaimed," in *Fidel Castro Speaks*, 78–79, 81.

41. For the following discussion of the origins of the MLN, see Juan de Dios Vargas Sánchez, with Donald C. Hodges, "La resistencia popular en México 1940–1976" (unpublished *licenciado* thesis in sociology, Universidad Nacional Autónoma de México, 1986), 88–89.

42. Movimiento de Liberación Nacional, *Programa*, 5.

43. Ibid., 68–71.

44. Ibid., 22–51.

45. Ibid., 65, 67.

46. The following discussion of the failure and eclipse of the MLN is based on the discussion in Vargas and Hodges, "La resistencia popular," 91–95.

47. Castro, "Turn toward Socialism," 78–79.

48. Cited in an editorial comment by Martin Kenner and James Petras, *Fidel Castro Speaks*, 116.

49. Fidel Castro, "The Latin American Communist Parties and Revolution: 'Their Attitude toward the Guerrilla Struggle Will Define the Communists in Latin America,'" *Fidel Castro Speaks*, 131.

50. Ibid., 131–132.

51. Fidel Castro, "Discurso pronunciado en la clausura de la primera conferencia de la Organización Latinoamericana de Solidaridad, el día 10 de agosto de 1967," *Discursos*, 160.

52. Cited by Luis E. Aguilar, ed., *Marxism in Latin America* (New York: Knopf, 1968), 222.

53. Castro, "The Latin American Communist Parties," 127.

54. Castro, "Discurso . . . el día 10 de agosto de 1967," 153–154.

55. Ibid., 154.

56. For an appreciation of Castro's anarchism, see Abraham Guillén, *Philosophy of the Urban Guerrilla: The Revolutionary Writings of Abraham Guillén*, ed. and trans.

Donald C. Hodges (New York: William Morrow, 1973), 292–293; and Rafael Santiago, "Si la guerrilla anarquista hubiese existido," *El Machete*, no. 13 (May 1981), 35–37.

57. Bartra, "*Regeneración*," 327.

58. Ernesto Che Guevara, "Notas para el estudio de la ideología de la Revolución Cubana," *Obras 1957–1967*, 2 vols. (Havana: Casa de las Américas, 1970), 2:92.

59. Ibid., 95, 100–101.

60. Castro, "The Latin American Communist Parties," 130–131.

61. Castro, "Discurso . . . el día 10 de agosto de 1967," 129.

62. Letter from Rodríguez to me, 3 October 1992.

63. Robledo, "Toda la verdad," 36.

64. Godines, *¡Que poca mad . . . era!*, 53–54, 59, 68. Compare with Jan Valtin, *Out of the Night* (New York: Alliance, 1941), and Eudocio Ravines, *The Yenan Way* (New York: Scribner, 1951).

65. Godines, *¡Que poca mad . . . era!*, 5, 7, 148, 166.

66. Ibid., 6, 50–52, 162.

67. Ibid., 50–54, 59, 70–71.

68. Ibid., 39, 106–107.

69. Ibid., 129–132.

70. Ibid., 53.

71. Ibid., 102–105.

72. Ibid., 74–77, 107, on the Cuban desertions. On the desertions from Jaramillo's October 1953 planned takeover of the Government Palace in Cuernavaca, Morelos, I am indebted to the testimony of Gorgonio Alonso, 13 July 1975. Alonso was a leading participant in the events.

73. López, *10 años de guerrillas*, 25, 27.

74. Ibid., 25; and Godines, *¡Que poca mad . . . era!*, 94.

75. Natividad Rosales, *¿Quién es Lucio Cabañas?*, 82; and Hirales Morán, *La liga comunista*, 92.

76. Suárez, *Lucio Cabañas*, 70.

77. Ibid., 34.

78. Ibid., 44.

79. See Vargas and Hodges, "La resistencia popular," 137.

80. "Ernesto," *El guerrillero*, 61–62; and Suárez, *Lucio Cabañas*, 46–47.

81. Suárez, *Lucio Cabañas*, 55–58, 63–64.

82. Ibid., 276.

83. Ibid., 45.

84. Ibid., 279.

85. Ibid., 53.

86. Ibid., 54.

87. Ibid., 175. See also 325–327.

88. Ibid., 115, 127–131, 186, 195.

89. Baloy Mayo, *La guerrilla*, 47.

90. The following review of the main exploits of the Party of the Poor is based on Vargas and Hodges, "La resistencia popular," 140–147.

91. Suárez, *Lucio Cabañas*, 318.

92. Ibid., 86; and De Mora, *Las guerrillas en México*, 693–694.

93. Suárez, *Lucio Cabañas*, 87–92.

94. Ibid., 89.

95. See the discussion of these massacres in the next chapter, on the student rebellion and its aftermath.

96. Suárez, *Lucio Cabañas*, 288–290.

97. Ibid., 267.

98. Baloy Mayo, *La guerrilla*, 48.

99. Ibid., 92–93. See Enrique Maza, "Las discrepancias de sus militantes acabaron con la lucha armada en Guerrero," *Proceso* (8 July 1985), 13–17.

100. Rubén Figueroa wanted to "make sure that another Cabañas can't exist, and that no one else has a reason to go into the hills," while Pres. Luís Echeverría stated in 1974 that the causes of subversion should be addressed rather than its effects. See Juan Miguel De Mora, *Lucio Cabañas: Su vida y su muerte* (Mexico City: Editores Asociados, 1974), 7–8. But the causes were only partly addressed and, contrary to government claims, the PDLP was never wiped out. See Miguel Cabildo et al., "Hasta ancianos y bebés detenidos en acciones llenas de arbitrariedades," *Proceso*, no. 701 (9 April 1990), 12–16.

101. Baloy Mayo, *La guerrilla*, 46.

102. Ibid., 35–38, 57.

103. Ibid., 58.

104. López, *10 años de guerrillas*, 62.

105. De Mora, *Las guerrillas en México*, 35–36.

106. López, *10 años de guerrillas*, 62.

107. De Mora, *Las guerrillas en México*, 36. See Regis Debray, "'El castrismo': La larga marcha de América Latina," in Departamento de Filosofía de la Universidad de Habana, *Lecturas de filosofía*, 2 vols. (Havana: Instituto del Libro, 1968), 2:481–526.

108. De Mora, *Las guerrillas en México*, 36–37.

109. Ibid., 37–38.

110. Ibid., 36.

111. López, *10 años de guerrillas*, 64.

112. Orlando Ortiz, *Genaro Vázquez* (Mexico City: Diógenes, 1973), 196.

113. Ibid., 196, 198.

114. López, *10 años de guerrillas*, 54.

115. Ibid., 55–57; and Baloy Mayo, *La guerrilla*, 81.

116. Baloy Mayo, *La guerrilla*, 74–75.

117. Interview with Cristóbal Rojas, owner and editor of *¡Presente!*, 10 December 1977.

118. See the contributions by these apostles of guerrilla warfare in Donald C. Hodges and Robert Elias Abu Shanab, eds., *National Liberation Fronts, 1960–1970* (New York: William Morrow, 1972), 222–310; and Donald C. Hodges, *The Legacy of Che Guevara: A Documentary Study* (London: Thames and Hudson, 1977), 100–197.

119. Bartra, "*Regeneración*," 31.

120. Martin Ebon, *Che: The Making of a Legend* (New York: Signet, 1969), 59–60, 61–62, 66.

121. Guevara, "Diario en Bolivia," *Obras 1957–1967*, 1:583.

122. Ebon, *Che*, 65.

123. Ernesto Che Guevara, "Guerra de guerrillas: Un método," *Obras 1957– 1967*, 1:165–166, 169. See idem, "Mensaje a los pueblos del mundo a través de la Tricontinental," *Obras 1957–1967*, 2:593–596.

124. Ernesto Che Guevara, "La guerra de guerrillas," *Obras 1957–1967*, 1:31– 34, 46–48.

125. José Carlos Mariátegui, *Defensa del marxismo. Obras completas*, 3d. ed., vol. 5 (orig. pub. 1959; Lima: "Amauta," 1967), 21, 59–61. For Mariátegui's intellectual indebtedness to Sorel, see Hodges, *Intellectual Foundations*, 180–182.

126. Hilda Gadea, *Ernesto: A Memoir of Che Guevara* (Garden City, N.Y.: Doubleday, 1972), 5.

127. Georges Sorel, *Reflections on Violence*, trans. T. E. Hulme and J. Roth (orig. pub. 1908; Glencoe, Ill.: Free Press, 1950), 57, 141–145.

128. Sorel, *Reflections on Violence*, 145; and Mariátegui, *Defensa del marxismo*, 59–62.

129. Sorel, *Reflections on Violence*, 253; and Mariátegui, *Defensa del marxismo*, 59–60.

130. Guevara, "La guerra de guerrillas," 1:61, 62–63.

131. Guevara, "Guerra de guerrillas: Un método," 1:165–167.

132. Guevara, "El socialismo y el hombre en Cuba," *Obras 1957–1967*, 2:372, 379, 381–383.

133. Rolando E. Bonachea and Nelson P. Valdés, eds., "Introduction" to Ernesto Guevara, *Che: Selected Works of Ernesto Guevara* (Cambridge: M.I.T. Press, 1969), 21–22, 35.

134. Michael Lowy, *El pensamiento del Che Guevara*, 2d. ed. (Mexico City: Siglo XXI, 1972). See Hartmut Ramm, *The Marxism of Regis Debray: Between Lenin and Guevara* (Lawrence: Regents Press of Kansas, 1978), 222.

135. Guevara, "La guerra de guerrillas," 1:43, 46.

136. De Mora, *Las guerrillas en México*, 259–260; and Ramón Pimentel Aguilar, *El secuestro: ¿Lucha política o provocación?* (Mexico City: Posada, 1974), 11–16.

137. Guevara, "La guerra de guerrillas," 1:62, 98, 116–118.

138. See James Kohl and John Litt, eds., *Urban Guerrilla Warfare in Latin America* (Cambridge: M.I.T. Press, 1974), 118, 211, 214, 358–364.

139. For a minibiography of Guillén, see my "Introduction" to his *Philosophy of the Urban Guerrilla*, 2–49. There is a brief discussion of Guillén in Hodges, *La revolución latinoamericana: Política y estrategia del apro-marxismo al guevarismo* (Mexico City: V Siglos, 1976), 321–325, 329–332.

140. Fidel Miró, *El anarquismo, los estudiantes y la revolución* (Mexico City: Editores Mexicanos Unidos, 1969), 153, 154.

141. Omar Costa, *Los Tupamaros* (Mexico City: Era, 1971), 149–159.

142. Abraham Guillén, *Estrategia de la guerrilla urbana*, 2d. ed. (Montevideo: Liberación, 1969), 158. An earlier edition published in Montevideo by Manuales del Pueblo appeared in 1966.

143. Santiago, "Si la guerrilla anarquista hubiese existido," 35.

144. Guillén, *Philosophy of the Urban Guerrilla*, 221–226.

145. Ibid., 91, 167.

146. Ibid., 31–32.

147. Guillén, *Estrategia*, 148, 160.

148. Ibid., 160.

149. Guevara, "Notas para el estudio de la ideología de la revolución cubana," *Obras 1957–1967*, 2:92, 95.

150. For the following discussion, see Abraham Guillén, "Lecciones de la guerrilla latinoamericana," in Donald C. Hodges and Abraham Guillén, *Revaloración de la guerrilla urbana* (Mexico City: El Caballito, 1977), 69, 76–77.

151. Ibid., 70, 129–130.

152. Ibid., 87–96.

153. Hodges, "Introduction" to Hodges and Guillén, *Revaloración*, 14.

5. THE STUDENT REBELLION AND ITS AFTERMATH

1. For the special usage of the Spanish *anarquisante*, see Sergio Zermeño, *México: Una democracia utópica* (Mexico City: Siglo XXI, 1978), 211, 215 (table 2), 225, 235 (table 3), 273–274.

2. Marta Harnecker, *Cuba: Dictatorship or Democracy?* trans. Patrick Greanville. (Westport, Conn.: Lawrence Hill, 1980), xxvii–xxviii, 45–46, 56–57.

3. For this information I am indebted to John Hart, who took part in some of the early demonstrations.

4. Zermeño, *México*, 13. For a day-to-day account of the main events from 22 July to 2 October, see Ramón Ramírez Gómez, *El movimiento estudiantil de México*, 2 vols. (Mexico City: Era, 1969), 1:145–397.

5. Elena Poniatowska, *Massacre in Mexico* (New York: Viking, 1975), 33; and Revueltas, *México 68*, 142–143.

6. Cited by Cockcroft, *Intellectual Precursors*, xviii.

7. Zermeño, *México*, 13.

8. Ramírez, *El movimiento estudiantil*, 1:153–154.

9. Ibid., 153, 157.

10. Ibid., 187; 2:182, 184.

11. Zermeño, *México*, 29–30.

12. Ibid., 28, 33–34.

13. Ibid., 30–32; and Ilán Semo, "El ocaso de los mitos," 118, 143.

14. Zermeño, *México*, 31.

15. Ibid., emphasis deleted.

16. Ibid., 13.

17. Ibid., 32, nn. 12, 13.

18. For a periodization of the movement, see Carr, *Marxism and Communism*, 258–264.

19. Zermeño, *México*, 13; and Ilán Semo, "El ocaso de los mitos," 126, 146.

20. Carr, *Marxism and Communism*, 260.

21. Ibid., 263.

22. Ibid., 261, 263–264.

23. Ibid., 267–268.

24. Zermeño places the Marxist-Leninist current to the left of the anarchizing current. See *México*, 37–40, 210–211, 234–235, table 3.

25. Ibid., 214, 234–235, table 3.

26. Ibid., 8.

27. Ibid., 38, 210–211.

28. Elena Poniatowska, *La noche de Tlatelolco* (Mexico City: Era, 1978), 37.
29. Cited by Ramírez, *El movimiento estudiantil*, 1:315–316.
30. Ibid., 2:196.
31. Carr, *Marxism and Communism*, 263.
32. Robert Simón Crespi, "José Revueltas (1914–1976): A Political Biography," *Latin American Perspectives* (Summer 1979), 94.
33. Cited by Revueltas, *México 68*, 312–313.
34. Crespi, "José Revueltas," 110.
35. Revueltas, *México 68*, 44.
36. Ibid., 48.
37. Ibid., 136, emphasis deleted.
38. Ibid., 142.
39. Ibid., 153.
40. Ibid., 21.
41. Ibid., 22.
42. Ibid., 163.
43. Ibid., 326, emphasis deleted.
44. Ibid., 326–327, emphasis deleted.
45. Cited by Ramírez, *El movimiento estudiantil*, 2:503.
46. For the following account of the student rebellion in Monterrey and its repercussions in the nation's capital, see Vargas and Hodges, "La resistencia popular," 162–173.
47. Antonio Solís Mimendi, *Jueves de Corpus Sangriento* (Mexico City: Talleres Alfaro Hermanos, 1975), 95.
48. See Gerardo Medina Valdés, *Operación 10 de junio* (Mexico City: Universo, 1972), 74–106.
49. Solís Mimendi, *Jueves*, 105.
50. For the following details concerning the *porros*, see Vargas and Hodges, "La resistencia popular," 150–161.
51. Medina Valdés, *Operación*, 210.
52. Solís Mimendi, *Jueves*, 37–38.
53. Conversation with Juan de Dios Vargas, Cuernavaca, Morelos, July 1975.
54. Medina Valdés, *Operación*, 220.
55. Vargas and Hodges, "La resistencia popular," 155.
56. Medina Valdés, *Operación*, 87.
57. In a report by journalist José Luis Mejías, *Contenido* (October 1977).
58. Revueltas, *México 68*, 160–161.
59. Ibid., 160.
60. Ibid., 162, 163.
61. Ibid., 178.
62. Hirales Morán, *La Liga Comunista*, 92, 94.
63. Carr, *Marxism and Communism*, 267–268; and Robledo, "Toda la verdad," 34–38.
64. Robledo, "Toda la verdad," 43–44.
65. López, *10 años de guerrillas*, 108.
66. Ibid., 118–119.
67. Ibid., 118; and Carr, *Marxism and Communism*, 268.
68. Pimentel Aguilar, *El secuestro*, 12.

69. López, *10 años de guerrillas*, 101, 108–111, 113–114, 116–117.

70. Paquita Calvo Zapata, "Urban and Rural Guerrillas Have the Same Importance," in Hodges, *The Legacy of Che Guevara*, 130 and 131; from *Punto Crítico* (June 1972), 28–29.

71. Cited by López, *10 años de guerrillas*, 114.

72. Calvo Zapata, "Urban and Rural Guerrillas," 132.

73. López, *10 años de guerrillas*, 110–111.

74. Robledo, "Todo la verdad," 47–48.

75. Hirales Morán, *La Liga Comunista*, 13–15. See Guillén, *Estrategia*.

76. Hirales Morán, *La Liga Comunista*, 17–18.

77. Mario Menéndez Rodríguez, "'Los procesos' y la guerrilla en México," *¡Por Esto!*, no. 94 (19 January 1984), 9; and Gustavo Hirales Morán, "La guerra secreta, 1970–1978," *Nexos*, no. 54 (June 1982), 40.

78. Robledo, "Todo la verdad," 34–35.

79. Ibid., 36.

80. López, *10 años de guerrillas*, 105.

81. For the account of the Revolutionary Action Movement, see Robledo, "Todo la verdad," 35–36, 38–42.

82. On the Revolutionary Student Front, see López, *10 años de guerriilas*, 91–99.

83. Robledo, "Todo la verdad," 43.

84. Ibid.

85. López, *10 años de guerrillas*, 140–142, 146–147.

86. Pimentel Aguilar, *El secuestro*, 144–147.

87. Robledo, "Todo la verdad," 44.

88. Ibid.

89. For the following account of the September 23 Communist League, see Vargas and Hodges, "La resistencia popular," 180–184.

90. Robledo, "Todo la verdad," 44.

91. Ibid., 44–45.

92. Hirales Morán, *La Liga Comunista*, 18–19.

93. Ibid., 18.

94. Carl Davidson, "A Student Syndicalist Movement: University Reform Revisited," *New Left Notes* (9 September 1966). See Kirkpatrick Sales, *SDS* (New York: Vintage, 1973), 290–297.

95. Herbert Marcuse, *An Essay on Liberation* (Boston: Beacon, 1969), 89. For a discussion of Marcuse's alleged kinship with anarchism, see Douglas Kellner, *Herbert Marcuse and the Crisis of Marxism* (Berkeley & Los Angeles: University of California Press, 1984), 279, 456 n. 4, 457 n. 6, 457–458 n. 9.

96. Hirales Morán, *La Liga Comunista*, 22.

97. Joe Foweraker, "Popular Movements and the Transformation of the System," in Wayne A. Cornelius, Judith Gentleman, and Peter H. Smith, eds., *Mexico's Alternative Political Futures*. Monograph Series, 30 (La Jolla: Center for U.S.–Mexican Studies, University of California, San Diego, 1989), 109; Francisco Pérez Arce, "The Enduring Union Struggle for Legality and Democracy," in Joe Foweraker and Ann L. Craig, eds., *Popular Movements and Political Change in Mexico* (Boulder: Lynne Rienner, 1990), 105, 119–120; and Ann L. Craig, "Institutional Context and Popular Strategies," *Popular Movements*, 271, 284.

98. Joe Foweraker, "Introduction" to *Popular Movements*, 7.

99. Pérez Arce, "The Enduring Union Struggle," 108.

100. Craig, "Institutional Context and Popular Strategies," 284.

101. Kathleen Logan, "Comment," *Mexico's Alternative Political Futures*, 173 – 174; Carr, *Marxism and Communism*, 237 – 238.

102. Carr, *Marxism and Communism*, 230, 237.

103. Jeffrey W. Rubin, "Popular Mobilization and the Myth of State Corporatism," *Popular Movements*, 262.

104. Elena Poniatowska, *Fuerte es el silencio* (Mexico City: Era, 1980), 197 – 198, 238, 256, 267.

105. Carr, *Marxism and Communism*, 237, 383 n. 31.

106. Lewis S. Feuer, *The Conflict of Generations: The Character and Significance of Student Movements* (New York: Basic Books, 1969), 193.

107. Ibid.

108. Mao Tse Tung, *A Critique of Soviet Economics*, trans. Moss Roberts (New York: Monthly Review, 1977), 47.

109. Hodges, "Introduction" to Guillén, *Philosophy of the Urban Guerrilla*, 39.

110. See Jeffrey W. Rubin, "State Policies, Leftist Oppositions, and Municipal Elections: The Case of the COCEI in Juchitán," in Arturo Alvarado, ed., *Electoral Patterns and Perspectives in Mexico* (La Jolla: Center for U.S.–Mexican Studies, University of California at San Diego, 1987).

111. Poniatowska, *Fuerte es el silencio*, 259.

112. Ibid., 275.

113. Víctor Orozco, "Las luchas populares en Chihuahua," *Cuadernos Políticos*, no. 9 (July–September 1976), 49–66.

114. For the following account of the genesis of the Chihuahua CDP, see Vargas and Hodges, "La resistencia popular," 199–209.

115. Fabio Barbosa, "Izquierda radical: Las utopias cambiantes," *Nexos*, no. 68 (August 1983), 35–47.

116. See Hodges, *The Latin American Revolution*, 108–111.

117. G. P. Maksimov, "The Soviets of Workers', Soldiers', and Peasants' Deputies," in Paul Avrich, ed., *The Anarchists in the Russian Revolution* (Ithaca, N.Y.: Cornell University Press, 1973), 103. See in the same volume the editor's comment on p. 108; and Peter Kropotkin, "Message to the Workers of the West," 151–152.

118. "To All Peasants and Workers of the Ukraine" (Makhnovist Proclamation, 1920), in Avrich, *The Anarchists in the Russian Revolution*, 134.

119. Guillén, *Philosophy of the Urban Guerrilla*, 77.

120. Ibid., 76.

6. THE REVIVAL OF ANARCHIST THEORY

1. "Mexico's Ripped-Off Revolution" is the English title of a paper I read at the 11th International Congress of the Latin American Studies Association in Mexico City, October 1983, in a symposium with Arnoldo Martínez Verdugo, Enrique Semo, and Arnaldo Córdova representing the three main currents in the Partido Socialista Unificado de México (Unified Socialist Party of Mexico)—the

PCM's successor, founded in November 1981. The symposium was a product of Barry Carr's fertile imagination.

2. Among the works celebrating this legacy of direct action that have yet to be mentioned in the notes, see Adolfo Gilly, *La revolución interrumpida* (Mexico City: El Caballito, 1971); Ramón Martínez Escamilla, *La revolución derrotada. México, revolución y reformismo* (Mexico City: Editores Asociados, 1977); and Salvador Hernández Padilla, *El magonismo: Historia de una pasión libertaria 1900–1922* (Mexico City: Era, 1984). As part of the revival, books originally published in English also appeared in translation, notably those by John Womack, Jr. (1969), James D. Cockcroft (1971), David Ronfeldt (1975), and John Hart (1980).

3. See José Porfirio Miranda's effort to salvage the radical content of Marx's theory, *Marx en México: Plusvalía y política* (Mexico City: Siglo XXI, 1972); and Enrique González Rojo's critique of its conservative content in *La revolución proletario-intelectual* (Mexico City: Diógenes, 1981).

4. For the essentials of Ivan Illich's communitarian anarchism, or anarcho-communism, see *Tools for Conviviality* (New York: Harper & Row, 1973); *Energy and Equity* (New York: Harper & Row, 1974); and *Medical Nemesis: The Expropriation of Health* (New York: Pantheon, 1976).

5. In a little more than a decade, the following works by anarcho-Marxists were translated and published in Mexico: Karl Korsch, *Marxismo y filosofía* (Mexico City: Era, 1969), and *Teoría marxista y acción política* (Mexico City: Pasado y Presente, 1979); Daniel Cohn-Bendit et al., *La rebelión estudiantil* (Mexico City: Era, 1969); Andre Glucksmann, *Hacia la subversión del trabajo intelectual* (Mexico City: Era, 1976); Noam Chomsky, "Notas sobre el anarquismo" and "Los intelectuales y el estado," in *Antología anarquista* (Mexico City: El Caballito, 1980); Donald C. Hodges, *Marxismo y revolución en el siglo veinte* (Mexico City: El Caballito, 1978); and Douglas Kellner, *El marxismo revolucionario de Karl Korsch* (Mexico City: Premia, 1981).

6. Revueltas, *Ensayo*, 41–45.

7. V. I. Lenin, "What Is to Be Done?" in Tucker, ed., *The Lenin Anthology*, 19, 20; emphasis deleted.

8. Revueltas, *México 68*, 21–22, 33.

9. Andrea Revueltas et al., "Prólogo" to Revueltas, *Ensayo*, 31.

10. Revueltas, *México 68*, 312.

11. Revueltas, *Ensayo*, 112–114.

12. Ibid., 140.

13. Ibid., 157–158.

14. Ibid., 160.

15. Norma Castro Quiteño, "Oponer el ahora y aquí de la vida, el ahora y aquí de la muerte," in José Revueltas, *Conversaciones con José Revueltas*, ed. Jorge Ruffinelli (Mexico City: Universidad Veracruzana, 1977), 88. Revueltas owed a special debt to José Carlos Mariátegui's *7 Ensayos de interpretación de la realidad peruana* (orig. pub. 1928; Lima: "Amauta," 1969).

16. Revueltas, *Ensayo*, 178–179.

17. Ibid., 186–187, 192–193; original emphasis.

18. Ibid., 195; original emphasis.

19. Ibid., 224, 231.

20. Ibid., 206, 207; original emphasis.

21. Ibid., 209–210.

22. Ibid., 208. For a brief account of the 1923 strike, see Hart, *Anarchism*, 164–166.

23. Aguilar Mora, *La crisis*, 98–99, 130–133. For a further tribute to Revueltas, see idem, *El bonapartismo mexicano*, 2 vols. (Mexico City: Juan Pablos, 1982), 1:12–13, 106–107. For Trotsky's critique of the Soviet bureaucracy, see *The Revolution Betrayed* (orig. pub. 1937; New York: Merit, 1965), 123–127, 135–142, 235–244; and idem, "The USSR in War," *In Defense of Marxism* (New York: Pioneer, 1942), 9, 15.

24. Aguilar Mora, *La crisis*, 13, 15.

25. Ibid., 24, 26.

26. Ibid., 24–25.

27. Leon Trotsky, "Burguesía nacional y bonapartismo en América Latina," in *Por los Estados Unidos Socialistas de América Latina* (Buenos Aires: Coyoacán, 1961), 15.

28. Trotsky, "La administración obrera en la industria nacionalizada," in *Por los Estados Unidos Socialistas*, 25–26.

29. Aguilar Mora, *El bonapartismo*, 1:42; and idem, *La crisis*, 24.

30. Aguilar Mora, *El bonapartismo*, 1:119. See Gilly, *La revolución interrumpida*, 299–301, 332–334, 337–338, 388.

31. Gilly, *La revolución interrumpida*, 44, 76–77, 277–278.

32. Ibid., 329–330, 393, 395.

33. Ibid., 332–334, 387–389, 392–393.

34. Aguilar Mora, *El bonapartismo*, 1:30–37, 200.

35. Adolfo Gilly, *Sacerdotes y burócratas* (Mexico City: Era, 1980), 51–52, 57.

36. Lenin, "The State and Revolution," 375–378, 381–384.

37. Miranda, *Marx en México*, 1–2, 7–8, 63–68, 100–115.

38. José Porfirio Miranda, *Marx against the Marxists: The Christian Humanism of Karl Marx*, trans. John Drury (orig. pub. 1978; Maryknoll, N.Y.: Orbis, 1980), 106, 224, 261–263 n. 2.

39. Miranda, *Marx en México*, 4–5, 132–133.

40. Ibid., 13–16.

41. Ibid., 15–16.

42. Ibid., 18, 19.

43. Ibid., 19–20.

44. Ibid., 21–22.

45. Ibid., 23.

46. Ibid., 24.

47. Ibid., 133.

48. José Porfirio Miranda, *Being and the Messiah: The Message of St. John*, trans. John Eagleson (orig. pub. 1973; Maryknoll, N.Y.: Orbis, 1977), 15, 21; my emphasis.

49. Ibid., 66.

50. Miranda, *Marx en México*, 117, 117–118.

51. Ibid., 42, 80–85, 106.

52. Ibid., 106.

53. Miranda, *Being and the Messiah*, 7, 8, 10.

54. Ibid., 12, 22.

55. Ibid., 23. For the citation in Miranda's *Marx against the Marxists*, 107, see Friedrich Engels, *Anti-Dühring*, 2d. ed. (Moscow: Foreign Languages Publishing House, 1959), 249–250.

56. Miranda, *Marx against the Marxists*, 26, 27.

57. Miranda, *Marx en México*, 83; and idem, *Comunismo en la biblia* (Mexico City: Siglo XXI, 1981), 15–16.

58. Marx and Engels, "Manifesto of the Communist Party," 484–485, 497.

59. Miranda, *Being and the Messiah*, 12, 22.

60. Miranda, *Marx en México*, 42. See Marx, *Capital*, 1:66 n. 1.

61. Miranda, *Being and the Messiah*, 15.

62. Ibid., 224.

63. Ibid., 40.

64. Ibid., 36, 37, 38.

65. José Revueltas, "Libertad del arte y estética mediatizada," in José Revueltas, *Cuestionamientos e intenciones*, 2d ed. (Mexico City: Era, 1981), 182–183, 184; emphasis deleted.

66. Revueltas, "Esquema teórica para un ensayo sobre las cuestiones del arte y la libertad," *Cuestionamientos e intenciones*, 189.

67. Revueltas, "La situación de los judíos en la Unión Soviética," *Cuestionamientos e intenciones*, 212.

68. Revueltas, "Prólogo," *Cuestionamientos e intenciones*, 147; emphasis deleted.

69. Ibid., 137, 152.

70. Revueltas, "La libertad y el socialismo, por que no vuelve a suicidarse Mayakovski," *Cuestionamientos e intenciones*, 279–280.

71. Revueltas, "Literatura y liberación en América Latina," *Cuestionamientos e intenciones*, 309.

72. Revueltas, "Notas," *Cuestionamientos e intenciones*, 374, 376.

73. See Marx and Engels, "Manifesto of the Communist Party," 477–483; V. I. Lenin, "Imperialism, the Highest Stage of Capitalism," and "Communism and the East: Theses on the National and Colonial Questions," in *The Lenin Anthology*, 243–244, 621–624; and Joseph Stalin, *Economic Problems of Socialism in the USSR* (New York: International Publishers, 1952), 26–30.

74. González Rojo, *La revolución proletario-intelectual*, 27–28.

75. For the citation from Bakunin, see Max Nomad, *Apostles of Revolution*, rev. ed. (New York: Collier, 1961), 203.

76. Waclaw Machajski, "On the Expropriation of the Capitalists," in V. F. Calverton, ed., *The Making of Society: An Outline of Sociology* (New York: Modern Library, 1937), 428, 434. For a discussion of Machajski's theories, see Max Nomad, *Aspects of Revolt* (New York: Bookman, 1960), 96–117.

77. González Rojo, *La revolución proletario-intelectual*, 9, 129, n. 9. For González Rojo's sources, see Henry Mayer, "Prólogo," *Notas marginales sobre la obra de Bakunin, El estatismo y la anarquía, de Carlos Marx* (Bogotá: Controversia, 1973), 6–30; S. V. Utechin, *Historia del pensamiento político ruso* (Madrid: Revista de Occidente, n.d.), 194–196; and Nico Berti, "Anticipaciones anarquistas sobre los 'nuevos patrones,'" *Vuelta* (Mexico City), vol. 1, no. 6 (1977), 28–36.

78. González Rojo, *La revolución proletario-intelectual*, 95–96, 132, nn. 47, 48.

79. Ibid., 102–103, 105.

80. Ibid., 109–110; emphasis deleted.

81. James H. Billington, *Fire in the Minds of Men: Origins of the Revolutionary Faith* (New York: Basic Books, 1980), 79–83.

82. González Rojo, *La revolución proletario-intelectual*, 95, 103, 105. On "absolute equality" in labor and distribution, a "Republic of Equals," and a "community of goods," see "Babeuf to Dubois de Fosseaux" (8 July 1787), Maréchal's "Manifesto of the Equals" (April 1796), and the "Analysis of the Doctrine of Babeuf by the Babouvists" (1796) in Albert Fried and Ronald Sanders, eds., *Socialist Thought: A Documentary History* (Garden City, N.Y.: Anchor, 1964), 46, 49–50, 52–54, 55–56.

83. Marx, "Critique of the Gotha Program," 530.

84. Trotsky, *The Revolution Betrayed*, 244, 248–250.

85. Trotsky, "The USSR in War," 9.

86. Nomad, *Aspects of Revolt*, 113–114.

87. Trotsky, *The Revolution Betrayed*, 101–102, 115–143, 258–259, 276.

88. Revueltas, "Notas," *México 68*, 338; and Andrea Revueltas et al., "Prólogo," in Revueltas, *Ensayo*, 26–27.

89. See Barry Carr, "The Left and Its Potential Role in Political Change," in Wayne A. Cornelius et al., eds., *Mexico's Alternative Political Futures*, 371, n. 11.

90. Carlos Sirvent, *La burocracia* (Mexico City: EDICOL, 1977), 12–15, 41–42, 49–51.

91. Ibid., 43–46, 50–51.

92. Ivan Illich, *Deschooling Society* (New York: Harper & Row, 1971), was the first to appear and made him famous.

93. Illich, *Tools for Conviviality*, xxiv–xxv.

94. Illich, *Energy and Equity*, 7, 8. See also 30–33, 67.

95. Illich, *Tools for Conviviality*, 23, 122.

96. Ibid., 49–50.

97. Illich, *Medical Nemesis*, 261.

98. Maréchal, "Manifesto of the Equals," 52, 53.

99. Illich, *Tools for Conviviality*, 13, 69.

100. Illich, *Deschooling Society*, 9.

101. Illich, *Tools for Conviviality*, 16.

102. Leo Gabriel, *Levantamiento de culturas: Las zonas de conflicto en Centroamérica*, trans. Angelika Scherp (orig. pub. 1987; Mexico City: Edivisión, 1988), 25–27, 182–183, 188, 217, 266. I was a frequent visitor at the Grupo Informe's apartment in Cuernavaca and later at its rented house on the city's outskirts, and intermittently assisted Gabriel in his propaganda. See my references to him in *Argentina 1943–76: The National Revolution and Resistance* (Albuquerque: University of New Mexico Press, 1976), vii, and *Intellectual Foundations*, 282.

103. Gabriel, *Levantamiento de culturas*, 26, 183.

104. Ibid., 15–19, 23–27, 77–82, 275.

105. Hart, *Anarchism*, 19, 53–54, 55, 64, 75–76.

106. Ibid., 104, 111–114.

107. See the table on p. 117 of Donald Hodges and Ross Gandy's expanded English version of their 1976 book, *Mexico 1910–1982: Reform or Revolution?* (London: Zed, 1983).

108. Marx and Engels shared the anarchists' goal of a stateless society, but

rejected their strategy for arriving at it. See Friedrich Engels, "Socialism: Utopian and Scientific," in *The Marx-Engels Reader*, 713.

109. In riding the wave of anti-imperialist sentiment in the early 1970s, El Caballito published an anthology of labor articles and editorials edited by Rodolfo F. Peña, *Insurgencia obrera y nacionalismo revolucionario* (1973), followed by *La economía mexicana y el nacionalismo revolucionario* (1974) by Salvador Carmona, a leading theorist of the ruling party.

110. López Gallo was much taken with Pres. Juan Domingo Perón's third position in Argentina and my discussion of it in *Argentina 1943–1976*, a work he briefly considered translating. See pages 125–137 and the further discussion of it in my book coauthored with Ross Gandy and published by El Caballito, *El destino de la revolución mexicana* (1977), 202–211.

111. Hodges and Gandy, *Mexico 1910–1982*, 115–116.

112. Discussions with López Gallo at his weekend retreat in Cuernavaca, November 1977 and February 1978.

113. Pierre-Joseph Proudhon, "An Anarchist's View of Democracy," from "Solution du problème social" (1848), in Robert Hoffman, ed., *Anarchism* (New York: Atherton, 1970), 59. See also Proudhon's *General Idea of the Revolution in the Nineteenth Century* (orig. pub. 1848; London: Pluto, 1989), 136–169.

114. José Riera, "Presentación," *Antología anarquista*, 7–8.

115. Gino Cerrito, "El movimiento anarquista internacional y su estructura actual," in *Antología anarquista*, 9, 24–26.

116. Ibid., 25.

117. Marc Paillet, *Marx contra Marx: La sociedad tecnoburocrática* (Barcelona: DOPESA, 1972); Cornelius Castoriadis, *La sociedad burocrática*, 2 vols. (Barcelona: Tusquets, 1976); and Heleno Saña, *El anarquismo, de Proudhon a Cohn-Bendit* (Madrid: Indice, 1970), 17–20, 22–24, 104, 139, 148–149.

118. From a political discussion with López Gallo, Cuernavaca, January 1980.

119. Manuel López Gallo, *Economía y política en la historia de México* (Mexico City: El Caballito, 1965). The book went through twenty-five printings over two decades. He also wrote a sequel, *La violencia en la historia de México* (Mexico City: El Caballito, 1976).

120. López Gallo identified Mexico's fundamental enemy as imperialism, not bureaucracy, and was sympathetic to a variety of currents on the Left that could be called anticapitalist. Sharing common ground with Hodges and Gandy, *¡Todos los revolucionarios van al infierno!* (Mexico City: Costa-Amic, 1983), he supported revolutions from above as well as below, and the theory and practice of revolutionaries as diverse as Bakunin, Kropotkin, Villa, Zapata, Stalin, Trotsky, and Perón.

121. Hodges and Gandy, *Mexico 1910–1982*, 114–115.

122. Conchello et al., *Los partidos políticos*, 323, 330, 344. The Popular Socialist party and its Marxist-Leninist precursor, the Popular party, opted for a peaceful road to socialism that excluded the Trotskyist and anarchist reliance on direct action.

123. See the discussion of both books in Hodges and Gandy, *Mexico 1910–1982*, 111–114.

124. Ibid., 121.

125. See López Gallo, *La violencia*, 475–476. On the premise of an advancing bureaucratic mode of production geared to replace capitalism, there was a Leninist basis for López Gallo's pragmatic leftism. See my interpolation and updating of key passages from Lenin's "Two Tactics of Social-Democracy in the Democratic Revolution" in *Revaloración*, 52–53. "Since the rule of the . . . [bureaucracy] over the working class is inevitable, it can well be said that a . . . [bureaucratic] revolution expresses the interests not so much of the proletariat as of the . . . [bureaucracy]. But it is just absurd to think that a . . . [bureaucratic] revolution does not at all express proletarian interests . . . [On the contrary,] seeking salvation for the working class in anything save the further development of . . . [bureaucracy] is *reactionary*. . . . The more complete, determined, and consistent the . . . [bureaucratic] revolution, the more assured will the proletariat's struggle be against . . . [bureaucracy] and for . . . [communism]."

126. For the foregoing account, I have relied on Ross Gandy's report on the Mexican political situation in a thirteen–page letter from Cuernavaca dated 20 November 1988.

127. Ibid.

128. Hodges and Gandy, *Mexico 1910–1982*, 115–117.

129. Ibid., 116.

130. An activist in Students for a Democratic Society (SDS) during the mid-sixties, Ross Gandy (1935–   ) taught at CIDOC from 1972 to 1974. In radical circles in Mexico, he is best known for his widely read *Introducción a la sociología histórica marxista* (Mexico City: Era, 1980). Used as a text at the National University, Gandy's book sold over thirty thousand copies between 1980 and 1990.

131. Letter to me dated 20 November 1988.

CONCLUSION

1. Guillén, *Philosophy of the Urban Guerrilla*, 37.

2. Carol J. Adams, *The Sexual Politics of Meat: A Feminist-Vegetarian Critical Theory* (New York: Continuum, 1991), 37–38, 186–190; and Jeremy Rifkin, *Beyond Beef: The Rise and Fall of the Cattle Culture* (New York: Dutton, 1992), 9–33.

3. Rifkin, *Beyond Beef*, 116–145.

4. Ibid., 165–169.

5. Diego Abad de Santillán, "Prólogo," Fidel Miró, *El anarquismo*, 9, 16–17; emphasis deleted.

6. Juan Gómez Casas, *Anarchist Organization: The History of the F.A.I.*, trans. Abe Bluestein (Montreal: Black Rose, 1986), 82–86, 156–163.

7. Abad de Santillán, "Prólogo," 13–14.

8. Cited by Gómez, *Anarchist Organization*, 83.

9. See Diego Abad de Santillán, *Ricardo Flores Magón: El apóstol de la revolución social mexicana* (Mexico City: Grupo Cultural "Ricardo Flores Magón," 1925).

10. Gómez, *Anarchist Organization*, 85. For Abad's subsequent defense of programmatic anarchism, see 162–163.

11. Abad de Santillán, "Prólogo," 20.

12. Ibid., 20–21.

13. Irving Louis Horowitz, ed., "Introduction," *The Anarchists* (New York: Dell, 1964), 27.

14. Cited by Guillén, *Estrategia*, 159.

15. Ibid., 160.

16. Guillén, *Philosophy of the Urban Guerrilla*, 221.

17. Abraham Guillén, *Socialismo libertario: Ni capitalismo de monopolios, ni comunismo de estado* (Madrid: Ediciones Madre Tierra, 1990), 411–445.

18. Gómez, *Anarchist Organization*, 252.

19. Ibid., 253.

20. Hart, *Anarchism*, ix, 175–177, 182–183.

21. Ibid., 170, 172–173, 175.

22. Marjorie Ruth Clark, *Organized Labor in Mexico* (Chapel Hill: University of North Carolina Press, 1934), 274.

23. Enrique Flores Magón, *Peleamos*, 2:147, 504, 515–516; see also 341, 455, 471–472, 499.

24. Ibid., 517.

25. Taibo, *Arcángeles*, 69.

26. Enrique Flores Magón, *Peleamos*, 2:509.

27. Ibid., 510–511, 513–514.

28. Abraham Guillén, *Economía libertaria: Alternativa para un mundo en crisis* (Madrid: Fundación de Estudios Libertarios Anselmo Lorenzo, 1988), 89–90, 155, 160–162, 199; and idem, *Economía autogestionaria: Las bases del desarrollo económico de la sociedad libertaria* (Madrid: Fundación de Estudios Libertarios Anselmo Lorenzo, 1990), 128, 158, 232–235.

29. Ross Gandy brought this line to my attention. The interpretation is mine. See Pierre-Joseph Proudhon, *What Is Property*, trans. Benjamin R. Tucker (London: William Reeves, n.d.), 37–38, 264–265; and Patrick H. Hutton, *The Cult of the Revolutionary Tradition: The Blanquists in French Politics, 1864–1893* (Berkeley & Los Angeles: University of California Press, 1981), 45, 118, 132.

30. Cited by Dirk J. Struik, *Birth of the Communist Manifesto* (New York: International Publishers, 1971), 31.

31. Jaramillo, *Autobiografía*, 31.

32. Ravelo, *Los jaramillistas*, 114–115.

33. Hirales Morán, *La Liga Comunista*, 34–35.

34. Alanís, Pichardo, and Ambriz, "Anecdotario."

35. For a possible scenario of the future of Mexican anarchism, see the conclusion to Donald C. Hodges, *Sandino's Communism* (Austin: University of Texas Press, 1992), 155–177.

POSTSCRIPT

1. From the epigraph to the concluding section of chapter 7, "The Guerrillas," in César Romero Jacobo, *Los Altos de Chiapas: La voz de las armas* (Mexico City: Planeta, 1994), 140.

2. Poniatowska, *Fuerte es el silencio*, 275.

3. Paco Ignacio Taibo II, "¡Zapatista! The Phoenix Rises," *The Nation* (28 March 1994), 407; Michael S. Serrill, "Zapata's Revenge," *Time* (17 January 1994),

32. For the references to Bakunin, see Sam Dolgoff, ed., *Bakunin on Anarchy* (New York: Knopf, 1972), 41-42, 69, 100, 152, 177-179.

4. Guillermo Correa et al., "Película del diálogo," *Proceso* (28 February 1994), 18; and Romero, *Los Altos de Chiapas*, 46-47.

5. Guillermo Correa and Ignacio Ramírez, "A Emiliano Zapata y su Plan de Ayala atribuye el Ejército Zapatista de Liberación Nacional su inspiración ideológica," *Proceso* (10 January 1994), 10.

6. Romero, *Los Altos de Chiapas*, 38; Froylán M. López Narváez, "Marcos: Conversación al alba," *Proceso* (21 February 1994), 39; Tim Golden, "Rebels Determined 'to Build Socialism' in Mexico," *The New York Times* (4 January 1994). For an understanding of the role of Indian millenarian movements in Mexico, see Margarita Zárate, "Apéndice: Algunas aproximaciones a los movimientos indígenas," in *Movimientos indígenas contemporáneos en México*, ed. Arturo Warman and Arturo Argueta (Mexico City: Centro de Investigaciones Interdisciplinarias en Humanidades UNAM, 1993), 227-230.

7. Jorge G. Castañeda, *Utopia Unarmed: The Latin American Left after the Cold War* (New York: Knopf, 1993), 90-94. On MR-13, the Maoist precursor of the EGP and the ORPA, see Hodges, *La revolución latinoamericana*, 118-125.

8. Gabriel, *Levantamiento de culturas*, 46.

9. Tim Golden, "Mexican Troops Battling Rebels," *The New York Times* (3 January 1994).

10. Tim Golden, "The Voice of the Rebels Has Mexicans in His Spell," *The New York Times* (8 February 1994).

11. Romero, *Los Altos de Chiapas*, 107-108.

12. Cabildo et al., "Hasta ancianos y bebés detenidos," 12-13.

13. Romero, *Los Altos de Chiapas*, 108, 140-141.

14. Ibid., 33-34, 138-139.

15. Enrique Maza, "Juntas, la acción política y la acción pastoral concientizaron a los indígenas en la búsqueda de su redención," *Proceso* (7 February 1994), 23, 25.

16. Ibid., 25.

17. Ignacio Ramírez, "Grupos de izquierda de Torreón utilizaron la infraestructura religiosa y radicalizaron a los catequistas," *Proceso* (28 February 1994), 6, 10.

18. Antonio Jáquez, "Los apoyos políticos de Línea de Masas," *Proceso* (24 January 1994), 26-29.

19. Vicente Leñero, "El Subcomandante se abre," *Proceso* (21 February 1994), 9-10, 12-14; and Guillermo Correa et al., "Representantes zapatistas concretan su demanda fundamental," *Proceso* (28 February 1994), 12-13.

20. Leñero, "El Subcomandante se abre," 10, 15.

21. Ibid., 14-15.

22. Ibid., 10, 15.

23. Tim Golden, "Jungle to Peace Talks: Mexican Chronicles Revolt," *The New York Times* (21 February 1994).

24. Romero, *Los Altos de Chiapas*, 41.

25. Sonia Morales, "Exdirigentes guerrilleros: La estrategia del Ejército Zapatista, inédita en México y Latinoamérica," *Proceso* (10 January 1994), 12.

26. *Zapatistas* (Westport, N.J.: Open Magazine Pamphlet Series, 1994), 13-18.

27. Comunicado del Comité Clandestino Revolucionario Indígena, Comandancia General del Ejército Zapatista de Liberación Nacional, 20 January 1994.

28. Hodges and Guillén, *Revaloración*, 77, 78, and 84–100. There is a reference to this work in Romero, *Los Altos de Chiapas*, p. 138.

29. Romero, *Los Altos de Chiapas*, 127, 146–147, 149.

30. Ibid., 146.

31. Marc Cooper, "Starting from Chiapas: The Zapatistas Fire the Shot Heard around the World," in *Zapatistas*, 5.

32. Taibo, "¡Zapatista!" 409–410.

33. Serrill, "Zapata's Revenge," 34.

34. Bill Weinberg, "From an Anti-Authoritarian Perspective: Interview with Insurgent Subcommander Marcos of the Zapatista National Liberation Army." From the Love and Rage New York News Bureau, April 1994. (Love and Rage is a revolutionary anarchist federation in the United States, Canada, and Mexico.)

INDEX